BACK FROM THE DEAD

BACK FROM THE DEAD

One woman's search for the men who walked off
America's death row

JOAN M. CHEEVER

WILEY

Published in 2006 by   John Wiley & Sons, Ltd, The Atrium, Southern Gate
                          Chichester, West Sussex, PO19 8SQ, England
                          Phone (+44) 1243 779777

Copyright © 2006   Joan M. Cheever

Email (for orders and customer service enquires): cs-books@wiley.co.uk
Visit our Home Page on www.wiley.co.uk or www.wiley.com

This publication is designed to provide accurate and authoritative information in regard to
the subject matter covered. It is sold on the understanding that the Publisher is not engaged
in rendering professional services. If professional advice or other expert assistance is
required, the services of a competent professional should be sought.

Joan M. Cheever has asserted her right under the Copyright, Designs and Patents Act 1988,
to be identified as the author of this work.

Other Wiley Editorial Offices

John Wiley & Sons, Inc. 111 River Street, Hoboken, NJ 07030, USA

Jossey-Bass, 989 Market Street, San Francisco, CA 94103-1741, USA

Wiley-VCH Verlag GmbH, Pappellaee 3, D-69469 Weinheim, Germany

John Wiley & Sons Australia, Ltd, 33 Park Road, Milton, Queensland, 4064, Australia

John Wiley & Sons (Asia) Pte Ltd, 2 Clementi Loop #02-01, Jin Xing Distripark, Singapore
129809

John Wiley & Sons Canada Ltd, 22 Worcester Road, Etobicoke, Ontario, Canada,
M9W 1L1

Wiley also publishes its books in a variety of electronic formats. Some content that appears
in print may not be available in electronic books.

CIP catalogue records for this book are available from the British Library and the US Library
of Congress

ISBN-13   978-0-470-01750-0 (HB)

Typeset in 10.5/13.5pt Photina by MCS Publishing Services Ltd, Salisbury, Wiltshire.
Printed and bound in Great Britain by T.J. International, Padstow, Cornwall.
This book is printed on acid-free paper responsibly manufactured from sustainable forestry
in which at least two trees are planted for each one used for paper production.
10 9 8 7 6 5 4 3 2

Dedication

For my parents, Sally and Charlie, for bringing me to life
and for Dennis who enriches it.

"Joan Cheever takes us on a journey of personal stories that will help bring about the abolition of the death penalty. The unusual path she takes to collect these stories gives the reader a rare view not only of our justice system, but of life, death, love, rehabilitation and forgiveness. *Back from the Dead* shows us that there is hope."

Bill Pelke, Co-founder of Journey of Hope ... From Violence to Healing.

"When death takes a holiday, investigative journalist Joan Cheever goes to work. What she uncovers should shock our entire system of justice."

Sherry Sontag, co-author, Blind Man's Bluff, the Untold Story of American Submarine Espionage.

"*Back From The Dead* is a riveting, intense narrative of one woman's search for former Death Row inmates, a group of Dead Men Walking, right out of prison to freedom. After witnessing an execution in Texas, Joan M. Cheever felt compelled to find the answer to a distressing question: What did these killers do with their second chance at life? Cheever tells of her long journey and the results of the 33 years of post-release data she's discovered about this group. Theirs is a story we should hear."

Sister Helen Prejean, Author, Dead Man Walking: An Eyewitness Account of the Death Penalty in the United States and The Death of Innocents: An Eyewitness Account of Wrongful Executions.

"In *Back From The Dead* Joan M. Cheever tells a compelling story of what happened to hundreds of Death Row inmates who won the lottery of life. In *Back From The Dead*, we travel with Cheever, a journalist and mother of two, to find these former residents of Death Row, many of whom don't want to be found. These graduates of Death Row took their second chance at life and turned their lives into success stories; it's a story about redemption and rehabilitation.

"An execution will never mend the hole in our heart; there is no such thing as closure. Healing can only begin when we turn the hate and revenge into compassion and understanding. I've been on the journey from rage to reconciliation. We will never forget those we love and lost."

Bud Welch, president of Murder Victims' Families for Human Rights and father of Julie, 23, who was killed in the 1995 Oklahoma City bombing.

CONTENTS

ACKNOWLEDGEMENTS

I am lucky to have had a lot of midwives who helped me birth this book. It was an arduous labor and I thank them for their patience and loyalty.

I am most grateful to the graduates of Death Row – most especially for their courage in sharing their stories. Thanks to all the members of the Class of '72 whom I interviewed and especially William Henry Furman, Elmer Branch, Chuck Culhane, Moreese Bickham, Freddie Pitts, Wilbert Lee, Mike Turczi, Leroy Johnson, Jim Bryson, Monty Powell, Lawrence Hayes, Calvin Sellars, Willie Stafford, and Rusty Holland. And to the memory of Gary McGivern, William "Sarge" Wallen, Bennett Belwood, and Joseph Cerny.

I am inspired and awed by the indefatigable spirit of Sister Helen Prejean and thankful; and I am truly blessed for the friendship and love of Lea and Roger Liepold.

Much appreciation to the "other Sally" in my life, my editor Sally Smith of John Wiley & Sons UK, for taking a chance on me and The Class of '72. Thanks also to The Wiley team: Rebecca Dimery, Julia Lampam and Felicity Roberts, Ian Campbell, Kate Stanley, Jamie McOuat, Martin Tribe, Grace O'Byrne and Roger Hunt. Thanks also to a writer's true best friends, copyeditor Kate Santon and proofreader Sarah Nawrocki.

And thanks to photographer Daniel Borris.

A heartfelt thanks to Betsey and Jim Hedges, who epitomize the true meaning of friendship; they moved not only mountains, but offices, houses and storage units and kept safe eight years of research as it traveled across the Atlantic and across the country. A thank you just isn't enough.

Updating the "alumni" directory was an overwhelming task and I am deeply indebted to my former co-worker and friend for life, Ed Frost of the Mintz Group in New York City.

Special thanks to Charles Salzberg, my teacher, editor, and friend for his encouragement and great ideas on the manuscript; and to the support and enthusiasm of Edward L. Beck, a gifted writer, good friend, and hand-holder. Thanks also to the Passionists of Riverdale, N.Y. who gave me a quiet place so I could meet a deadline.

Much appreciation to my agent, Jeff Kleinman, and to the earlier hard work of Denise Marcil and Maura Keyes.

I am grateful to Cathy "Cat" Bennett, a friend wise beyond her years who left us much too early, and to her partner and my friend, Robert Hirschhorn, who wouldn't take "No" for an answer and turned a "one year" death penalty case into nine long years.

Many thanks to my sister, Jean, and brother, Charlie, and my other brother, Jack, and the twins, Susan and Kara, for keeping me company on this journey; and to all those who kept my children company while I traveled.

Thanks also to Professor Anthony Amsterdam, Michael D'Amelio, Professor Hugo A. Bedau and Professor Michael Meltsner, for your 11th-hour edits, advice and review of the manuscript regarding the history of the death penalty, specifically the Furman ruling. I am grateful to attorneys Mel Bruder and Andy Ryan Jr. for their time, and to the late Professor Charles Alan Wright and Bobby Hill.

My appreciation to Author Gary M. LaVergne and David Messmore and to all those officials in corrections and parole who helped to fill in the blanks on the Death Row list of 1972 and then patiently provided 33 years of updated information; and to James W. Marquart and Jonathan R. Sorensen, authors of *A National Study of the Furman-Commuted Inmates: Assessing the Threat to Society from Capital Offenders.*

I am appreciative of Attorney Paul Burnham for explaining, to a certain government agency, the difference between a "hobby farm" and a book. And thanks to lawyer friends Mike Von Blon, Kathleen Curry, Diana Geis and the late Monique Berryhill, for such good advice.

Thanks also to my colleagues at *The National Law Journal*: Doreen Weisenhaus, Anthony Paonita, Sherry Sontag, Doug Hunt, Rosemary Olander, Randall Samborn, Hal Davis, Victoria Slind-Flor, and Marcia Coyle.

A thank you to Laurissa James for helping me compile the Class of '72 list, and to Kathryn Oliver for number-crunching, Excelling, and friendship. And to Bill at MBE for patience.

Thanks to those friends who read countless drafts and had great suggestions and just listened: Guy Barresi, Karen Nemiah, Wendy Burnham, Carol Sebastian, Susan Taylor, Cynthia Stix, and Kelly Newton, Cecile and the Cindys[2].

I am blessed, too, to have special people in my life who provided a peaceful retreat to write and reflect: Virginia and Lee Lahourcade, Moya Doherty and John McColgan, Gail Cornell and Franco Bianchi.

Finally, there are no words to express my profound appreciation and love to Dennis, my best friend, whose patience and unwavering support is without bounds, and thanks to our children who gave up a lot in sharing their mother with the Class of '72. I am truly grateful.

PROLOGUE

"For God's sake, Joan. If you are there, just close your eyes. You don't need to watch."

I stared back at my boss, sitting behind his expensive oak desk in the expansive corner office on New York City's tony Park Avenue, in disbelief. We were having this discussion on the ninth floor offices of *The National Law Journal*, a national weekly newspaper covering court cases, lawyers, and legal issues across the United States, but we might as well have been sitting in an ivory tower.

"Why would I want to do that? Newspaper reporters have been covering executions for over 100 years. Why in the hell would I close my eyes?"

"Because you just don't *need* to watch it. Besides, you're not going there as a journalist. You're a witness. His lawyer. It's different. Just close your eyes and keep them closed. You don't need to see this," he answered, in an annoyed and dismissive tone.

There are days and many sleepless nights when a part of me wishes I had taken my boss' advice. But I knew in my heart that he was wrong. I did need to see it. I needed to be an eyewitness to the execution of Walter Key Williams, my client of nine years. On that warm autumn night in Huntsville, Texas, I did keep my eyes open – wide open. And, during the six years I have spent researching, interviewing, and writing this book, I have worked hard to keep open the eyes of an objective journalist.

On October 5, 1994, I no longer had a client on Death Row. Walter was my one and only. I should have felt some sort of relief;

there were no more execution dates for me to worry about. There were no more 11th-hour races to the post office or the Federal Express drop box with babies strapped into car seats, while I clutched a manilla envelope of endless motions, hoping to stop an execution. There were no more notes to a federal judge disclosing details of my honeymoon plans or telephone numbers where I could be reached on long-awaited and carefully planned family vacations. There were no more trips to Texas during the brutally hot months, carrying a laptop in one hand and a crying baby and diaper bag in the other. There were no more ruined holidays with deadlines hanging over my head for legal briefs that hadn't been started, much less finished.

There was no reason to escape to the bathroom, lock the door, and turn on the bathtub to drown out the sound of my sobs. I didn't want my children to see or hear how scared Mommy was. In the months before Walter's execution, I cried a lot; I was terrified that we would lose this case and, in doing so, that Walter would lose his life. When the tears fell on those nights before Walter was executed, I never knew that those crying jags behind locked doors were just beginning.

I should have felt some sort of release now that Walter was gone. After all, now I could surf the web for Christmas presents instead of frantically searching legal websites looking, many times well past midnight, for the latest "gift" from a federal appellate court – a ruling that I just knew would free Walter from the Death House.

After Walter's execution, I found myself walking out of movies with scenes of gratuitous violence; I stopped reading newspaper reports of executions. I found myself crying through Death Row movies and documentaries. In 1998, on the afternoon of Karla Faye Tucker's execution in Texas, I ran out of my office after a well-meaning colleague at *The National Law Journal* began "Instant Messaging" me every five minutes, reminding me that "time was running out."

Time did run out for Karla Faye Tucker and for Walter, but in the summer of 1972 time was a gift for the 587 men and

2 women who were facing execution in the United States. At that moment those 589 people were in the right place at the right time.

They were spared execution because of a narrow 5–4 ruling by the United States Supreme Court in a legal case called *Furman versus Georgia* that, for a short time, abolished the death penalty in America. Five of the nine justices of the Supreme Court, in one of the longest written opinion in U.S. history, agreed that the death penalty was unconstitutional and therefore illegal, but their reasons differed: it was racist, arbitrary, unfairly applied, wanton, and freakish and cruel and unusual.

To those on Death Row, the reason wasn't important. The "whys" didn't matter but, later on, the "wheres" did. What turned out to be the most important factor in determining an inmate's future and possible release was location. If you were housed on Death Row in a state such as Louisiana or Massachusetts where a life term meant exactly that, your natural life, chances were you'd die behind bars.

But if you were in the state next door to Louisiana, housed in the overcrowded prisons of Texas, which, in the 1980s, was under a federal court order to cut its prison population, a life term was 60 years or less. If you were on your best behavior, you could cut that down to 20 years or less; under the "good time" laws, an inmate could earn three days of time served for every day behind bars.

You had even a better chance of a much lighter sentence if you weren't physically on Death Row the day *Furman* was handed down. If you were sitting in a local jail, usually in the county where the murder occurred, and were either waiting to go to trial or be sentenced, you might get a plea bargain, resulting in the dismissal, reduction, or resentencing of your capital murder conviction.

For many on Death Row, the court's ruling and its timing was a double-edged sword. It was both a victory – being saved from Death Row and a lifetime exemption from a sentence of death, and a defeat – being resentenced to a term much longer than

3

those defendants who committed capital murders in the post-*Furman* period of abolition.

Regardless of its interpretation, for the brief moment in the history of the United States, death took a holiday and the lives of 589 inmates were spared. In the months that followed *Furman*, while politicians were frantically rewriting their state's death penalty laws to withstand the scrutiny of the Supreme Court, several men who had been on Death Row since the late 1950s walked out of prison as free men. These inmates were released either because they had already served their time and their sentences ended or they became eligible for parole.

It is this group who, on a daily basis, undergoes a series of tests: Can they be law-abiding? Can they adapt to life in the Free World? Will they remain free? What makes some fail and others succeed?

Of those 589 former Death Row inmates, I chose to focus only on those 322 who have been released from prison.

This book is about these men and my journey with them – those inmates who "won" America's Death Row "lottery" in the summer of 1972 when Death Rows closed and electric chairs were unplugged and dismantled.

The executioners' vacation was short lived, however. Death Rows reopened in 1976, when the United States Supreme Court approved more stringent death penalty laws that provided "constitutional protections" such as narrowing the list of capital crimes only in cases of murder or murder during the course of another felony, such as rape, robbery, and kidnapping; laws that instituted a separate, post-verdict phase to determine sentencing, and laws that implemented the constitutional right of a defendant to a jury trial.[1]

But even with these constitutional safeguards, the United States is still one of the leaders in executions around the world. In 2004 the U.S. was among the four countries which make up 97 per cent of the total of executions, according to a report from London-based Amnesty International.

China accounted for 3,400 executions in 2004; Iran had at least 159; Vietnam executed at least 64, and, in the U.S., 59 prisoners were put to death.[2] The criminal justice systems in China, Iran, and Vietnam lack the constitutional protection and rights afforded defendants in the United States – trials are conducted in secret, without a jury, with limited or no appellate review, and defendants are sentenced to death for crimes other than murder, such as drug trafficking, embezzlement, and corruption.[3]

Since the death penalty returned in 1977 with the execution of Gary Gilmore by a Utah firing squad, executioners in America have been busy. The United States recently achieved a milestone when it carried out its 1,000th execution on December 2, 2005, of Kenneth Lee Boyd, a Vietnam vet with a history of alcohol abuse, who had no prior criminal record.[4]

For *Back from the Dead*, more than 125 of the approximately 250 of these "lottery winners" who are still alive and out of prison were interviewed; most of the interviews were conducted outside prison walls. Many interviews were conducted in person. I interviewed many more over the telephone and a few were interviewed through a series of letters. And I've kept track of all 589, through correspondence with parole and corrections officials for the past eight years.

This group of 589 former Death Row inmates, many of whom are living and working in communities across the United States, represents the largest unexamined social experiment in U.S. criminal justice history. They have the answer to one of the most troubling and controversial questions in the debate on the death penalty: Can convicted killers be rehabilitated? Will they kill again?

These men were freed not because of innocence or faulty lab work; as far as I know, their convictions were not based on perjured testimony or coerced confessions. These men missed their appointment in the Death House only because, for a brief moment in the history of the United States, the death penalty was abolished.

The search for this group of former Death Row inmates wasn't easy. It would turn out to be both a labor of love and of frustration. This book tells the story of my travels across America in search of these men and how, as a journalist, wife, and mother of two, I confronted and mostly conquered my fears when meeting these killers, one on one, face to face – without the watchful eyes of prison guards. Often times, while armed with only a cell phone, a tape recorder, and a note pad, I met these men behind closed doors, in private, where anything could have happened.

When I began my search, I was surprised how difficult it was to find out who was on America's Death Row the day of the landmark ruling. I spent many months trying to put together a list: reading court opinions and old newspaper articles, and talking to a few of the lawyers of these inmates. Some states kept meticulous records. Many did not.

Once I was able to determine who was on Death Row back then and whether they were still incarcerated or on parole, I worked with (and at times, for) a private investigative agency to find them. Sometimes I called parole officers, the inmate's former lawyer, his relatives, or former cellmates. My task was made more difficult because some of these men had changed their names; others had changed their birthdates.

None of these men had anything to gain by talking to me. In fact, they had, and have, everything to lose by going public. They would now be identified by their past – as former inmates on Death Row. No one was paid for an interview. If they didn't want to talk to me, they didn't have to. But each man I talked to said he felt as though he had a duty to tell his story, especially in light of the increased number of men who have been executed since 1976 when the death penalty was reinstated. These men know how close they were to the Death House. They know how lucky they are. They know second chances at life are rare.

There are some men who didn't want to talk about their experience. Several said they have been able to stay out of prison by looking ahead – to the future, not the past. A few said revisiting Death Row would stir up too many painful memories. I understand why a few just couldn't talk about it.

Except as noted, every former inmate spoke freely and on the record. Many told the truth, but there were a few who lied. Some of the con men of 1972 are the con men of 2006. Only older and a bit wiser.

This book is not about angels because angels don't end up on Death Row. There are many good reasons why these men landed there. And almost everyone in The Class of '72 – with the exception of the seven who have been exonerated by the courts – are most probably guilty of the crimes for which they were accused.

Not everyone has done well. There are those who failed, some miserably, when they got their second chance. Some stumbled on the road of freedom; others came crashing down. Some men are unrepentant and incapable of rehabilitation. Others are just downright evil.

It is an almost impossible task to predict who will succeed and who will fail. Even the so-called "experts" can't do it. But we ask jurors every day in death penalty trials across the United States to make those predictions.

The reasons for success are as varied as the facts of the crimes that sent them to Death Row. But there are some common denominators in the success stories:

- Faith. There was only one book allowed in the cellblock on Death Row that wasn't considered "contraband." The Bible. For those who had grown up with the "good book," Death Row provided a time (and they had plenty of it) to get reacquainted. For those who did not have religion or a religious influence in childhood or during their teenage years, there was plenty of time to explore it on Death Row. Faith is not limited to a belief in God or a higher being, however. In addition to religion, some men had faith in themselves and/or a belief that the U.S. criminal justice system would, eventually, dispense justice. Most all of those who were paroled and have been successful outside of prison have a high self-esteem – a belief so strong in themselves and the justice system that they never envisioned their death in the electric chair.
- Family. Several inmates attribute their success to loyalty and devotion from family. The weekly prison visits from their

mothers, wives, and siblings gave them hope and a reason not to give up. Once released, they moved in with family members who sheltered, fed, and clothed them and provided a basic support system to help insure their success.

- Friendship. But for those men who were either abandoned by their family or chose to distance themselves from their dysfunctional one, they created their family inside. Many men chose to adhere to the old saying: "You can pick your friends but not your family." And so, on Death Row, their friends were their family.

Despite the segregation and isolation of Death Row, deep and long-lasting friendships with other Death Row inmates were created and continued, even after their release. The saying "misery loves company" was especially applicable to the men of Death Row. Even though the crimes which sent them there differed greatly, the men on Death Row shared a common bond – each one had a date with the executioner. When they were eventually transferred to the general prison population and physically separated from each other, the stigma of being under the sentence of death followed them. Wardens, guards, and even fellow inmates all knew where they once lived – many inmates were forced to keep and wear the "Scarlett Letter" of Death Row: the original number that identified them as former residents there.

The former Death Row inmates didn't just limit "family" to blood relatives or even fellow prisoners. Some regarded those wardens, guards, and prison support staff who took an interest in them and their case as members of their "family." Often times they maintained those decades-old friendships with corrections officials, even in the Free World.

- Education. Another common denominator is education. It's not surprising that a majority of those sent to Death Row in the 1960s and 1970s were either elementary or high school dropouts. If they could write or read, the only book allowed in their cells back then was a prison-issued Bible; even the newspaper was considered contraband. It was a waste of money to educate men who would wind up in the electric chair. No one ever thought this group of killers and rapists would leave prison in anything other than a pine box. But when they were eventually released, these former Death Row inmates all had a high school degree and/or a vocational skill to help them make a lawful living on the outside.

Many took college courses while inside, several earned college degrees, and a few more hold Master's degrees. These former Death Row inmates credit their success to prison education programs. Researchers agree. Studies show that the rate of recidivism is reduced significantly when prisoners participate in educational, vocational, or work programs, and participants earn higher wages upon release.

But in the "tough on crime" agenda of the 1990s, politicians decided that providing college courses to prisoners was unfair to their law-abiding constituents. In 1994, Congress eliminated federal financial aid, called Pell grants, to 28,000 prisoners. With funding cut, more than 250 college prison programs closed. By 1997, only eight college prison programs remained.[5]

Friends have asked me why I embarked on this search. And there have been many times, most often when I found myself in a cheap motel room with faulty locks on the door late at night, gearing up for yet another interview in a town or city thousands of miles away from home, when I have asked myself the same question. At times this journey put a strain on finances; the trips and interviews resulted in high anxiety on the home front, sometimes resulting in a bit too stressful marriage. Health wise, I developed high blood pressure (controlled by medication) and insomnia (controlled by something stronger than a glass of warm milk).

But I stayed the course because I believed I would find the answer to an unrelenting question that has kept me focused and, some friends and family say, made me obsessed: Could convicted killers be rehabilitated? Would Walter have killed again? Did these men get a second chance to kill?

I had to find the answer for myself. To do that I had to find them.

I ignored my boss' advice back in 1994, when I kept my eyes open on that hot morning as I stood in the Death House in Texas. And I have tried hard to keep them open since then, in telling the stories about the 587 men and 2 women whose return address in 1972 was Death Row, U.S.A.

CHAPTER ONE

A DATE WITH DEATH

It was 85 degrees that night in Huntsville, Texas. I sat alone in a booth at the McDonald's, off IH-45, drinking coffee and picking at a plate of greasy French fries, staring at the clock on the wall. The clocked ticked too slowly for me, but too quickly for Walter Williams, my 32-year-old client, who also sat alone just a mile away, in his cell on Death Row. We were both waiting for midnight.

Two thousand miles from my home in Connecticut, I felt awkward in this fast-food joint, filled with late-night highway travelers. I took out a yellow pad of paper and wrote "To Do" at the top. The page remained blank during the next hour and a half as I cried silently, bit my fingernails, and quietly asked myself: What was I doing here? There was nothing left for me "To Do." I was killing time before it was time to kill.

I had left Walter in the Death House an hour earlier. Walter had been my only client for nine years. I signed onto the case in 1985 shortly after I graduated from Columbia Journalism School and I was looking for a reporting job. I was back in San Antonio when an old law school friend and the newly appointed appellate attorney for Walter Williams pleaded with me to look at the transcript.

"Please, Joan. You worked for the Court of Criminal Appeals a year ago. You know these guys," Robert Hirschhorn said. "You know what they are looking for. Please. Just a little look?"

When I graduated from law school, I took a job as a briefing attorney for the Texas Court of Criminal Appeals – the first and last stop for death penalty cases in Texas. The TCCA is the equivalent of the state supreme court.

Each of the nine judges on the court have both a briefing attorney and a staff lawyer. A briefing attorney is usually hired by one of the appellate judges for a one-year term and is most often a recent law school graduate. The job involves reviewing motions, appeals, and writs of habeas corpus, spending countless hours in the law library conducting research, and writing memos on the legal issues raised in the appeal. The cases are either assigned to the judge by the presiding judge (or Chief Justice), or the judge is allowed to pick which case he wants to review if his briefing attorney or staff lawyer are successful in the traditional ceremonial roll of the dice which occurs in the court's conference room immediately after oral arguments.

After years as a courthouse newspaper reporter, I gravitated towards criminal trials. During law school, I worked as a part-time law clerk for Roy R. Barrera Jr., a criminal district judge, watching murder trials and writing briefs. The death penalty cases in Judge Barrera's courtroom were mesmerizing. The 28-year-old Republican judge, the youngest jurist in the state when he was appointed in 1980, was media-savvy; he ran on a "law-and-order" ticket. While on the bench, Barrera took every opportunity to "run for office" by giving impromptu press conferences during courtroom breaks to the TV and newspaper reporters that hung out in the courtroom during sensational death penalty trials, like that of Jesse De La Rosa, whom Barrera sentenced to death.

On May 15, 1985, two years after I graduated from law school, Barrera witnessed the execution of 24-year-old De La Rosa, then the youngest man in the nation to be executed and the first Hispanic in Texas to face execution, since the death penalty was reinstated in 1976.[1]

During the one and a half years as his law clerk, I turned into a death penalty junkie. I think Barrera was one, too.

And when Court of Criminal Appeals Presiding Judge John F. Onion offered me a job at the highest criminal court in the state in 1983, I didn't take more than 30 seconds to accept.

But when Hirschhorn asked me to look at Walter's transcript, I didn't take any time in turning him down. I said "No" 10 different times in 10 different ways. My reasons were good: I wasn't practicing law and had no intention to do so. I went back to my first love – working as a newspaper reporter. And I lived 2,000 miles away.

I ended up telling Hirschhorn I'd take a look. Three hours later I signed on as co-counsel in the case of the *State of Texas v. Walter Key Williams*. It was 1985. I thought this would be an easy appeal – a total slam dunk. The trial lawyers failed to introduce any evidence on Walter's behalf, at either the one-day guilt/innocence or the two-hour punishment stage; it was a clear case of ineffective assistance of counsel and his conviction would be reversed within a year. But that one year turned into nine and there was nothing "easy" about Walter's appeal.

During those nine years I represented Walter, I read and re-read the transcript of *State v. Williams* many times. The file was thin, very thin. Walter didn't have much in the way of a prior record. There was some juvenile joy riding; pot smoking, possession of a gun (not unusual in Texas), and one other more serious but understandable incident regarding his father – an assault.

After reading the transcript, I was shocked at the speed of his trial on capital murder charges stemming from a botched robbery of a convenience store and the cold-blooded killing of the store's clerk. His trial attorneys failed to object to damaging evidence – one objection, I found out later, would have been an automatic reversal and grounds for a new trial.

Walter's lawyers testified at one of the three evidentiary hearings that it was their strategy not to put on any witnesses and not to introduce any mitigating evidence that might explain what led up to the events on that murderous night.

The lawyers said that they were worried that if they put Walter's mother on the witness stand, they would risk opening the door – and allow the prosecution to bring in damning evidence about the altercation between Walter and his father. They said that if the jurors heard that story they would think that Walter had a propensity for violence and would be incapable, in the eyes of the jury, of rehabilitation. But had those lawyers questioned Mrs. Williams, Mr. Williams, or even Walter himself about the incident, they would have discovered – weeks before the trial and not years later – that Walter hit his father that night to protect his mother from Lucian's regular beatings, which most often occurred after a night of heavy drinking. Those lawyers never asked any questions about what triggered the assault and Walter never volunteered any information.

I never understood why Walter's lawyers didn't put his mother on the witness stand. I met Melba Williams in February 1986, during an evidentiary hearing; she was small and frail and deeply concerned about Walter, or "Dino" as she called her only child. "Miz Cheevah. I don't have any money to pay you for you and Mr. Hirschhorn's time. Maybe I could get a loan," Mrs. Williams told me in the hallway of the San Antonio courthouse. "They just can't kill him. You won't let them, will you?"

Of course not, I assured Walter's mother, breaking one of the cardinal rules of criminal defense law – never promise something you cannot deliver. I was so sure Walter's death sentence would be changed to a life term for many reasons, but the primary one was because the state of Texas had offered him a sweetheart plea bargain on the eve of his trial – after good time credits, Walter would be out of prison in nine years. And then there were the number of character witnesses that came to Judge Ted Butler's courtroom for the evidentiary hearing who finally got a chance to tell the court what they would have testified to five years earlier at Walter's trial. If they only had been asked.

Our witness list included Sister Mary Boniface O'Neill, a highly respected nun who ran the Catholic high school Walter attended and who is an expert in working with troubled kids. "As far as I could see and in my association with him, he was absolutely nonviolent," Sister Boniface testified. "And that's God as my witness, you know. There are a lot of kids I could not say this for, I can say it for him."

Father Maurice Abadie, the priest who baptized Walter and taught him how to play basketball, had years of experience working with juvenile delinquents, but said that in his opinion,

Walter was "a good kid" and "not violent." Walter's aunt, "Honey," and uncle, "Wax," recently retired as a police officer in Brenham, Texas where Walter spent every summer during his youth, said they were surprised at the charges because their nephew was such a quiet, passive but polite young man. There were countless neighbors, family friends, and cousins who told Judge Butler that they were "shocked" to hear of the capital murder charges.

Hirschhorn and I also had reviewed the testimony of six jurors, who, while they were being questioned during jury voir dire, warned Walter's attorneys that the jurors needed to hear some "background information" about Walter at the punishment phase.

"What if I told you I was going to sit back for a ride on this one, and not present any evidence?" Walter's lawyer asked one juror. The juror answered bluntly: "I think you'd have a losing case."

We had more. Hirschhorn and I introduced evidence from three psychologists who said they would have testified that Walter Williams would not pose a continuing threat to society.[2]

Even the county's own shrink, Dr. John Sparks, Bexar County's chief psychiatrist who is often used by the prosecution in death penalty trials but was not called in Walter's case, said in an affidavit that "it (the death sentence) was not appropriate in this particular case." Dr. Sparks added: "I don't believe he would be a threat to society if he were required to serve a life sentence in prison."[3]

The lack of a prior record was a home run, we thought.

While on Death Row, Walter had converted to Islam and went by the name of "Abdalla Hashim." I told him that I'd met him as "Walter" and that was the name I would always call him. He returned my admonition with a smile. He spent his years on Death Row praying and reading about his religion; reading about the law and thinking about his adolescence and the crime that landed him on Death Row.

During the nine years that we talked, through letters and face to face, I could see that he was a changed man. Every time we talked, Walter expressed deep remorse for his crime. I wanted him to write the victim's family and express that sorrow, but I never told him so. While I knew that a letter to the Liepold family would have been the "right" and honorable thing to do, it was dumb legal advice and a direct violation of another cardinal rule of criminal law that goes after "never ask a witness a question unless you know the answer." The one I was about to break was "never put something in writing that you might regret later." If we were able to get his conviction reversed, a letter from Walter expressing remorse and guilt could be introduced against him at a new trial. I knew Hirschhorn was probably relieved that I lived 2,000 miles away and there was a reason I didn't practice criminal law; I probably would have been disbarred for malpractice for giving advice like that.

Walter wrote often during those nine years. We corresponded on a variety of subjects. Never death.

The last night of Walter's life was the first time we talked about death. We spent two and a half hours talking, praying, laughing, and crying. And asking for forgiveness. He, for killing Daniel Liepold, the 18-year-old convenience store clerk he shot in the head. I for not being a better lawyer – for being unable to get him off Death Row.

During the years when I visited, Walter and I talked about much more than his case. We talked about how we both grew up in the same town – San Antonio – just three miles from each other, but worlds apart. Walter was from the city's poor East Side, a neighborhood rife with gangs, drive-by shootings, and drugs. I grew up on the city's wealthy North Side, where the homes were impeccably maintained and the lawns carefully manicured, thanks to the men and women who came from Walter's neighborhood, and worked in our home and our neighbors' as maids and yardmen.

Walter's father was a janitor. Every Saturday morning as a child, Walter accompanied his father to his job at the Menger Hotel. Every Saturday morning, from 1965 through 1969, my sisters and I and our mother went to the Alamo, next door to the Menger, to attend meetings of the Children of the Republic of Texas (descendants of those who fought and died in the Alamo). And very often after the meeting, as a reward for good behavior –

for having suppressed those giggles during our recitation of the Texas Pledge of Allegiance and for nicely belting out the state song, "Texas, Our Texas" – my mother treated us to a Shirley Temple "cocktail" at the Menger Hotel. Walter was there. And so was I. We must have passed each other in the hallway. We must have looked right at each other.

Several years later Mrs. Williams enrolled Walter, her only child, in the Catholic school in her neighborhood – St. Gerard's. Mrs. Cheever enrolled her four daughters and two sons in St. Peter's, a Catholic school just three blocks away from home, in the upscale North Side.

The two schools were great rivals on the basketball court. My twin sister and I were cheerleaders for the St. Peter's Tigers. At St. Gerard games, Walter sat in the stands, rooting for his team. We must have passed each other at the concession stand or in the hallway of the gymnasium when the Tigers played the Baby Royals of St. Gerard's. We must have looked right at each other.

Like Sally Cheever, Melba Williams sent Walter to St. Gerard's because she wanted him to be under the watchful eyes of the nuns – Sisters from the Order of the Incarnate Word. Unlike the North Side, Mrs. Williams knew the streets of the East Side were deadly. She wouldn't know how deadly until October 5, 1994. Like my mom, Mrs. Williams wanted Walter to learn more than reading, writing, and arithmetic. Both women wanted their children to learn about God and His teachings; about morals and values and the Ten Commandments.

While in law school, I still maintained my junior membership at the San Antonio Country Club, a private and exclusive club, where my sisters, brothers, and I spent many hours in our youth – swimming, sunbathing, playing tennis and golf. I also worked there as a lifeguard and swimming instructor. But in the summers during college, I worked at *The San Antonio Light* newspaper. And from that summer on, I never felt comfortable at the club.

Perhaps it was because as a newspaper reporter – on general assignment, sent to the "cop shop" or the courthouse – I saw real life outside the vine-covered walls of the clubhouse. I wrote about burglaries and robberies and the occasional story about some tourist who was stabbed on the Riverwalk. I sat through the seemingly never-ending Thursday "Citizen" nights at the San Antonio City Council meetings when lines of angry residents would air a myriad of complaints about San Antonio's poor drainage system, or the inadequate transit authority, or the water quality and the hot-button issue of big-name developers versus the destruction of San Antonio's primary water source, the Edwards Aquifer. Those developers were our neighbors. They were club members. Could they really be as sinister as the activists portrayed them to be?

Maybe I was just uneasy because of the blatant discrimination. The SACC was a "whites-only" club and one that generally excluded Jews. I don't remember San Antonio being like any typical "Southern" town back in the 1950s and 1960s. The population was predominantly Hispanic, with only a handful of blacks. I don't ever remember seeing "whites-only" water fountains, restrooms, or lunch counters back then. But we didn't mix once we drove through the club gates. I wasn't comfortable with the country club scene. And neither were my parents. My father grew up on military bases – where men were segregated by the number of stripes on their sleeves or the stars on their hats. A military wife did not initiate a conversation with the wife of a higher-ranking officer; she did not speak until spoken to.

My mother was not a lady who lunched. She didn't play bridge, thought golf was too slow, and picked up a tennis racket occasionally only because it was "a good cardiovascular exercise." She preferred to spend her time with the Girl Scouts or rummage through someone's "trash" working on her "estate" sale business or to spend the lunch hour as a volunteer at St. Peter's where, in an assembly-line fashion, she'd slap a slice of tasteless pizza, which the government supplied free of charge, on the brown plastic cafeteria trays. Mom was paid handsomely for her volunteer lunch work – every Friday she brought home the pizza.

Perhaps we joined the country club because it was the "correct" business decision; it probably "wouldn't look good" if my father, a community leader and prominent banker who both loaned and protected these club members' money, wasn't a member himself. He grew up going to the officers' clubs on several military bases. Weren't all clubs alike?

Like many, this one was steeped in Southern tradition. The men had their own "grill" room: No ladies allowed. There wasn't a reciprocal deal for women. Female golfers were barred from teeing up on weekend mornings and were allowed to play only under the hot afternoon sun, to give those "hard-working" club men the first opportunity to play 18 or 36 holes without being unduly delayed by any female foursomes up ahead.

The dress code was strictly enforced. Men and boys had to wear a coat and tie in the main dining room and women were required to wear dresses or skirts.

And, all the waiters were men. Black men. And, as I recall, they were required to wear white gloves with those crisp, starch-filled uniforms that seemed so uncomfortable, especially in the brutal Texas heat.

One of those white-gloved young men who cleared the tables in that stuffy dining room had been that little boy I had seen on Saturday mornings years ago, working at that downtown hotel dutifully helping his father with the push broom. Over the years, that little boy grew up and now he was a young black man, dressed in that scratchy, starched, white uniform. In 1981, Walter Key Williams was a busboy at the San Antonio Country Club and I was a club member.

The next time Walter and I would meet, officially, would be four years later, in 1985. This time we didn't pass each other in the hallway at the Menger Hotel; he with a broom, I with a soda pop. We didn't pass by each other on the basketball court. This time I didn't glance up from the dining room table at the club while my water glass was being poured and quickly look away. This time we looked directly at each other. We stared through the cold, gray prison bars of Death Row, the unit known as Ellis I. This time, for the first time, we spoke.

I was the lawyer and Walter Williams was my client. And we were both scared.

In our last hours together, we talked a lot about Walter's troubled childhood. I had a list of "what ifs" on my mind.

What if Walter had better lawyers? What if those character witnesses Hirschhorn and I found for his evidentiary hearing had testified at his original sentencing trial?

My list of "what ifs" was endless. What if Walter had never found out, at the difficult age of 14, that he had been adopted? That troubling revelation came as the result of a conversation Walter had with his cousins at a family reunion. Walter learned he was the product of an extra-marital affair. His father's wife, Melba, who was unable to have children, showed up at the hospital two days after Walter was born and took him home.

Both Walter's parents were alcoholics; Melba was a battered wife. Upon learning the news of his unique "adoption," Walter rebelled against his mother. That is when he started drinking, using drugs, and hanging out with gangs.

I often wondered what would have happened had Walter been surrounded by siblings growing up, like I had been with three sisters and two brothers. He might never have felt alone. He might never have joined a gang for companionship.

There were more what ifs. What if his parents had the kind of money mine did? Walter and his parents, like more than 90 percent of defendants charged with capital crimes, were too poor to hire an experienced criminal defense attorney to represent them. At trial he had to rely on underpaid court-appointed lawyers. Until recently, defense attorneys in three Southern states, Alabama, Louisiana, and Mississippi, were paid a flat fee of $1,000 for death penalty cases – which translates into about $5 an hour.[4]

The death penalty punishes the poor. As Justice William O. Douglas wrote in *Furman*: "One searches our chronicles in vain for the execution of any member of the affluent strata in this society."

What if Walter had been white? There are 1,411 black men on Death Row – just over 42 percent of the Death Row population, even though black males represent only seven percent of the population in the U.S.[5]

A report by Amnesty International USA in 2004 found that murderers of whites are about six times more likely to be executed than those murderers of blacks, although about equal numbers of blacks and whites are homicide victims. Nationally, the majority of the 4,220 prisoners executed in the U.S. between 1930 and 1996 were black. [6]

Would a "white" Walter have gotten the death penalty?

But in the hours before he was to be put to death, Walter and I didn't talk about the what ifs. We spent some of the time silently standing side by side, separated by the cold gray steel bars, quiet in our own thoughts.

Walter was a light-skinned black, of slight build, about 5'6". When he first came to Death Row, he sported an Afro haircut. Tonight, his hair was very short, almost like a military cut. He looked the same as he did the day we met. He had hardly aged, yet throughout the years I did notice that his skin had changed color. It was almost as gray as the steel bars that caged him. Over the years, the circles under his eyes grew darker. But then here, on Death Row, sleep must have been almost impossible. His skin was in need of sun. Even in the Texas heat, sunlight is a rare commodity here on Death Row. Residents are entitled to only one hour of fresh air and sunshine a week.

Walter's life stood still during those nine years. But not mine. I had a successful career; I got married and had two children. Unlike Walter, I had aged. Flecks of gray now lightened my once dark-brown hair.

Stress was my partner during those years – financial, marital, and child rearing. I had a long commute into the city each day and what seemed like a longer one at night. Writing and editing deadlines were never-ending. And then I lived with the unrelenting pressure of having a client on Death Row. My life was planned around execution dates. In October 1991, I was home on maternity leave, awaiting the birth of my daughter. And while most soon-to-be mothers used the time to decorate the nursery, shop for baby clothes, or finish writing baby shower thank you notes, I sat hunched in front of my computer for hours on end, with photocopies of recent court opinions scattered on the floor, dashing off yet another endless brief and motion to delay the execution scheduled in three weeks.

Wednesday nights were especially memorable. I always called Hirschhorn at midnight from the lobby of the Columbia University Law School library on Manhattan's Upper West Side. I'd go there at 10 p.m., after putting the business section of the *The National Law Journal* to bed. On Wednesdays, I stayed in New York City at my sister's apartment because of the late deadline at work and the deadline that was always looming over me with Walter's appeal.

After finding the federal court ruling I just knew would reverse Walter's conviction, I'd wake up my co-counsel. His answer was either: "Joan, wrong circuit. We're in the Fifth, not the Eleventh," or "You've got to distinguish that case from the one they've used," or "Have you forgotten what state we're in? The Killing Fields of Texas." He would end the conversation quickly with "It's late. Call me tomorrow. *In the office.*"

We were able to stop four execution dates and I felt as though I could have lived with that stress of having a client on Death Row forever if it meant I could put off tonight – to postpone forever this appointment in the Death House.

As we stood next to each other, Walter and I watched the hustle and bustle of the prison guards. A card table was set up, just a few feet from Walter's cell, laden with homemade cookies, pies, and cakes. There was an urn for coffee and a pitcher of ice-cold fruit punch.

"Party food," Walter whispered to me through the bars of the Death House cell. It was a party – to celebrate the state's victory – and we were not invited. No one offered us any food or drink and neither Walter, the evening's "guest of honor," nor myself dared ask.

That night, countless numbers of people walked through the first set of steel doors that led from the warden's office to the holding cell. We looked up and both glanced at the second set of doors. Those led to the chamber of death where, we both knew, the inevitable would happen in just a few hours.

Walter would walk through those doors shortly before midnight and the execution team would help him get on the gurney. He would then lay down onto the "cross-like" table and extend his arms. The team – four guards who had been specially trained for the task – would pick up the wide white leather belts and strap him down. The leather belts would hold his arms, feet, and upper and lower torso in place. He would be unable to move. A medical technician would then insert a needle into a vein in his left arm. The needle would be attached to a tube and the tube would lead to an opening behind a black partition. Soon, the execution would begin.

I hadn't planned on being here tonight. But when I visited Walter at the Ellis Unit earlier that day, shortly before he was moved to the Death House, I asked him one question that would change my life forever.

In the visiting room at Ellis, I looked right at him through the screen mesh that separated us and asked what family members would be there with him tonight as he faced the executioner. Both his parents were dead. Aunt Honey had died in 1992; his uncle, "Wax," was too ill to travel.

"No one," he said, trembling, his eyes darting around the small cubicle.

"Do you want me to be there?" I asked, not really sure that I wanted to hear his answer.

"Would you? *Could* you? I didn't want to ask you," he said, his eyes fixed on mine.

"I will if you want me to."

"Yes, I do. I'm really scared, Joan. I'd feel a lot better if you were there."

With that, I raced out of the visiting room to call a lawyer friend who had offered to contact the governor's office. I returned for a note from Walter to the warden asking that I be put on the list of witnesses.

The governor's office had no objection; neither did the Office of the Attorney General, my adversary for nine years. The warden's office was not so generous. Both the wardens at Ellis I and the warden at the Walls Unit, where the execution would take place, turned down Walter's request. My personal appeal to the head of the entire prison system, Texas Department of Corrections director Wayne Scott, fell on deaf ears.

"Rules are rules, Miss Cheever," Mr. Scott said. "You were supposed to be on that list 14 days ago. What if I let everyone, at the last minute, show up for an execution? It'd be absolute bedlam. That's why we have rules. And you and Mr. Williams didn't comply."

"Yes, I know that. But Walter did not know I would be here. And no one from his family will be there for him tonight. You can't let him die alone, sir. Please."

I had tried to adhere to the 14-day rule. In early September, I had written Walter a letter about our last appeal to the U.S. Supreme Court, but I received no reply. A week before his execution, I made three telephone calls to him on Death Row, but they went unanswered. Walter told me he hadn't received those telephone messages until the day before his execution. He also thought we'd deserted him because Hirschhorn and I sent Walter's file and our nine years of work to an out-of-state death penalty resource center for an independent evaluation as to whether we had been ineffective in our representation.

In a letter to Walter, Hirschhorn wrote: "Joan and I are not abandoning you but we feel that another pair of eyes are needed," to see if we had committed malpractice.

The lack of communication and hurt feelings were the reasons I wasn't on Walter's witness list.

But TDC Director Scott responded to my pleas with a barrage of what, I thought, were terribly inappropriate questions. "What do you do for a living if you don't practice law? Where is Mr. Hirschhorn, your co-counsel? And why isn't he here? You're from New York City? How do I even know you are a real lawyer?"

His purpose was clear – to get me to surrender. But our 25-minute conversation succeeded only to provoke a silent rage. I was determined that Walter would have one final victory at the end of a 13-year-ordeal marked by five execution dates but only four successful stays.

Before I called Director Scott, I placed a call to a federal judge in Huntsville and let him know that I might have to knock on his door late tonight with a temporary restraining order in hand, asking to be allowed to witness an execution. I asked if there might not be some way to resolve the issue without litigation.

"I don't know Mr. Scott," the judge said, never hinting at how he might rule. "I don't know what to tell you, but I'll be here at home tonight if you decide this is what you want to do."

I hung up and took a deep breath and called Mr. Scott. I let him know that I was prepared to delay "his perfectly scheduled execution" – by filing a temporary restraining order with the judge with whom I just spoke.

Scott was livid. "Wait a minute, Miss Cheever. Are you threatening to sue me? You are *threatening* me?"

"Oh, no, sir. I am *informing* you that I will sue you tonight at 10 p.m. so that my client doesn't have to die alone."

There was silence on the other line. I knew then that I'd probably pushed too far. But there was no going back.

Finally, he spoke. "Well, I've decided to give you 90 minutes with your client tonight. I never do that for anyone. Real lawyers compromise, Miss Cheever, and if I were you, I'd take the 90 minutes," he said. "I suggest you get over to the prison right now. Your time is running."

The 90 minutes turned into two and a half hours, simply because no one tapped me on the shoulder and asked me to leave. We spent those hours talking like old friends. We laughed, we cried, and at times we just fell silent. Occasionally, we both looked at the door that stood only 10 feet away – the one to the Death House.

And then we talked about a subject that was never taught in law school. Earlier that day in Houston, before my one-hour trek to Death Row, I made a last-minute telephone call to Sister Helen Prejean, the spiritual adviser to inmates on Death Row in Louisiana. She was not at home and her answering machine recorded my frantic plea for help.

"Hi, Sister Helen. My name is Joan Cheever and I have a client on Death Row in Texas. And he's going to be executed tonight.

And I don't have a clue as to what to say to him. And I was hoping you could help me out. Or give me some advice. I'll be at this number for the next couple of hours."

I knew what to say. At the airport, I walked into the bookstore there looking for a trashy, "beach" read. Instead, a book with cherubic angels on its gold cover jumped out: Sophy Burnham's *Book of Angels*.[7]

Tonight I was prepared to talk to Walter about life, death, and the afterlife. I told him I didn't understand why, but that I knew it had to be part of God's plan. If he asked for forgiveness, he would be forgiven.

We both began to cry. I reached into the cell and held his hands. And then we both prayed. I hoped that I would find the strength to get through tonight.

That afternoon, as I tried to prepare myself for the impending execution, I remembered feeling how this execution could have been avoided – if someone had just knocked some sense into the then-cocky 19-year-old who was strung out on drugs and alcohol and convinced him to take a plea bargain.

Even the prosecutors didn't think the evidence justified a death sentence in this case. That's why they were pushing so hard for Walter to take the plea. Despite the fact that he confessed to the murder on three separate occasions, and all three confessions were going to be admitted at his trial, the just turned 19-year-old heard what he wanted to hear. His lawyer told Walter he could "beat it." So, why not go for it?

It was a suicidal move. Walter didn't take the plea and now they were going to take his life.

If Walter had played the system, he would have been outside of prison, on parole, and free – probably eating dinner with friends at a fast-food restaurant like McDonald's, but far away from Texas' Death Row. Instead, his last meal ordered by the warden, a double cheeseburger with fries, sat untouched on the aluminum tray outside his cell at the Death House while prison officials were in the next room preparing the vials of poison that would kill him.

My time was up. As I left the Death House, the warden at the Walls Unit stopped me to say that Mr. Scott had reconsidered. I would be allowed in.

I asked him if Walter had been told. He said he was on his way to break the news, but that I needed to sign some papers in his office. I didn't feel triumphant. Now I was scared silly. I knew that this was real. Walter's execution was proceeding exactly on schedule.

As we walked back to his office, the warden told me the rules: be back and standing outside the Walls Unit, also known as the Death House, at 11:45 p.m., carrying nothing but a driver's license and my Texas Bar card.

He kept talking as we walked into his office. Nervous chatter. I don't even remember much of what he said. I was struck by the table in his office that was crammed with pastries, cookies, coffee thermoses, and a bowl filled with punch. He then asked me to fill out some paperwork in order to take custody of Walter's personal belongings once the execution was over. I tried to concentrate on the task at hand – reading over what I was about to sign, when I was interrupted. In a patronizing tone, this middle-aged corrections official told me that he'd never, ever allow his wife or daughter to witness an execution, a not so subtle insinuation that I was either fatherless or husbandless, or that both men had beans for brains.

Quietly seething, I politely thanked him for his "concern," emphasizing the word "concern,' and told him I'd be back at the appointed hour. Shortly before midnight, I returned to his office. This time I was in the front of the line, leading a group of my colleagues, journalists who had the misfortune of getting this grim assignment. Only this time, I didn't have a reporter's notebook in my hand. I was carrying my identification, stuffed in a packet of Kleenex.

My thoughts turned to a conversation I had with my mother on the pay phone outside McDonald's, only an hour earlier.

In the first 30 seconds of the call, Mom proceeded to tell me that she knew tonight was "the night" because she had heard the news about Walter's execution broadcast all day long on her "Number One" radio station – the same one that hosts two of her favorite conservative radio personalities, Paul Harvey and Rush Limbaugh. After the first broadcast, my mother decided to go to two Masses that day, instead of her usual one, the 8 a.m. at St. Peter's. She wanted to pray for Walter. And for me.

She kept talking and talking. I still hadn't gotten a word in edgewise. She asked about the health of my two-year-old daughter and my newborn son. A week earlier in Connecticut, I had rushed my daughter to the emergency room in the middle of the night because she had difficulty breathing – an undiagnosed case of asthma. I was scared but I felt safe. After all, I was in a hospital, surrounded by medical professionals whose job it was to help my daughter breathe. Never did I anticipate that in a few short minutes, I would, once again, be watching someone else's child struggle to breathe. He, too, would be surrounded by medical professionals. But their job was different. They were not paid to heal, but to kill. Soon, Walter's struggle for air would be over, forever, within minutes.

"The kids are fine, Mom. I haven't seen them in a couple of days though. They're at home. I'm down here."

"What do you mean, *here*? Where in the Sam Hill are you at this hour, for Lordy's sake?" she barked into the phone.

"Where else? Huntsville. Don't give me a lecture. Please. He asked me to be here. He doesn't want to die alone," I whispered into the pay phone, as travelers passed me, carrying bags stuffed with quarter-pounders and fries. Again, I started to cry.

"Oh, good God. I really wish you weren't there. Damnit to hell. Okay. I'll just stay up and say some more rosaries for the both of you. Listen, sister," she said, emphasizing the sister, "just get home." And then she hung up.

For nine years, across the dining room table, when the dinner conversation turned to the issue of crime in America, invariably the "great death penalty debate" began. Despite her deep and devout religious conviction, this mother of six, who grew up on a ranch in West Texas and proudly displays on her refrigerator door a photo of herself with President George Bush Sr., is a staunch supporter of capital punishment.

And like most Texans, Sally Cheever is a talker. And a good debater. During our arguments, Mom would always quote the Bible – the Old Testament.

Like many Catholics my age, I didn't grow up reading the Bible. We had the Baltimore Catechism and that was it. But I'd memorized the Ten Commandments and reminded her of Number Five – "Thou Shalt Not Kill." I also pointed out that she was quoting the Old Testament, not the New, and that she needed to "get with the Pope's program" of abolition.

But before the discussion ever escalated into a war of words my father, the negotiator and peacemaker, surfaced. He'd jump up at the dinner table or run into the kitchen when he heard the abolitionist battle cry: "But, Mom. Killing is wrong. All kinds of killing are just plain wrong."

My military-trained father issued an order – an immediate cease and desist in the discussion; a white-flag surrender from both sides. There was not going to be a free-spirited debate because he knew we were both passionate on the issue of the death penalty and we would never agree. And on that warm October night in 1994 we were still on opposing sides, but that night we kept our thoughts to ourselves.

When I replayed our conversation earlier that evening, I also thought about another mother, Lea Liepold, whose son's life had been ended so abruptly and brutally by the man I had represented, counseled, and befriended for the past nine years.

Her son had two days left before leaving his job at the convenience store where he worked as a clerk on the late shift. When Walter and Ted Edwards walked into the Circle K that night and demanded money, Daniel Liepold complied. Walter and Ted killed Daniel before he ever had a chance to open the cash register.

Daniel knew Walter as a friend; he had installed a radio in Walter's car a few months earlier and had sent him a birthday card a few weeks before.

It didn't make any sense.

I've often wondered if Mrs. Liepold was awake that night, waiting for the midnight hour when her son's killer would himself be killed. For her, it had been a 13-year appellate nightmare. I wondered during those years if Mrs. Liepold had ever circled her calendar – marking the five times the state of Texas had scheduled the killer's death – and how she felt when four of those executions were postponed. I had many questions for Mrs. Liepold.

During most of those nine years with Walter, I had been only a journalist and a lawyer. Tonight I had another role, one that was relatively new. I was a mother. And as a mother, for the first time I realized that the large hole in Mrs. Liepold's heart would never, ever heal regardless of what happened in the room where Walter would be strapped down on the gurney. I knew Lea Liepold would carry that searing pain with her for the rest of her life. A day would not go by when she wouldn't think about Daniel, her child, who was brutally murdered by the hands of the man I had been holding tonight as we both prayed to God – he for forgiveness and I for not being able to legally postpone this evening, forever.

My heart was heavy as I left Walter in the cell, next door to the death chamber. I was escorted out by a female guard, about my age. As the guard and I – both mothers, one black, the other white – sat on the bench outside the office waiting to meet with the warden, she asked me about Walter's childhood and his family. She wanted to know where his mother was. I told her that Melba died several years ago.

She told me she'd be with Walter tonight, standing guard, while he waited for midnight. She was a member of the execution team. She had a job to do, one that she admitted was painful. She said that she'd try to make it as easy as she could for him.

I saw that guard again, shortly before I walked back into the Death House. That same guard was now assigned to me – for a search. She led me to a small bathroom in the waiting area for a pat-down. She did not speak but her eyes did. This was painful for both of us.

She then introduced me to David, a burly assistant warden who looked like he'd been a linebacker 20 years ago for the Huntsville Hornets, the local high school football team. I was David's charge. He read the list of instructions. He told me what I would see. He forgot to tell me how I would feel.

It won't be bad, he said. It looks like a hospital. Pea-green walls. Very antiseptic-looking.

I had about 30 seconds to talk to Walter and say goodbye, David said. There would be a microphone hanging above my head and one dangling above the gurney where Walter would be lying. And then the press would come in followed by the visiting dignitaries – lawyers from offices of the Governor and Attorney General. Walter would make his last statement. And then "the procedure," David said.

You mean "poison?" I interrupted.

"Look, little lady. If you're feeling faint, just fall back and I'll catch ya," David said. "Or hold onto that rail in front of the window. It'll be over soon."

But not soon enough. As I walked through the long corridor, past the holding cell where I'd spent the last hours with Walter, through two steel doors and then outside, I looked down to see a ceramic pot filled with white chrysanthemums. It looked like it was planted just for the festivities.

Another assistant warden joined me in my somber walk to the Death House. "Whereabouts are ya from?"

I didn't know if he meant where I lived, where I worked, or where I was born. Native Texans usually call Texas home even if we haven't lived in the Lone Star State for 20 years. Tonight I hated everything about my home state.

So my reply was quick. "New York City."

"Oh, heck. We just had a New Yorker here last month. Fella named Ron Kuby. Snappy dresser, that guy."

I know that Ron Kuby, a criminal defense attorney who practiced law with the legendary civil rights lawyer William Kunstler, wouldn't want to be known for the Armani suit he may have worn on August 2, 1994, the night he witnessed the execution of his client, Robert Drew.

I looked down at my own outfit. A wrinkled sleeveless white linen shirt and black skirt, both sale items from Ann Taylor. I wondered what they'd say about me next month.

When I walked into the Death House, I was struck by the starkness of the room. There was the gurney and there was Walter, already lying on top of it, bound by those six thick white leather straps. We were separated by only five feet. His head immediately turned to the glass window. He seemed to have been waiting for me. I looked up and the microphone, as promised, was directly above. It seemed to be dangling in mid-air. It was time to say goodbye.

"God bless and Godspeed, Walter. You're almost home," I said, choking back the tears.

"Thank you, Joan."

And then the warden asked if Walter had any last words. Dressed in blue pants, a short-sleeved prison shirt, wearing a prayer cap and the new hi-top basketball shoes he had recently purchased at the prison commissary, Walter looked up at the microphone and said he was grateful that he had converted to Islam. And then he asked the family of Daniel Liepold for forgiveness. He closed his eyes and a tear rolled down his right cheek.

There was nothing I could do to stop the machinery of death. I asked God to forgive the executioner and the State of Texas. I prayed that Walter's angels would take him and take him quickly. The room was silent. The only sound was that of the scratching of pens of my fellow journalists as they scribbled in their notebooks.

In the reflection in the glass that separated Walter and me, I watched myself watch the murder. It was eerie. The scene was surreal. I felt as though I was an actor in a bad B-movie.

I was filled with hope that he would go quickly and this nightmare would end.

Silently, I was seething. I saw the murder unfold before my eyes and I felt angry at my own helplessness. I stood on the front row and steadied myself by hanging onto the metal railing in front. As

I watched, I wanted to scream, to slam my hands on the Plexiglas that separated us. To do anything I could to stop what was happening. But I knew that I couldn't. Instead, I just kept my eyes on Walter, never imagining that those few minutes would burn in my memory for a lifetime. At that moment, I knew that I would never be the same.

I watched as Walter, struggling to breathe, took one last gasp of air. Then his eyes opened. At 12:21 a.m., six minutes after the poison began to flow, Walter was dead.

David, my escort, put his hand on the small of my back and gently pushed me to the exit. But I wouldn't move. I turned around and held onto the rail with one hand and pointed my finger at David with the other. "I want his eyes closed. Make sure they close his eyes. Get Chaplain Pickett to do it. But please do it. Please close them."

David assured me it would be "taken care of."

I wanted Walter to be remembered by his few relatives and friends, who would bury him in two days, as dying peacefully in his sleep. It was certainly less bloody than the murder of Daniel Liepold, who was shot in the back of the head and died instantly. But Walter's death was painful, both physically and mentally. As the poison ran through his veins, I watched him suffocate; I saw as he tried, desperately, to hold onto one last breath. And then it was over. He just stopped breathing. The mental pain must have been almost unbearable for Walter as he sat on Death Row for 13 years, with five execution dates, waiting to die.

Nine minutes after I walked out of the Death House on that warm still morning, the belongings Walter had accumulated during his years on Death Row were out on the sidewalk, packed in orange nylon-mesh duffel bags. The guards, who just a few minutes earlier stood behind me, carefully watching my movements, helped lift the six heavy bags of Walter's books, letters, and photographs into my rental car. His body was sent to a funeral home in nearby Brenham for burial in a family plot.

It was 1:45 a.m. by the time I got back to Houston. Two attorneys from the Texas Resource Center drove me to my "hotel" – not the small room at the La Quinta motel where I'd spent two previous, sleepless nights, but at the home of Virginia and Lee, a childhood friend. Another lawyer drove my car back to his office.

I left my luggage and Walter's bags in my trunk with some hesitation. I had hoped it wouldn't be vandalized. But I didn't think it was proper etiquette, especially at 2 a.m., to lug Walter's personal belongings, stuffed in those six Day-Glo orange bags clearly stamped: "Texas Department of Corrections," into the posh River Oaks home where I was staying. My host had two small children, the same age as mine.

River Oaks is a neighborhood filled with wealthy businessmen – oil tycoons, investment bankers, doctors, and lawyers – whose wives, usually "stay at home" moms, fill their day with volunteer work. The prices for homes here in this rich, upscale neighborhood start in the high six digits, and property taxes are hefty. The residents of River Oaks pay plenty for extra police protection.

When the sun rose, my friend, Lee, headed downtown to make some more investment deals; I drove an hour to visit "Reverend Sarah," a United Methodist Church minister and Walter's spiritual adviser, to drop off his personal belongings. On the way back from her house, I stopped at a pay phone outside a convenience store and ordered flowers for Walter's casket. The funeral was scheduled for the next afternoon. My flight was leaving tonight. And my five-year wedding anniversary was tomorrow.

I was on my way home and Walter was, too. His remains were in a body bag. By now he would have arrived at the funeral home in Brenham, the small East Texas town famous for its "Blue Bell" ice cream, where Walter spent his summers.

On October 5, 1994, Walter Williams, aged 32, was the 11th inmate that year to be put to death in Texas – a state that executes about one man a month. In the next two and a half months, there would be three more executions in Texas. And the numbers have increased dramatically.

Nationally, Walter was the 82nd to be put to death since 1982, when the Lone Star state resumed executions. Since 1976, when states began executing inmates once again, there have been more than 1,000 executions in the United States; 359 from Texas alone.[8]

I've often wondered, during those nine years as Walter's lawyer and friend, what he would do when he was let out. If he was given a second chance at life, how would he spend it?

I asked him that question the night he died. He told me that if he had been paroled, he would've liked to work with inner-city kids like himself. He would've warned them of the dangers of the street and tried to help them stay off of drugs, away from alcohol and to steer clear of gangs.

Of course, Walter never had that second chance.

But there were 587 men and 2 women who did when the U.S. Supreme Court abolished the death penalty in 1972, changing all death sentences to life terms. If I found this group of former Death Row inmates, I knew they would be able to answer the question that has haunted me: What do convicted killers do with their second chance at life? Do they kill again?

In the early morning hours on October 5, 1994, my search began.

CHAPTER TWO

A "VISIT" FROM WALTER

Of the 322 who have been released from prison, at least 85 men have died in the Free World.

Those who have never been released from prison will most probably die there. To date, approximately 94 men in this group have died while incarcerated. One of those was Richard Speck, convicted of brutally murdering eight nurses in Chicago in 1966. The 48-year-old Speck died of a heart attack in 1991.

Some inmates kill themselves rather than endure a life term. There have been 10 reported prison suicides.

In the hours before his execution, I asked Walter for permission to write about him, his life, and the death penalty. I had so many questions about why people kill and if it was possible for killers to be rehabilitated. His reply: "That's fine, Joan. Just make sure you get it right."

Nine months later, I have the opportunity to see if Walter will come "back from the dead."

Bill Falk, a reporter for *Newsday*, is working on a profile of John Edward, a young, and then relatively unknown, psychic based in Huntington, Long Island. Falk and his editors at *Newsday* wanted to see if Edward is the real thing. I want to see if Walter has a message for me.

Falk has been following Edward for the past six months – watching him at work, interviewing clients, trying to figure out if he is the real thing or a real phony. The Pulitzer Prize-winning reporter has observed Edward in readings and even undergone one himself. Falk is impressed; he says Edward hit the mark.

Falk's editors are intrigued and convinced...almost. They want the psychic to be tested – on *Newsday*'s own terms. Edward tells the newspaper to go ahead and send anyone.

And that's why I'm here tonight.

Newsday wants someone who had "a death experience that was so unusual" it would be hard to figure out. After a series of calls through the journalism grapevine and without the knowledge of Edward, Falk calls me, convinced that my presence will make or break the story. And eventually John Edward.

I've never met Bill Falk. And I have never heard of Edward.

I agree, reluctantly, and am filled both with dread and curiosity about what might happen. I know that any secrets I have will be exposed. This entire reading will be "on the record." For 19 years, I had been in the comfortable position of being the interviewer. Now the tables are turned and I am the subject. I have no control over either what John Edward will say or what Bill Falk will write.

I don't say much during the 45-minute drive to Long Island, a large suburban area to the east of New York City; unbeknownst to Falk, I am in a heated discussion with my head and my heart. My head tells me to order Falk to turn the car around. My heart is more gentle. Keep going.

I do believe in life after death and in spirits and that it's possible for them to send messages through others. There is a good possibility that this trip will only increase my pain. I have spent two years trying to forget that horrible October morning in Texas.

We drive to Edward's house, on a cul-de-sac in a neighborhood full of ranch houses, and a 27-year-old guy in blue jeans and an old T-shirt greets us. A basketball game on TV is blaring in the background. We shake hands and we follow him into his office. He knows me only as Joan. No last names. And I make sure to keep my mouth shut and not to look at him during the reading. I decide I will only give him "Yes" or "No" answers because I don't want to let him coax information out of me. He is the one being tested tonight.

Immediately Edward tells me I am from the Southwest, although I don't have much of an accent. I figure it's a lucky guess. Then he says he is seeing the symbol for twins. For a few seconds, I stop breathing. I keep my head down and shake my head. "Yes. I'm a twin."

Then in a rapid-fire delivery, it all comes out. I ask him to slow down but John Edward is excited. He says it seems that whoever wants to talk to *me* won't stop talking to *him*.

"Is there someone around you who had a sudden passing? I'm getting a very sudden feeling. Is there someone whose actions led to their passing? It wasn't a suicide, but their actions brought about their own passing."

I dig my fingernail into my thumb so hard that it hurts. It gives me a moment to focus on the physical pain and not the mental one I am about to endure. I don't want Edward to see that he is getting close. Bill Falk and I are going to make him work. I don't respond to Edward's question but then again, he doesn't give me a chance to.

The person who is trying to talk to me is impatient. He wants to give me more clues. To make sure I know who is really coming through.

This person was "stabbed or impaled," Edward says. I guess an executioner's needle would do that, I think as I continue to keep my head down. I start taking slow, deep breaths. Then Edward gets excited. I sense that he is jumping out of his chair because I hear it squeak and I hear it knock into the large blonde oak desk that separates us. I refuse to look up.

"He's showing me headlines. Yes, that's it. It's headlines. His death and whatever he did to cause it is showing up in the newspaper. It's big. Big. That's it. It's headlines. That's what he's showing me."

I nod slightly because I have been warned that Edward won't stop repeating what he's seeing until you give him a signal. Walter's crime and his death did make headlines. In fact, shortly after his execution, members of the Texas legislature introduced a bill to sharply curtail the appeals of Death Row prisoners because they said justice delayed meant that justice had been denied for the 13 years Walter had been on Death Row.

Then Edward says there are two people with the spirit on "the other side" and these two are at a higher level than the spirit, indicating, in "psychic speak," either "a parent or grandparent."

He gives me initials only. One is an "M"; the other an "L." He continues: "They are with him. They are his parents. M and L, Joan. That's it. M and L. Do you know who these people are?"

I nod but do not talk. I am too busy digging my nail back into my thumb again. Walter's father's name was Lucian. His mother's, Melba.

"Did you do any work for this person, did you have a connection with work for him or with him?" Edward asks.

I don't answer. I don't know how to.

"I get the feeling that you worked together on a project, on a team. Not like you worked for the same company."

Again, I nod. Nine years of appellate work was *some* project.

Then the psychic says the spirit is acknowledging someone named "Bob" who has done television work. The spirit wants to "thank him for working for him, too."

That's when I start to have trouble breathing. I am thankful my jacket is covering my arms. Goose pimples are popping up like crazy. My co-counsel's name is Robert, but his friends call him Bob or Bobby. He's frequently on television, on *Larry King Live* or *Geraldo Rivera* or Court TV, as a legal commentator. He and his wife, Cathy Bennett (who died of cancer in 1992), are professional jury consultants. They picked the jury in the highly publicized William Kennedy Smith rape case in Palm Beach and the drug trafficking trial against automobile magnate John DeLorean. Both cases resulted in acquittals. Robert had been interviewed by Johnnie Cochran as a potential jury consultant in the O.J. Simpson trial.

"Who's the 'H'?" Edward asks. "It sounds like Hirsh. Hirshstein. Hirshfeld. Hirsch-something." Suddenly, I lift my head up. I feel as though I have been punched in the stomach. I stare at Edward. Breathless.

He returns my look with a wide, toothy grin. He knows he's just hit the mark.

I try to compose myself. I want to look cool but it is too late. It's a John Edward "gotcha."

Then I speak, trying to maintain a poker face but failing miserably. I start to smile and then stop myself before saying: "Yeah, sounds like. Close."

Robert's last name is Hirschhorn. I turn and look at Bill Falk, who is scribbling in his notepad. He stops momentarily, and catches my eye. I then motion for Falk to look down at my hands, which have been hidden from Edward. During the drive to Long Island, Falk and I had talked about how I would communicate.

A "thumbs up" would indicate that Edward was right. But he spoke so fast during the session, that I didn't have time for hand signals. That's until he said "Hirsh." This time, my hands didn't dig into my thumb. My right hand was busy giving Falk a very clear "thumbs up." [1]

Throughout the entire reading and during the few times I look up, I get the sense that Edward is talking to someone else. He isn't looking at me, but past me. Sometimes to the right, sometimes to the left. But never to me. He has a weird look, a dreamy glaze in his eyes. Edward is distracted and he won't stop talking. It seems that he is carrying on a conversation with a roomful of people even though it is just Bill Falk and me. [2]

The next thing Edward says makes me look up. Again. It is the way he says it. Edward has a message. This time he looks right at me. He wants to make sure I get it. "Are you writing something about him [the spirit]?" he asks, but it sounds more like "You are writing about him."

"Yes," I answer, and return his stare.

"Well, the spirit says okay. Just make sure you get it right."

That's when I stop breathing. That's when I know that Walter has delivered his message.

Edward repeats the same thing that Walter had told me shortly before his execution. I'd never told anyone about the details of that conversation. I'd never even repeated the "just make sure you get it right" conversation to my husband.

That's when I know I don't really have a choice.

It was time to find these former Death Row inmates.

CHAPTER THREE

WINNERS OF AMERICA'S 1972 DEATH ROW LOTTERY

Currently, there are 3,318 men and 55 women on Death Row – 1,411 black, 1,531 white, 353 Hispanic, and 78 "other" minorities.[1]

When the Furman ruling was handed down on June 29, 1972, the Death Row population stood at two women and 587 men – 323 black, 256 white, 9 Hispanic, and a Native American.[2]

Of the 589 former Death Row inmates whose death sentences were commuted to life, 224 men and 2 women are currently incarcerated: 123 blacks, 96 whites, and 7 Hispanics. Of those 226 now in prison, 62 are recidivists.

Of the original group of 589 inmates on Death Row, 164 (including the women) have never been released.

Those 164 who are still in prison will probably never be paroled because either the nature of the crimes which landed them there was too gruesome or notorious, or their behavior while incarcerated has made them ineligible. Or, in some states, a life sentence meant life in prison without parole.

On the evening of January 16, 1972, Mel Bruder, 29, tried to relax by watching the highlights of the Super Bowl, in which Roger Staubach and the Dallas Cowboys crushed the Miami Dolphins 24 to 3. But, most likely, Bruder's mind was elsewhere. The next morning the 1966 graduate of the University of Texas

Law School was to meet the NAACP Legal Defense Team – Anthony Amsterdam, Jack Greenberg, and Jack Himmelstein, and justices on the U.S. Supreme Court – to argue the Texas appeal in the case of *Furman v. Georgia.*[3]

The central issue in *Furman* and the three other cases argued with it concerned the constitutionality of the death penalty. Since 1967, no one in the United States had been executed because of a national moratorium on executions. The suspension would either be lifted or kept in place; whatever the Supreme Court decided would ultimately affect the lives of hundreds of men and women who sat on Death Rows across the United States.

On January 17, 1972, Bruder, the lawyer for convicted Texas rapist Elmer Branch, trudged through the early morning snow on his way to the courthouse. Inside the courtroom, the air was thick with tension, writes Michael Meltsner in his book, *Cruel and Unusual: The Supreme Court and Capital Punishment.* He described Anthony Amsterdam as the "tall, wiry, coffee-guzzling law professor" sitting at the counsel table lost in thought waiting for the justices to enter the courtroom. Next to him sat Jack Himmelstein, flipping through a file. And nearby was Jack Greenberg, a veteran of many legal battles including the landmark ruling in *Brown v. Board of Education,* the 1954 Supreme Court decision that ended legally sanctioned segregation in public schools. Greenberg was chatting with a newspaper reporter and Bobby Hill, the 27-year-old lawyer from Savannah who had represented convicted rapist Lucious Jackson.[4]

Hill, a Georgia state legislator and former associate at the prominent Washington, D.C. firm of Covington & Burling, would not be speaking before the high court. Instead, Greenberg, a man who had been mentored by Legal Defense Fund founder Thurgood Marshall until Marshall was appointed to the federal bench and then to the Supreme Court as its first black justice, would take the podium on behalf of Lucious Jackson.

Founded in 1940, the LDF, which was associated with the NAACP until the two groups separated in 1957, was known as Justice Marshall's "old law firm." This small group of New York-based lawyers had a reputation as the national leaders in the abolition movement, responsible for keeping the national ban on executions in place.

In the area of death penalty litigation, the NAACP was involved in the infamous case of "The Scottsboro Boys," a group of eight black teenagers who had been sentenced to death for rape; the ninth boy was 13 years old. The teenagers were rushed to trial in 1931 and to Alabama's Death Row, convicted of raping two white women. The NAACP joined several other organizations, including the International Labor Defense, the legal arm of the Communist Party, in creating the Scottsboro Defense Committee.

After Scottsboro, the NAACP and the Legal Defense Fund began to focus on death penalty cases in which there was evidence of racial bias, such as in the cases of black men being sentenced to death for raping white women.[5]

After the execution of Hispanic Luis Monge in Colorado in 1967,[6] Anthony Amsterdam said the LDF changed its "black-only" representation strategy and decided to intervene in all cases in which executions were imminent – regardless of the race of the defendant, the crime for which he was sentenced to death, or the state where he was housed on Death Row.

On that snowy day in Washington, D.C., the future of the entire Death Row population lay in the hands of the LDF's lawyers. One misstep by them – one misspoken word, one unplanned concession, one deviation from LDF's carefully crafted "script" – could result in a bloodbath. The Supreme Court might find reasons not to invalidate the death penalty and executions would resume.[7]

Amsterdam was the first to speak on behalf of California's Earnest J. Aikens Jr., convicted in two brutal murder-rapes. He told the court that executions are cruel and unusual because death sentences are not administered fairly but only to society's "outcast creatures." He said that because the death penalty had been assessed less and less frequently, the punishment had become "unusual" and that it had been repudiated and condemned by the conscience of the country. Amsterdam also argued that day on behalf of convicted murderer William Henry Furman; the facts in Furman's case differed greatly from those in Aikens. Furman accidentally shot the homeowner after he tripped over the cord to a washing machine.

The argument in the rape cases were next, and the LDF's Greenberg, appearing for Lucious Jackson, had to give a great deal of care in both his choice of words and in his line of defense. He had to convince the Supreme Court that the death penalty was not appropriate in cases in which no one died, such as in cases of rape. But Greenberg also didn't want to suggest that it was appropriate in cases of murder such as in the kinds of cases his colleague Amsterdam was defending. It was a slippery slope.[8]

When the arguments ended four hours later, it would be at least another six months – well into summer – before the court handed down its decision.

————

In the summer of '72, I had the perfect job for a teenage girl: getting paid to sunbathe while talking to my girlfriends and, at the same time, keeping a sharp eye on the diving area at the pool at the San Antonio Country Club. My twin sister Jean and I got jobs as lifeguards and our girlfriends kept us company by pulling up lounge chairs close to the lifeguard stands so we could gossip and work at the same time.

During our break, we joined them for a mid-afternoon lunch in the snack bar and ended up charging it to their parents' account. When our friends said they felt sorry for us because Jean and I "had to work for a living," we laughed.

Were they kidding? It was a great job – getting paid to sunbathe. The summer of '72 was a perfect one, except for the annoying Watergate hearings on TV that pre-empted our favorite soap opera, *All My Children*. Watching Maureen "Mo" and John Dean at the hearings just wasn't the same as seeing who else Erica Kane could bed down at the Pine Valley Inn. The blonde Mrs. Dean was pretty but she was no Erica. And all the

Deans did, on camera, was to hold hands. They were totally boring.

We were pretty much oblivious to what was going on in the world that summer. I was busy working on my tan and keeping a close watch on the good-looking high school golf team. From the lifeguard stand, I had a perfect view of the first tee.

While I was spying on the golfers, a dedicated group of men and women were anxiously waiting to find out what the Supreme Court was going to do in three death penalty cases known collectively as *Furman v. Georgia*.

The *Furman* decision, when it was finally handed down, was long; with five different opinions as to the reasons why the death penalty was unconstitutional. It was difficult to comprehend, but it was the law.[9]

I had heard about the Furman case during my first year in law school; I was always curious as to what happened to the key players in that historic ruling. When I worked for the Texas Court of Criminal Appeals in 1983 as a law clerk, the other clerks and I always talked about *Furman* and the group of inmates who were freed because of the ruling; we referred to the group as the winners of the "Death Row lottery." The death penalty returned to the U.S. four years later in the case of *Gregg v. Georgia*.

And in 1990, five years after I took on Walter's appeal, I was on vacation – driving through Savannah, Georgia on my way to a friend's wedding. But when you have a client on Death Row, you're never really ever on vacation. I felt that since I was passing through Savannah, the birthplace of the case that abolished the death penalty, I should try to find William Henry Furman or Lucious Jackson or at least one of their lawyers.

When I looked out the window of the motel and saw the sheets of rain, I decided to pass up the Savannah home tour we had planned for the day. When my husband discovered my plans, which included an interview with Savannah District Attorney

Andrew Ryan Jr. and a search for Furman, Dennis decided to join the busload of tourists. By that time, Dennis had already seen and heard enough of Death Row to know that visiting historic homes – even in a thunderstorm – would be less stressful.

With Dennis happily on the tour bus, I drove to the courthouse to meet Savannah's District Attorney Ryan, who had prosecuted the rape case against Lucious Jackson, one of the three other cases argued with *Furman*. Ryan bragged that Jackson was the first of his six death penalty trials; he got death sentences in all of them.

"At one time, there were more people on Death Row from here than any other circuit in Georgia," Ryan said.

The state of Texas has its own bragging rights. [10]

When I interviewed Ryan in 1990, Walter had been sitting on Death Row for seven years and while there, in Texas 37 men had been led to the execution chamber. Back then, I wondered how long my co-counsel and I could keep Walter's executioner waiting.

I peppered Ryan with a lot of questions about *Furman v. Georgia*, but of course my most pressing was "Where is he?" Ryan didn't know but he told me where to find Bobby Hill, the lawyer for Jackson, who was set to argue the biggest case in his career.

I walked up the sidewalk of this run-down old Victorian building, sidestepping needles, small glass drug vials, and empty cans of malt liquor. I thought I must have the wrong address or that Andy Ryan was mistaken. This couldn't be the home of the quick-thinking, eloquent lawyer who had a thriving law practice and who, at an age when most lawyers are just starting out, had a death penalty case which catapulted him into the national spotlight.

After knocking on the door, which was slightly ajar, and receiving no answer, I peered in. Hill, dressed in a coat and tie with his shoes on, appeared to be in bed, asleep. I didn't know what to do. So, I closed the door and knocked again. Loudly. A minute later, it opened.

"Bobby Hill? Hi, my name is Joan Cheever. I'm visiting from out of town. I'm working on a story about the *Furman* decision and if you have a minute I'd love to talk to you. I'm sorry for dropping in. I tried calling, but couldn't get through. I just spoke to Andy Ryan. He said to say hi," I lied.

His hair was unkempt, his dark suit rumpled, but Hill looked at me with blood-shot eyes and smiled.

"Sure, come on in. Sorry for this mess," he said, as he scurried around the small room, trying to find a place for me to sit. I pretended to be reading a magazine article about him I found on a plastic chair next to his desk. I looked up briefly to see him kick liquor bottles and newspapers under the bed.

"Sorry. I'm working on a big case and it's all over my office." I couldn't help but notice that it looked more like a bedroom than an office.

The man who sat across from me was not the same brilliant, gifted lawyer that I'd read about. At 23, Hill was the first black since Reconstruction elected to the statehouse from Chatham County; a skilled trial lawyer who won a landmark case in 1968 that desegregated the Savannah school system.

But on October 17, 1984, Hill was suspended from the practice of law by the state of Georgia for mishandling five clients' cases. Eight years later, Hill, then 50, was sentenced to a year in federal prison after being convicted on 34 counts of fraudulently obtaining $9,000 in federal job training money intended for the poor. [11]

Of course I didn't know any of that when I talked to Hill. I just knew he was in bad shape. Hoping to cheer him up, I started to ask about his 1972 death penalty victory in the Supreme Court. But Hill only wanted to talk about how he "should have never let" the New York City attorneys take over the case of Lucious Jackson. Jackson was his client, he reminded me. Giving up the chance to argue before the Supreme Court at the age of 27 was "the biggest mistake of my life," Hill said, his voice filled with bitterness. [12]

The only time Hill smiled was when I asked him about his other clients on Death Row. "I'll tell you one thing. I never lost one to the chair," he said, proudly. [13]

I wondered if I would be able to say the same.

———

Walter's case came to the Texas Court of Criminal Appeals a few months before I did; my first job out of law school. On June 22, 1983, when the decision in *State v. Walter Key Williams* was handed down by one of the court's most liberal members, I was feverishly studying for the Texas bar exam.[14]

On the first day in my new job, the other eight briefing attorneys and I took the oath of office – we acknowledged our obligation to the Court, to our judge, but most importantly, to the State of Texas, to uphold the Texas Constitution and the Constitution of the United States of America in carrying out our duties.

I took that oath and my job very seriously, although I didn't feel entirely comfortable reviewing death penalty appeals and then drafting a memo that usually helped to send a man closer to the Death House.

The evidence of guilt and reasons for the sentence of death were usually very clear, at least from what I saw on the typewritten pages of the record. And there were graphic, gruesome autopsy photographs attached, in case I or one of my fellow clerks might be unduly influenced by the arguments of the defendant. We weren't allowed to "go outside the record;" the appeal was limited to those grounds raised in the defendant's brief. It wasn't our job to "lawyer" the case for him, the judges warned us, or to engage in a "theoretical retrial." If the defendant didn't raise all the points on appeal at the one chance he got at our court, then he was out of luck. And back in 1983, we were required to ignore claims of new evidence of innocence. In Texas, if a defendant did not raise claims of innocence (or any new evidence), on direct appeal, within 30 days of sentencing, it could *never* be considered by the state's supreme court. Once a case got to the Texas Court of Criminal Appeals, a defendant was one step closer to the Death House.

When I first opened Walter's file back in 1985, I read the court's decision and noted that the facts of Daniel Liepold's murder were particularly gruesome. Walter and his accomplice, Ted Edwards, walked into the convenience store where Walter had previously worked with Daniel and where Daniel had befriended him, and didn't even wait until the young clerk opened the cash register before shooting him.

On those black and white pages of the opinion, there was nothing even remotely sympathetic about Walter. There were no mitigating circumstances, no defense of temporary insanity, not even one character witness who testified at his sentencing hearing that his life was worth sparing. [15]

On its face, there appeared to be nothing illegal about the death penalty; the statute, that is. How it was applied was something else. By the time I had read Walter's transcript, 50 men had been executed in the United States under the new death penalty law; 10 in Texas, alone. [16] By the time he was executed in 1994, 75 men and one woman had been sent to the execution chambers across the United States.

Now that I had a client on Death Row, it was important to understand how the new and "improved" Texas death penalty statute differed from those laws that were reversed in 1972 – Furman, Jackson, and Branch – and why they were constitutionally flawed. [17]

William Henry Furman was dubbed "the bungling burglar;" Jackson and Branch were rapists. The fourth case argued on that snowy day in January 1972 was the case of Earnest Aikens of California, a rapist and murderer. [18] The facts in Aikens were especially brutal and his conviction was to be argued along with the somewhat different crimes in Furman, Jackson, and Branch. The LDF had no control over which cases the high court would hear, and in 1972 everyone on Death Row was their client. Including Aikens' case with the others caused Anthony Amsterdam and other death penalty lawyers many sleepless nights in the months before the high court arguments.

"We weren't overjoyed with the particular facts in Aikens. But the U.S. Supreme Court understood if they are going to invalidate the death penalty, there are going to be some gruesome cases. The infliction of the sentence of death was unconstitutional – pure and simple – regardless of who was killed, how they were killed or how many were killed," Amsterdam said in an interview.

Aikens committed two brutal, cold-blooded rape-murders, making it difficult for even the most die-hard death penalty opponents to argue his side. In April 1962, a young mother was home alone with her two toddlers when the 17-year-old broke in shortly before midnight and forced her to a railway embankment close to her house where he raped her. She managed to escape and run but Aikens caught her and stabbed her repeatedly in the driveway of a neighbor's house. Between 1962 and 1965, Aikens was in prison, convicted of other offenses. But on April 26, 1965, shortly after being paroled, he broke into the home of another woman whom he raped and stabbed to death. Before leaving her lifeless body, the killer took the woman's engagement and wedding rings and later gave them to two of his girlfriends. [19]

I had never read the facts in *Aikens* because his case wasn't discussed in *Furman*. And I know I didn't read it in law school since our professors advised us to skip the California opinions in the casebook for two reasons: There was a feeling that Texas was "the center of the universe," and, therefore, there was no need to cite to an out-of-state ruling. And, secondly, everyone knew the California appellate courts had a "questionable" national reputation and their legal reasoning was half-baked, the teachers joked, because of all the dope-smoking out there. The reasons weren't important; I was just happy to lighten my workload.

I must have been asleep during my constitutional law class when we talked about the rape cases of Jackson and Branch. When I first read the decisions carefully, after Walter's execution, I was shocked to find out a man could be executed solely for rape.

Between 1930 and 1967, of the 455 men executed for rape in the United States, 405 were black. All but a dozen of the executions for rape occurred in the South, with the greatest number of rapists on Texas' Death Row – 82 blacks, 14 whites, and 3 Hispanics. The race of the victim was also a determining factor as to the sentence. In Texas rape cases in which the defendant was sentenced to death, 95 percent of the victims were white and if the defendant was a black man, convicted of raping a white woman, the death sentence was a guarantee. No white man has ever been executed for raping a black woman.[20]

But in 1981, during my first criminal law course, I do remember being more shocked to find out that Section 1225 of the Texas Penal Code gave any man who found his wife in *flagrante delicto* with another man permission to kill either one or both of them. Under the defense of "justifiable homicide," a husband could legally murder his wife or her lover, but she could not do the same.

The facts in the cases of Texas' Branch and Georgia's Jackson differed greatly, but two elements were identical – both victims were white and the defendants were black. Branch was convicted of raping an elderly woman and then having a "polite" conversation with her after; Jackson, an escapee from a prison work gang, broke into a young woman's house and, with a pair of scissors to her neck, brutally raped her while her infant child lay sleeping in the next room.

The pro-death penalty members of the Supreme Court were pleased that the Aikens case from California had to be argued with the other three, according to Bob Woodward and Scott Armstrong, authors of *The Brethren*, a book about the inner workings of the high court. The public could support capital punishment in crimes such as Aikens, some members of the court reasoned. The grisly facts made the death penalty more palatable.[21]

Shortly after the Supreme Court arguments, the California high court decided, based on its own constitution, to abolish the death penalty – thereby releasing more than 100 inmates from California's Death Row, including celebrated serial killer Charles Manson and Sirhan Sirhan, the assassin of presidential hopeful Robert F. Kennedy, brother of President John F. Kennedy. The inmates were moved from San Quentin's Death Row into the general prison population. The California court's action is said to have infuriated several justices on the U.S. Supreme Court, according to authors Woodward and Armstrong.[22]

On June 29, 1972, after months of speculation and grueling behind-the-scenes maneuvering, hand wringing, writing, and rewriting, the Court handed down its 5–4 decision – with nine separate opinions, totaling more that 50,000 words, it filled 243 pages.[23] The ruling made the case of *Furman v. Georgia* not only a household name in the 34 years since it was handed down, the decision was also the most controversial and one of the longest in the Court's history.[24]

It was the last day of the term, shortly after 10 a.m., when the Supreme Court justices entered the courtroom and took their seats. The crowded room was silent. Moments later, Chief Justice Warren Burger read a one-paragraph court order.

"This Court holds that the imposition and carrying out of the death penalty in these cases constitutes cruel and unusual punishment in violation of the Eighth and Fourteenth Amendments."[25]

The five in the majority seemed to agree that the U.S. Constitution prohibited the execution of those on Death Row but their reasons differed greatly. The Class of '72 were entitled to new sentences of life, to a term of years, or – in some cases – to new trials.

Justices William J. Brennan Jr. and Thurgood Marshall said the death penalty violated the Eighth Amendment regardless of the crime or circumstances involved. Justice William O. Douglas wrote that it was unconsitutional because of the discriminatory nature in which it was applied. Justice Potter Stewart said it was unconstitutional because it was so infrequently and arbitrarily imposed. The fifth justice, Byron White, ruled that because the death penalty is so seldom enforced, it is ineffective in controlling conduct and fails to deter individuals.[26]

The announcement shook the nation.

On the 31 Death Rows across the nation, the reaction was jubilant.

In Louisiana, 45 Death Row inmates were showering in relays following their mid-morning exercise period when a guard shouted, through the bars of a cellblock door, the Supreme Court news.

"I just stood there and let the water wash away the smell of death," said the then 30-year-old Joseph Vernon of New Orleans, a five-year-veteran of Death Row. "I could feel it running down my body. I feel good now. I feel real good." [27]

In the South, politicians were angry.

Georgia Lieutenant Governor Lester Maddox called the *Furman* decision "a license for anarchy, rape, murder." The police chief in Memphis, Tennessee, predicted that those criminals who "hesitated to pull the trigger before just might go ahead and do it now." [28]

In nearby Alabama, Lieutenant Governor Jere Beasley was livid. "A majority of this nation's highest court has lost contact with the real world." [29]

———

In the summer of 1972, I was spending most of my days lounging by a swimming pool. I had no idea nor did I care one iota that the country's criminal justice system was in chaos. Even though there was frantic movement in both Washington, D.C. and in state capitals, no one moved off Death Row.

The summer ended, and with it my perfect job. I entered my sophomore year of high school, as 589 inmates – 505 murderers, 80 rapists, and 4 armed robbers – sat on Death Row.

Prosecutors and politicians were hoping that *Furman* was just a bad dream. Many refused to integrate this group into the general prison population. There were no automatic reversals, en masse. Some inmates waited on Death Row for years. Others only a few months.

State legislatures responded in two ways: some enacted mandatory statutes, making the death penalty automatic upon conviction of defined capital offenses. Other states passed "guided discretion statutes," giving jurors some guidance in sentencing. [30]

Only a few years later, the Supreme Court was the stage for yet another battle – the constitutionality of five new death penalty laws. [31]

On July 2, 1976, the death penalty was back on the books in

the U.S. And on Dec. 7, 1982, Texas resumed executions when it sent Charlie Brooks Jr., a 40-year-old black man, to the Death House. But instead of the electric chair, Texas had "modernized" its method of execution – Brooks would be the first man in the United States to die by lethal injection. [32]

———

On that historic morning in June 1972, I was teaching a gaggle of five-year-olds how to swim. Hundreds of miles away on Georgia's Death Row, inmates there began clanging their metal cups on the bars of their cells in celebration.

It was a sound that William Henry Furman, the man whose case is synonymous with abolition, could not hear. A few miles from Death Row, Furman was locked up in the mental hospital, undergoing more tests to determine his IQ.

———

Twenty-five years later, I was determined to find Furman and the other former Death Row inmates. I wondered about Furman's current mental state. If he was retarded in 1972, was he still? More importantly, was he dangerous?

Did I *really* want to find William Henry Furman?

CHAPTER FOUR

CLASS OF '72: WHERE ARE YOU?

As of June 2005, 322 men in the Class of '72 have been released from prison. Of that number, 111 were reincarcerated either because they were convicted of committing a new crime or because they were accused of violating a provision of their parole.

Of those 111, prison officials count 33 as "technical violators," but the violations were so minor that officials decided either not to send them back to prison or they were reincarcerated for only a few months. In addition to committing misdemeanor crimes, other kinds of parole violations that are considered "technical" include failure to notify the parole officer of a change of address before moving, being around places where alcoholic beverages are served, or associating with persons of "questionable" character, failure to pay parole administrative fees, or racking up unpaid parking tickets.

Of the remaining 78 recidivists who returned to prison, 42 did so for non-violent crimes, such as drug or alcohol offenses, burglary, or possession of a firearm, and 29 were reincarcerated for more violent felonies such as armed robbery or aggravated assault. Two parolees were convicted of attempted murder, two of manslaughter, and three returned to prison for murder. One parolee committed suicide before he was charged with murder.

Iam desperate to find William Henry Furman and curious as to what has happened in the intervening years. I wonder if he is even alive.

I call Anthony Amsterdam, now a professor at New York University Law School, after hearing that there is a list of the names of all those who had been on Death Row in 1972 when Amsterdam argued *Furman*.[1]

Amsterdam has searched his office, the basement in his home and through boxes of papers and books in storage at NYU, and in both his home and summer home. Several times either Amsterdam or his assistant, Michael D'Amelio, call or write, apologizing that they haven't been able to find it – yet.

My initial frustration turns to amusement after I find out a little bit about Amsterdam. His mind is like a steel trap; he has a reputation for his uncanny ability to remember minute details about every death penalty case he's ever read.[2] But, somehow, he can't seem to remember where he has put the list.

When I started on this journey, I don't know where the former Death Row inmates are, but I do know the names of their lawyers and where to find them. The state of Texas was represented by the legendary Charles Alan Wright, a constitutional law professor from the University of Texas Law School. He was Mel Bruder's adversary and a formidable one at that. "Here I am arguing against a guy who gave me grades four years ago. He'd been the attorney for the President of the United States *and* Howard Hughes. *And* he had turned down an appointment to the U.S. Supreme Court!" Bruder tells me over the phone.

Charles Alan Wright must be intimidating, I think, after my own father, who had taken Wright's class while at the University of Texas Law School in the 1950s, pummels me with questions about whether I am adequately prepared to interview this "con [constitutional] law legend."

It has been 42 years since my father sat in Wright's classroom, but the memories are vivid. "I hope you're ready. Charles Alan Wright is extremely bright," my father says as we eat breakfast together. "You know what you're going to ask him? You have the questions written down, don't you?"

Only a few, I think, as I nod enthusiastically and then stop eating the cereal. My time would be better spent studying for Professor Wright's death penalty "test" that I will take in a few hours.

Both my father and Mel Bruder are right. I'm not prepared. During our interview, I feel as though I am back in law school. I immediately regress to the role of law student. My questions are turned around so that Wright can determine whether I really understand the nuances of the *Furman* ruling. I am glad that the grade the professor probably gave me that morning will never appear on any transcript.

Even on summer break, Professor Wright looks every bit the law professor. And even in the Texas heat, Wright is wearing a gray wool suit, with a purple handkerchief carefully placed in his left breast pocket.

I look around Wright's office as he scans the brief he wrote in *Branch* almost 30 years ago. I notice the Christmas card from Vice President George Bush on his wall; a sign, "Honest Lawyer," and the clock in the shape of the state of Texas perched on a bookshelf overflowing with books of federal court decisions. His small, cluttered office is illuminated by the light of two computer screens. Several times during our interview, Wright picks up his bright yellow Motorola walkie-talkie and asks his secretary to bring in yet another legal document for me to read.

I am surprised when he tells me he was against the death penalty in 1972 and still feels the same. But as Texas' hired gun, that was not the position he was being paid to argue.

"I don't take on a case unless I believe it has constitutional merit. I believe in what I argue," Wright says. "Even though I'm opposed, I still think *Furman* is bad law. If a state uses capital punishment for misdemeanors, now that would be cruel and unusual punishment. But that's not the case."

Momentarily distracted by something on his computer screen, the professor stops and then picks up the attack on *Furman*. "The court had to read something into the Constitution. That it did not allow the death penalty," Wright says. "And that was just wrong. The fact that we make death a possible penalty. Well, it has a deleterious effect, because death is different."

I nod and for a moment, I stop taking notes. Death is certainly different. Watching Walter die has changed me. I feel very different.

Wright is cerebral, soft-spoken, and almost dispassionate about the very issue that has kept me awake at nights. His approach to abolition is methodical. He dismisses my hypotheticals such as DNA tests that later prove an innocent man has been executed or increased activism and pleas to spare the lives of killers by groups such as Murder Victims' Families for Reconciliation.

Wright shakes his head. "Might help, but it's not enough."

It's all about money, Wright assures me. "It [abolition] will be based on economics." The cases are costly, he explains, and have already threatened to bankrupt small counties, which is why only large cities in Texas such as Houston and Dallas can afford to indict and prosecute death penalty cases. [3]

"When the taxpayers get tired of footing the bill, when there are alternatives like life in prison, that's when it will end." [4]

And so the case for abolition has been reduced to dollars and cents. Not innocence claims or arguments based on morality or humanity or even pleas by the families of murdered victims. It is all about money.

With that, Wright stands up and our interview has ended. Class is over. I am summarily dismissed.

When I leave Wright's office and fly to Dallas to meet Melvyn Bruder, Wright's adversary in 1972, the issue of money is very much on my mind.

Bruder's office is only blocks from the well-manicured, very monied, well-endowed campus of Southern Methodist University, my alma mater. But now, the only kind of criminal law Bruder practices is DWI defense. He says that 95 percent of his criminal practice is devoted to drunk drivers. I wondered how many of his clients I knew between 1975 through 1979 – frat rat friends from SMU.

Bruder's expensively decorated office is filled with commemorative plaques, newspaper clippings, diplomas, and books. A large Leroy Neiman oil painting – *Silverdome* – hangs behind his desk. A 1991 book, *Adams v. Texas*, by his former client, Randall Dale Adams of *Thin Blue Line* fame, is on Bruder's desk.

Bruder doesn't stop talking during our two-hour interview and, after my encounter with Professor Wright, I am grateful that I'm not being quizzed on the nuances of death penalty litigation and am no longer a victim of the Socratic method as I had been earlier that morning. With his reading glasses perched on the top of his bald head, I wait for the glasses to fall and for the 52-year-old attorney to lose his train of thought. But neither happens.

Bruder, who looks like a stocky version of the police detective Kojak, has represented 15 men on Death Row – none of whom have been executed. "I won all of them. No death penalty. After that I decided I had tied the Miami Dolphin's record so I quit."

Bruder says the years of defending killers has been exhausting. "No matter what anyone says, a death penalty case is different from anything else in the world. I stopped because I like to win too much. And it takes too much to win," Bruder says. "I don't have the drive to generate new issues in death penalty case law."

As I sit listening, I feel as though I'd been punched. I don't see death penalty litigation as a "game" of win–losses and I sure wouldn't compare it to a winning season of the Miami Dolphins. I didn't represent Walter because I "liked" to win; I just believed that I had a duty as a card-carrying member of the Texas bar to volunteer my time and that in the end, the law would prevail over the misplaced emotions of Walter's jury and the suicidal strategy of Walter's trial attorneys.

When I hear Bruder say "it takes too much to win," I wonder if he knows how much it has taken out of me – to lose.

He keeps talking, oblivious to my internal pain. And then his next statement stops me. I put down my pen.

"If you have an infected part of society, you cannot allow them to damage and inflict pain on the rest of society. You need to make as certain as you possibly can that these people are indeed guilty, but it's an imperfect world," Bruder says. "There are those who deserve to die."

It is a one–two punch. I wonder if he would have felt the same if he had witnessed an execution of someone he might have spent almost a decade trying to keep alive. Mel Bruder is a lucky man. He got out of the death penalty business at just the right time, long before men were being executed in the United States at a rate of 98 a year.[5] In the early 1980s, when Mel Bruder represented men on Death Row, the U.S. Supreme Court carefully reviewed each death case from Texas, instead of dismissing them outright.

I forgave Mel Bruder that afternoon because I knew that he had never looked death in the face through the bars of the holding cell of the Death House, hours before an execution. He never spent the later years locked in a solitary mental game of second guessing, wondering what he might have done differently to stop an execution. Mel Bruder has never heard the whispered "thank you" from a terrified young man, with tears streaming down his face, as he faced the executioner. Bruder has never had that moment burned in his memory. I wouldn't wish it on anyone.

I didn't begrudge Mel Bruder that day in his law office, surrounded by his plaques of commendations and awards; the magazines, newspaper articles, and books naming him "Attorney of the Year" and his entry into the *Best Trial Lawyers in America* book. He's earned those awards. After all, he's still practicing law, criminal law, and if comparing his track record to the Miami Dolphin's win–loss record is what keeps Bruder in the profession, then he should be commended. I don't envy his success; I just wish I could have kept Walter off the gurney.

———

My search for Furman has now become an obsession. Every day I "google" him on the Internet; I've paid $29.95 to an online national search database and periodically scan obituaries from online newspapers, as well as the Social Security Administration Master Death index database. I know he's alive. I just don't know where.

Furman doesn't have a phone or a permanent address. Since he's been released from prison in 1984, he's moved around a lot. While on parole, he had to check in periodically with his parole officer, but when he was discharged in 1988, he just vanished from the law-enforcement radar screen.

Furman has disappeared and I don't have a clue how to find him, except to travel to Georgia and retrace his steps. And ask a lot of questions.

I begin to plan my trip to Atlanta, reorganize the children's schedule, and call in some carpool favors. I explain to Dennis that I have an interview with Furman – "well, kind of," I quickly answer when he presses for specifics. I am one mouse click away from buying an airline ticket on the Internet, when a letter arrives from the Georgia Parole Board. In it is the name and address of Furman's former parole officer.

I write Dan Welton and enclose a letter I'd written to Furman but never mailed. The officer promises to keep a copy of the letter in his back pocket and if he ever runs into Furman, he'll deliver it in person. I don't hold out much hope.

Dear Mr. Furman,
I am a journalist and a former practicing attorney who is writing a book about the group of inmates who were on Death Row when the Supreme Court declared the death penalty to be unconstitutional...

But you were given a second chance at life when the Supreme Court reversed the death penalty...I am interested in talking with you about what you have done with your life since being released.

Like me, Welton has no idea where to find him. I am hoping my toll-free number will prompt a response from Furman and the other ex-Death Row inmates. I am glad that I didn't limit the 800 phone access to the 31 states that had the death penalty in 1972. Since he is no longer on parole, Furman could have moved anywhere in the United States. Or the world.

"My, you must have a lot of family," the nosy AT&T operator replied when I called asking to sign up for the "Friends and Family" 800 line for nationwide access. "Every state? Are you sure you want Alaska and Hawaii, too?" prompting me to get into an unplanned and unnecessarily lengthy explanation that I was one of six children and my husband was one of ten and that I was sure we had "relatives" in every state in the country and we didn't want to exclude anybody.

"That's so nice to have so much family scattered across the country. How do you all celebrate Thanksgiving and Christmas? It must be so much fun!"

While I listened to the one-sided giddy conversation, I couldn't help but think how this exchange might be different if this woman only knew who I was including in my "friends and family." Would it increase the 25-cent a minute advertised rate? Would the truth be met with a stony silence or the same kind of passionate "eye for an eye" lecture that I got from my own mother?

At that point, I didn't care. I knew that if I had a free-phone number, I had a better chance of hearing from more ex-Death Row inmates. Many had no phone, but with a toll-free number, they could use a friend's phone or call me from a pay phone.

But first I had to get the letter to Furman. And that was proving to be impossible.

In the meantime, I set my sights on those men whose names and few addresses I had, and wrote them the same letter.

The first interview was set up by phone. An anti-death penalty activist in New York City called me at work, saying she had heard I was looking for former Death Row inmates from 1972 and she knew of one who was willing to talk.

I tell my boss I have a dentist appointment even though about 20 news stories are waiting to be edited. The stories need to move to the copy desk if the newspaper is going to meet its deadline this week, but today I don't have the time. I can put the stories off a few hours; I have waited years to find a member of the Class of '72. As I begin to press the elevator button, I hesitate for a moment and walk back to the desk where Ed, my friend and colleague, sits.[6] He knows I am lying because I never make medical appointments on "deadline day."

"Hey, will you do me a favor?" I whisper. "If I don't come back in five hours, call the police. No, make that Dennis first and then the police. But make sure it's at least five hours. Okay?" He looks puzzled, then worried when I slip him a piece of paper with the name "Bubba" and a phone number and address. Ed is either too scared or too polite to ask questions. He knows where I am going; Ed's a first-rate reporter and a very good eavesdropper.

While on the subway to Brooklyn, I know that a visit to the dentist would probably have been less painful than going back to Death Row. But I don't really have a choice. And Lawrence "Bubba" Hayes, the first man on New York's Death Row, is only a 20-minute subway ride away.

When we set up our first meeting, Hayes explained that it would have to be early. He had a full caseload at NBI, the social service agency where he was a case manager.

The quickest way to Bed-Stuy is by subway and he insists on meeting me there. I am equally adamant – that he does not. I don't want to worry that he'll be waiting in a cold station for a train that might be delayed. He is obstinate that I call his beeper when I arrive and he will escort me to his office, six blocks away.

Since I have never been to Bed-Stuy, I can't figure out why Hayes is so worried. Maybe it is because he knows I will stick out in this neighborhood. I don't want to look like an outsider, so I memorize the directions. But it is hard to look like I belong; mine is the only white face around here.

I make it to Hayes' office and am embarrassed that I'd been so nervous. The only thing I had to fear were taxicabs running red lights. Everyone has ignored me.

Hayes greets me at the receptionist's desk: "Hey, you didn't call me. I was starting to get worried."

"Oh, sorry about that. Cell phone. Out of juice," I lied. "And who carries around quarters for the pay phone? That's if you can find one." We walk to his office, down a hallway lined with women sitting in metal folding chairs waiting to see a caseworker.

Lawrence Hayes is a good-looking, articulate man. He doesn't look or act like a killer – the way he was described in newspaper articles in the *New York Daily News* in 1971.

He works as a crisis counselor for low-income women at a state agency in the heart of this crime-ridden neighborhood and Hayes is the first Death Row survivor I have met. I have so many questions, I don't know where to start. He suggests June 29, 1972. That's the day, Hayes says smiling, he started to live.

His life would have been much different had he not been sent to Death Row. He says he probably would have been killed by rival gang members or died from a fatal drug overdose.

Hayes was 19 when he, his nephew Cornelius Butler, and Rudolph Graham walked into Joe's Confectionery in Queens, New York, intent on robbing the store. He describes the August 20, 1971, "Robin Hood-esque," robbery as one that quickly went awry. He says he hadn't counted on the arrival of Kenneth Nugent, a 13-year-veteran of the New York City Police Department, who stopped off at Joe's to buy a pack of cigarettes before starting the midnight graveyard shift at the 103rd Precinct in Jamaica, Queens.

When Officer Nugent, a 40-year-old father of seven, entered the store, a woman started shouting that three men near the counter were robbing the bodega. Officer Nugent drew his revolver and ordered the men to raise their hands. Hayes said that at that moment, his friend and fellow Black Panther Rudolph Graham turned around and started shooting. Nugent returned fire and hit Graham in the chest. Graham staggered out the door and died on the sidewalk. Officer Nugent lay fatally wounded inside the store. Hayes and Butler ran; Nugent was rushed to a nearby hospital and died two hours later.[7]

Hayes and Butler, also 19, were captured within days. And even though the two weren't armed, they were charged as accomplices – and faced death in the electric chair. Armed or not, Hayes and Butler[8] acted in concert, the court ruled. And that's why they ended up at Sing Sing. The only way to get to the Death House in New York State in 1971 was to kill a cop. You didn't even have to pull the trigger.

When I search through the pages of the May 13, 1972, edition of the *The New York Times*, looking for what I thought would be a lengthy article about the man who was the first to be sent to New York's Death Row under its new death penalty law, I am shocked that Hayes' death sentence merits only two paragraphs under "Metropolitan Briefs," buried on page 35.

I am surprised at the brevity and placement of the death sentence article, but I shouldn't have been. On May 13, 1972, the United States was focused on a war raging thousands of miles away in Vietnam. The front-page headline – "Raid Said To Cut One Line Linking Hanoi With China" – described a U.S. fighter-bomber attack on the North Vietnamese rail system in a campaign to cut off the flow of military supplies to North Vietnam.[9]

But I *am* surprised when the 50-year-old Black Panther (who quickly reminded me that there is no such thing as a former Black Panther) actually credits New York's Death Row with saving his life. Hayes says his experience as a militant (before, during, and after his release from prison) and the skills he acquired as an activist kept him focused on an inherent belief that he would be released. And when that day came, as it would surely, Hayes says he knew that he had to have the education and job skills in order to survive on the outside.

Hayes will be the first of many former Death Row inmates who tell me that the college courses they took in prison gave them not only an education with marketable skills, but the self confidence that accompanies a college degree – both of which are crucial for post-release success. Hayes earned a Bachelor of Arts degree from SUNY/New Paltz and a Master's of Divinity degree from

New York Theological Seminary and the skills he needed "to make it."

He describes June 29 as his second birthday – the day he was reborn. On that day, Lawrence Hayes was just days away from his scheduled execution.

"It was like a home run in a ball park. I knew the game wasn't over. But, boy, was it sweet." Hayes says smiling, as he seems to remember the day clearly. He talks non-stop and, unlike my conversations with Walter, Hayes never looks down or allows silence to take over the small conference room. Dressed in dark golden corduroy pants, a green and blue Navajo Indian print shirt, he wears a black beret, tipped cockily off to one side of his closely-cropped head.

For the next two hours, I hear of Hayes' three years on Death Row and the next 19 years he spent in Greenhaven Correctional Facility in Stormville, a maximum-security prison in upstate New York. When an all-white jury sent Hayes to Death Row in 1972, it was empty. The last man executed in New York was killer Eddie Lee Mays who died in the electric chair at Sing Sing on August 15, 1963.[10] Two years later, New York abolished the death penalty, except in cases involving the murder of a police officer or in cases of a prison murder by a murderer who was already serving a life sentence.

Then came *Furman* and Death Row was closed. New York tried to reinstate capital punishment in 1974, but the New York Court of Appeals struck it down as unfair. For years, politicians tried to pass a death penalty law but it failed – either because legislators could not get enough votes or because it continued to be vetoed by New York Governor Mario Cuomo. All that changed in 1994 when a state senator named George Pataki, a Republican from Peekskill, New York, 45 miles north of New York City, beat Cuomo in the election for governor. One of the hot-button issues in that race was bringing the death penalty back to New York.

Three years after Hayes and I spoke, an activist with the "Campaign to End the Death Penalty" called to tell me "Bubba" needed help. Lawrence Hayes was back inside and he wanted to contact me, but 800 numbers don't work behind prison bars. I told her to tell him to call me collect.

I couldn't believe that the first man on New York's "old" Death Row was back in prison because he tried to help keep another man from being the first to be sent to New York's "new" Death Row. Hayes had been on parole for almost eight years and had to check into his parole officer only four times a year. But when he was photographed at a death penalty protest on the courthouse steps, outside the trial of triple murderer Darrell Harris, Hayes' parole officer called him in the next day.

Hayes and Harris, a 42-year-old former prison guard also from Bed-Stuy, had a lot in common. Like Hayes, Harris was the first to be convicted of capital murder under Governor Pataki's new death penalty law. [11]

Hayes' friends and lawyers say his parole revocation was nothing more than "political payback" for the high-profile role he had played as a death penalty activist after being released from prison in 1990. Once out, Hayes, with his parole officer's permission, was invited by anti-death penalty groups in Europe to speak about his experiences on New York's Death Row. He gave a speech to the Italian Parliament and was soon a sought-after spokesman against the death penalty across the European Union. Hayes has spoken at colleges and universities across the United States and has addressed political and religious organizations around the world.

But it was his opposition to the execution of Darrell Harris that drew the attention of the parole board and some say, Governor Pataki himself. Shortly after Pataki took office in 1995, he dutifully kept his campaign promise and signed a death penalty statute into law. One of the death penalty supporters who stood beside the new governor as he signed the historic document was none other than the widow of Police Officer Kenneth Nugent, the victim in Hayes' case.

Hayes says a senior parole officer ordered that he be arrested for a parole violation. He was initially charged with missing one parole meeting, although he says he met with his parole officer several times, even when he was not scheduled to do so.

On April 28, 1998, Hayes was ordered to appear at the parole office. He came in as a free man and left in handcuffs, charged with a violation – refusing to check in with his parole officer on a daily basis, even after seven years with a clean parole record. In fact, Hayes was considered to be a low-risk parolee.

He was sent immediately to Rikers Island, New York City's 15,000-inmate jail, while waiting for his August 10, 1998 parole revocation hearing. At that hearing, his parole officer claimed that Hayes had missed 30 appointments. And, in a highly-unusual procedure, Parole Board Commissioner Sean McSherry[12] introduced victim-impact statements from Officer Nugent's widow, Barbara, a well-known pro-death penalty activist and her children, one of whom is an assistant district attorney in Brooklyn.[13] In an unrelated matter, two months later, McSherry was indicted and later convicted on charges relating to parole board corruption.[14]

Hayes says his parole revocation and McSherry's involvement is no coincidence. "There's no question it's politically motivated," he said in a telephone call from Woodbourne Prison. "No question at all. Pataki wanted someone in the Death House so bad for his re-election campaign. And that was Darrell Harris. They couldn't send me to Death Row so they did the next best thing. Prison. Five years. A trumped up parole violation. They knew in advance that I would object to that [daily parole meetings], so they were ready to lock me up. Took me right there in handcuffs."

In September 1998, the State of New York sent Lawrence Hayes back to prison for five years as a parole violator.

Despite the fact that Hayes never even pulled the trigger of the gun that killed Officer Nugent, he has already spent 20 years behind bars.

In December 1999, Hayes walked out of Woodbourne after forfeiting his right to sue the State of New York for "unlawful" imprisonment in exchange for a reduced sentence.

But that would not be the end of Hayes' legal troubles. On April 7, 2004, Lawrence Hayes returned to prison after missing another appointment with his parole officer. Supporters say he was again penalized after speaking at a press conference at the Sundance film festival in Utah, to promote an anti-death penalty documentary.

———

Chuck Culhane knows how hard it is to be an abolitionist and remain silent. He and Hayes were on Death Row together – dead men walking who won't stop talking.

CHAPTER FIVE

A DEAD MAN WALKING AND TALKING

The average length of time these former Death Row inmates served in prison before being released on parole is approximately 18 years and 3 months.

For this group of former Death Row inmates, the average length of time between release and the return to prison as a "technical" parole violator is four years; for a serious felony, it is approximately 10 years. The average length of time between release and return to prison for drug offenses is five years.

The average length of time for those parolees who killed again is approximately 2 years.

The recidivism rate for this group of ex-Death Row inmates is 34 percent, a little more than half of the 60 percent recidivism rate of the general prison population, according to the U.S. Department of Justice.[1]

"This house is really beautiful," Chuck says. "It has an incredible backyard and a great view, in the front yard, of Niagara Falls. Really neat stuff. A sauna and everything. It's awesome."

As I turn into the driveway with Chuck Culhane, a 55-year-old former Death Row inmate from New York, it is obvious that neither June nor Roger, the college professors who own the house, are here. That makes me nervous – as does the long patch of ice I have to navigate to get from the car to the back door. I slip

Chuck Culhane

and slide and, under my breath, say a dozen Hail Marys. I pray that I don't fall and break a leg on the ice, and that this lunch and house tour with a convicted killer is totally legitimate.

I thought we were on our way to church. But Chuck insists on the house tour. I feel safe in the kitchen. It is close to the back door and there is a phone within reach. We raid the freezer and find macaroni and cheese with some spicy peppers – an appealing meal for a jalapeño-starved Texan. While lunch is microwaving, I set the table. I open the utensil drawer and that's when it hits me. I see the collection of June's kitchen knives – shiny, sharp, lethal weapons. Chuck is standing over my shoulder. I know that he has seen them, too, and he seems confused by my reaction.

The lunch doesn't go down so well after that. I have lost my appetite. I quietly berate myself for getting into this situation. No interviews in a private home. I should know better. But how could I have anticipated that a house tour would be on the agenda? And of course the sauna he is eager to show me is in the bathroom, off the master bedroom. I follow Chuck to the bedroom and curse silently. When he turns around for my reaction, I have a plastic smile and a mouthful of enthusiastic compliments.

Chuck is oblivious to my discomfort. He will be horrified if he knows how I really feel. He is simply trying to be hospitable, a generous host, trying to go back seven years to show me the place where he could keep the light on all night and read, where he could take a sauna whenever he felt like it, where he wasn't on anyone's schedule, and where he had a refrigerator to raid. Where he found freedom.

Chuck is one of the lucky ones. He wasn't released to a half-way house but to a real home, to friends – college professors who taught him while he was in Sing Sing. They are respected community leaders and accomplished, law-abiding citizens. Chuck wants me to know that this is who he is now; he's not the same person he was in 1968. He's not an armed robber from the Bronx or a convicted killer on parole. He's a new man, an educated man. He wants me to see that he is a published poet who hangs out in the same circles, in the same house, with university professors.

But I can't see that. I am too worried about getting killed.

As soon as the house tour ends, I almost run to the car, murmuring something about wanting to meet his friends at church. I remind Chuck – who frequently loses track of time – that we are late. Once I get behind the wheel, I feel embarrassed that I have been so afraid. After all, this man is taking me to church!

My mother would be proud. Well, not really. Not with my escort or with the church. This is definitely not any house of worship I am used to. It is church – in the true sense of community. Congregants pray to God by walking through a forest on the edge of church property. We meet up with the group as they are ending a brisk, hour-long jaunt through six inches of snow, a pre-church warm up. Members of Riverside Salem gather inside a log cabin on the property, for the service. [2]

After it is over, the group assembles in the kitchen for a pot-luck supper and then ends the evening with an old-fashioned church meeting. The members review the church's bills, mention those members of the congregation who are sick and need a call or card. The group also discusses a proposal for an alcohol rehabilitation center they are considering to help fund. The center will be located in Chuck's neighborhood.

It is then that the soft-spoken Chuck speaks.

He tells them that it is long overdue and urges them to support the center. There is little conversation before a vote is taken. It gets the green light.

Chuck knows first hand of the need for a rehabilitation center. He had his own alcohol problem, before he went in and when he got out of prison. In January 1994, Chuck was stopped by police after running a red light. He was driving home from his brother's house where he had had dinner and two glasses of wine; he registered 0.08 on a breathalyzer test. Then a resident of Rennasuer, New York, Chuck had been working as a paralegal at the New York State Defenders' Association since he was paroled in 1992. He was given a 30-day sentence by the town judge. But the New York Parole Board hit him hard, sending him back to prison, in 1994, for 11 months.

He describes the Driving Under the Influence conviction as "an incredibly stupid mistake."

"Death Row and 26 years was nothing compared to that sentence. I was so depressed and so mad at myself."

He was paroled again and got a job teaching college, thanks to the intercession, again, of June and Roger, the college profs.

Tonight, almost a year after we first met, I'm back on a college campus to watch Chuck teach a course called "Criminal Justice in America" to 22 students at a state university in upstate New York.

This evening's lecture is on a subject he knows all too well – the Death Penalty in America. Though dressed like a college professor, in a blue-gray tweed jacket with a black beret, he looks more like a sparring partner for a boxer in the middle-weight category. He's a short man with sandy blonde-gray hair and thick wire-rimmed glasses.

Before class, the Bronx native nervously paces the hall waiting for his students. He glances repeatedly at his watch and steps outside into the crisp March air for a cigarette to calm his nerves. He knows the night will be difficult. His audience, made up of conservative and vocal Generation Xers, is tough. They know their professor was on Death Row for three years and in prison for 26, because that's the first thing he told them. No hurt feelings if they wanted to drop his class rather than be taught by a convicted murderer.

He's not embarrassed of his past and it doesn't seem to bother them either. From the exchange of greetings it is obvious they like Chuck. As the evening progresses, it is also obvious they like the death penalty, as well. [3]

Class begins at 7 p.m., but there are still students milling about. Chuck doesn't blow a whistle or yell. He's heard enough of that in prison. And it would be out of character. He's a quiet man who spent many years in prison meditating, beginning each morning by practicing yoga. He starts taking roll. Without a sound. He knows all of his students' names. Taking attendance is an administrative task Chuck loathes. He's a pushover when it comes to teaching. In prison Chuck says everyone starts out with an "F" – a failure – and they are never expected to progress. In Chuck's class almost everyone gets an "A" unless they "really screw up" or skip the entire semester.

Chuck's a bit stiff as he begins. Maybe he's nervous because he knows, after teaching this group every week for the past three months, that he doesn't have a sympathetic audience. He hesitates and then looks away. He clears his throat and then stammers. He seems to have lost his footing. For a minute, his nerve.

Where is the man who, on a daily basis, verbally and physically sparred with Death Row guards? Who stuffed newspapers and legal documents in the toilet in his cell causing it to overflow in order to break up the monotony of life on New York's Death Row?

Chuck is the middle child of seven; always the family's "black sheep." He attended St. Joseph's elementary school and then dropped out of Cardinal Spellman High in the 10th grade, because he was bored and he had "more fun hanging out in the neighborhood bars getting drunk."

His father, Joseph, now dead, was an alcoholic. Culhane says his Dad often drank a week's pay at a nearby Irish pub, leaving the family to fend, financially, for themselves. His mother, Catherine, who lives in Florida (not far from the rest of Culhane's siblings), worked hard to stay out of her husband's way and to save enough money from his dwindling paycheck to feed and clothe her children.

Chuck will be the first to admit that he's no saint. He was a neighborhood bully and had a juvenile criminal record. He escaped from an abusive home and found solace in the streets, particularly the bars.

In 1965, outside O'Malley's Bar in the Bronx, Chuck met Gary McGivern; McGivern looked like an Irish James Dean, very cool and very cocky. Chuck had just been released from prison where he served an eight-month sentence for armed robbery – holding up a taxi driver.

Chuck describes that meeting with a heavy sigh; the moment was one of adoration and envy. With his hair slicked back, McGivern, dressed in a leather jacket, drove up on a motorcycle with an attractive blonde hanging on. "He cut quite a romantic picture," Chuck says, laughing.

Chuck and Gary were inseparable. They terrorized the neighborhood. In 1966, Chuck returned to prison for robbing a gas station attendant at gunpoint and for wounding two police officers in the process. His accomplice was Gary, then 20, who had never been to prison. Chuck decided to take his chances at trial, but was convicted and given a 10- to 20-year sentence. Gary took a plea bargain and would be out in a couple of years.

Less than two years later, both men ended up on Death Row.

In September 1968, Chuck, Gary, and William Bowerman, convicted of armed robbery, as well – and an escape charge – were being transported from Auburn prison to a court hearing in Westchester, New York, by two deputy sheriffs in the deputy's private car.[4] During the drive, Bowerman attempted to escape and wrestled a gun from the deputy-driver. Both he and Bowerman were killed. Chuck and Gary said they had nothing to do with the escape and blamed it on Bowerman who they said shot the deputy.

At trial, the surviving police officer testified that Gary had killed his partner. Both Chuck and Gary also were shot in the ensuing gun battle, McGivern in the arm, Chuck in the chest. But there was medical evidence that Chuck had been crouched in the back of the car during the shooting and, therefore, could not have been involved.

The deputy disputed the defensive theory; he said Chuck had tried to choke him during the attempt – a claim that appeared to be at odds with the testimony of the Emergency Room physician who said he didn't find any marks on the deputy's neck. Chuck and Gary's first trial ended in a hung jury.[5] In 1972, after a second trial, they were convicted of capital murder and sent to New York's Death Row.[6]

The classroom is quiet as Chuck tells the teenagers of his life in the Death House. He describes the day he became an abolitionist.

While sitting in his cell in Greenhaven Prison, barely a month after his life had been spared by the *Furman* decision, he picked up the August 1972 issue of *Life* magazine. Flipping through the pages, Chuck stopped at the photographs taken in a field in Nigeria, of men only minutes from being executed. They were tied to wooden posts, held in place by oil barrels. Those men weren't killers. In 1972 more than 200 armed robbers – men who had never taken a life – were executed by the Nigerian government.

Chuck was hypnotized by the look in the eyes of one man who was photographed seconds before being executed. That picture changed his life. "His face had every kind of human expression. I could empathize with him. His eyes were filled with fear, hope, love, hate, and despair. Everything was there."

Chuck's lips begin to quiver, his eyes brimming with tears. "I saw myself in those eyes. He was *me*. I started crying. Over the next two days, I would pick up that magazine and look at his picture. We may have had different lives, but we were no different," Chuck says. "We were both convicted robbers. But for me this was a time when the door was opening. The Supreme Court said, "We're not gonna kill ya. You're going to live." So for me it was a time of hope. But looking at that picture, it certainly wasn't a time of hope for these people. I just started crying and crying. I broke down. In a good way."

It triggered a painful self-examination.

"The outcome for me was a series of deep probing questions. I had to ask myself, Why was I here? Why did I go through this experience? What did I learn from it?"

That was the moment, Chuck tells the class, when he decided he would devote his life to fight against the death penalty.

I look over at my twin sister, Jean, whom I have invited to the lecture. She's in Buffalo for business at a pharmaceutical company and we are sharing a room at the Radisson, a big step up from my usual $19.99 a night motel.

I can see Jean is teary. That's a good sign because she is fairly conservative on crime and punishment issues.

Two hours later, the lecture is almost over. Chuck refers to studies of recidivism, economic costs of life without parole versus execution, opinion polls, and is quoting failed U.S. Supreme Court Justice nominee Robert Bork, an arch conservative, writer Franz Kafka, and even some Victor Hugo, the nineteenth-century author of *The Hunchback of Notre Dame*. The class is moved, but they still favor the death penalty. Now it is time for questions.

Nineteen-year-old Nicole, a petite young woman with shoulder-length hair hidden in a Sox baseball cap, has a father who is a retired police officer. She tells Chuck she's glad his life was spared, but she still believes in capital punishment.

"I'm glad you didn't get it, but cops put their lives on the line every day. There has to be some way to protect them."

Another student applauds. Clad in a sweatshirt with a baseball cap bearing the name of his fraternity, Cole supports capital punishment and he spends the next few minutes picking apart the statistics and studies. "Look. You do the crime, you do the time. That's it. Pure and simple."

Not everyone agrees.

Mark is a Vietnam veteran and at least 25 years older than everybody else – except Chuck. He's been shaking his head throughout the discussion. His son, a second grader, sits next to him, doodling and periodically working on his homework while looking around. During a break, Mark explains that the baby-sitter didn't show up so he brought his son to class. Mark stares in disbelief at Cole, who wasn't even born when Mark was sent to the jungles of Vietnam.

"Give me a break. There's nothing *simple* about it. What about murder in the time of war?" Mark asks, his voice cracking. "I could have been one of the first to be executed in New York State. I did it over in 'Nam. I did it many times."

Chuck takes a deep breath. He doesn't want to put Mark on the spot, but he's helping to make the point. "Mark, did you feel good about what you were doing?" Chuck asks.

Mark glances at his son. He seems hesitant to answer.

"At that time it didn't really bother me. Heck, I was only 19. I was just following orders. Doing what I thought was right. It didn't hit me until I was discharged from the service. Thinking about it you realize you've killed a lot of innocent men, women, and children."

The issue of legalized murder stops the class. That's what the death penalty is, Chuck pleads. Government-sponsored murder.

For a moment the room is still. It doesn't last long. "It's not the same," one student shouts. "What about the rights of the victim?"

A young Asian woman, the only minority in the class, criticizes Chuck for ignoring the victim. She's a new mother, with twin girls. "You talk about the self-worth of these people and their families, but you seem to forget that the victims have self-worth. And their families. And they have lost their lives. What about them?"

Chuck explains that the death penalty creates more victims, specifically, the families of those who are executed. He says society is victimized when the government kills.

The class tells Chuck it is ludicrous to equate families of murder victims to families of Death Row prisoners. In an uproar, they reject Chuck's statement.

But he manages to find a common ground.

Chuck says he's in favor of Life Without Parole, or LWOP, for the "truly psychotic, the serial killers, the Ted Bundys, the Son of Sams, and the John Wayne Gacys." There seems to be a collective sigh of relief.

Then the discussion turns to the Bible and they begin quoting the Old Testament. "An eye for an eye," a few shout.

When one student talks about how expensive the death penalty is, Chuck smiles. This argument is a winner. But then a group says they are angry that taxpayer money is being wasted to house people who have no redeeming social value. Chuck reminds them that it costs $3 million to both house and provide legal representation to a Death Row inmate before executing him. He cites a Florida study that compares execution costs to the $750,000 to house a prisoner for 30 years.[7] Most of the students are unimpressed.

"Cut down the number of appeals and execute them within a year or two,' a student suggests. Others start clapping.

Cole talks the longest. And loudest. He talks as though he has some familiarity with the penal system, but he also appears to be parroting opinions from conservative political commentators. Cole has an opinion on just about every issue in the criminal justice system, yet he says he has never set foot in a jail or a prison. He boldly says he supports California's "three strikes and you're out" law – a statute designed to punish the habitual offender with a life sentence without parole, regardless of the severity of the felony.

"So what are we supposed to do?" Cole asks, angrily. "If a guy kills someone at age 20, we say, oh, he's young, he can be rehabilitated. We won't kill him. We'll let him out after 10 years?"

For the first time, Chuck loses his patience. "Where is this happening, Cole? Tell me where? Ten years? Fifteen years? Where is this happening? Where is this going on?" Chuck says, his voice a higher pitch, "I was never charged with killing anybody and I did 26 years. Do you know what it's like to do just one year in prison?"

"No, I don't. But you know what else, I'm not gonna do anything that's gonna land me in prison for a year," Cole replies. "I'm not going to go out and hold up a store." (A not-so-veiled reference to the armed robbery that sentenced Chuck to prison 31 years earlier.)

Chuck seems stunned. He fidgets with his glasses. He stops and looks out into the audience. His eyes meet Sister Roslyn's, his friend whom he met at Attica where she was the prison chaplain; she dropped in tonight to hear his lecture.

During the discussion, the nun sits silently; her hands are folded as if she is praying. She remains quiet until Cole's outburst. When Cole says he "will never, ever do anything" that will send him to prison, Roslyn turns in her chair and faces him.

"Cole, I hope I never see you in Attica. But, young man, there are people there who are doing 20 years for attempted murder. They did not take a life," she says calmly, but sternly.

Cole is not moved. "So what? If someone had attempted murder on my life, I'd want him in jail till he dies. Because I wouldn't want him to come back out and try to kill me again," Cole shouts. "And if someone else actually kills me, I would hope that someone else out there would make sure that justice is served. And in my mind and the minds of many people in this country, he should be killed."[8]

Chuck looks at the clock. The class is over, although he's not ready for it to be. Not on this note.

My sister is the first to leave; she seems to be in a hurry to get back to the hotel. She's exhausted. So am I.

And Chuck is depressed. He has so much more to say; he says he just needs a little bit more time to convert them. "I think it went badly. Don't you?" Chuck asks, once the room is empty. "What's with these students? Why are they in favor of the death penalty? Where are they *from*?"

Cole is the same age as Chuck when he first went to prison; Chuck was there for 26 years. For most of us, that is a lifetime.

The ex-con struggles, trying to understand that the teens of the 1960s were very different from those of today. Chuck knows that he has a lot of catching up to do. After all, he was in prison during the Vietnam War; he watched Watergate and the downfall of a president from a television set in prison. Chuck is a product of the generation that mistrusts everything about authority; he would never give the government – which he says is full of corruption – the power to execute. In prison he witnessed the abuse of power.

It's hard for Chuck to pack 26 years into the 5 years he's been living on the outside. He may be the teacher, but he says it's the students who teach him. A painful lesson is that the 1960s were over a long time ago.

But those years in prison turned Chuck into an activist. That was the only way he could survive. It is the same kind of activism Chuck says that keeps him and some of the other members of the Class of '72 going in their new lives outside of prison. His students don't seem to have an interest in politics. It is the 55-year-old professor who walks alone across the college campus with a stack of fliers and a roll of scotch tape, posting notices of rallies on a variety of political issues – Free Mumia Abu-Jamal, Battered Women in Prison, and the Plight of the Native Americans.

Chuck says he appreciates the diversity of opinion usually, but not on the death penalty. He's got a blind spot and he can't understand why *they* don't "get it." "The only way to eliminate the death penalty is to put a face on it," Chuck says, excitedly. "Then they will see who they are killing. Guys like me. People who can be rehabilitated. Who can make something of their lives. And have."

I met Chuck by phone a year earlier, after my letter was hand delivered by his parole officer.

He apologizes for the delay, explaining he's been in Florida over the Christmas holidays visiting his mother, brothers, and sisters.

We talk several times until I get up the nerve to invite myself for a visit. Chuck is enthusiastic and quickly gives me directions to his temporary home, the Western New York Peace Center in Buffalo, New York. Knowing that I have limited funds for travel, he offers me a bed at the Peace Center. I decline.

It is a freezing Sunday morning in February when I board an early flight to upstate New York. After renting a car, I drive to the Peace Center, a two-story brick building in a blighted area on the city's East Side. Chuck lives with "Star" and "Hungry," two stray cats he's adopted. He works at the center as a caretaker and an all-around handyman.

I drive up and see a white man, which is unusual because this neighborhood is predominantly black. Chuck is wearing a black wool beret and leaning on the side of the red-brick building smoking a cigarette in the 14-degree freezing temperature.

"Who better to live in this high-crime area than an ex-con?" Chuck says, half-joking, half-uncomfortable that he'll always be known as a convict.

Speaking in a low voice, Chuck rattles off the morning's itinerary. It makes me dizzy. "We have to go to the Wende Correctional Facility to see Gary [co-defendant McGivern], the hospice to see Herb, and then to church to see June, Roger, and the gang. And then we can do whatever you want to do."

During the drive to Wende in Alden, New York, Chuck tells me only bits and pieces of his 26 years inside prison. He's so soft-spoken, I can barely hear him. I steer with one hand and hold a tape recorder in the other, putting it close to his mouth. It's awkward. He seems nervous; maybe it's because of the way I'm driving. Or maybe he's just shy.

He wants to talk about Gary, his best friend and former co-defendant, who has been reincarcerated after being released seven years ago. Gary went back inside after being convicted of possessing a $10 bag of heroin. The judge gave him 90 days, but the New York Parole Board was not so forgiving, handing him a five-year term. The Board hadn't forgotten the first degree murder conviction that sent him to Death Row in the first place.

In 1985, when both Gary and Chuck first became eligible for parole, their case became a cause celebre in the abolitionist movement, supported by media heavyweights and strange bedfellows such as conservative journalist William Buckley, along with the poet Allen Ginsberg and folk singer Pete Seeger.

In 1989, Gary was the first to be paroled, amid angry protests by law enforcement groups. And even though he spent years learning the craft of prison activism, once Gary left Otisville state prison he turned his back on the anti-death penalty movement. Gary and his then wife, fellow activist Marguerite Culp, moved into the Woodstock, New York community and virtually disappeared from the public's eye.

That decision "was one of the biggest mistakes I made," Gary says, regretfully. "It was that kind of activism that kept me centered. And grounded. And out of trouble."

While on parole, Gary spurned offers of legal jobs or offers of employment from anti-death penalty groups. He took a job on a construction crew. For the first time in his life, Gary wanted to be anonymous. But in that anonymity, he says he "lost his center" and his "reason for being." He tried to escape the memories of those 18 years in prison, with drugs and alcohol. He forgot how long it took to achieve his freedom.

He forgot, that is, until 1994, when he was arrested for heroin possession.[9] With his parole revoked, he was sent to the high-security Wende, home to convicted Central Park, New York, murderer Robert Chambers.

This morning, Chuck and I are just a few miles from the prison entrance at Wende to meet McGivern when suddenly I feel sick. My stomach is churning. I stop talking. This is the first time I've been back to a prison since Walter's execution. I look up at the double barbed wire chain-link fence that surrounds this maximum-security prison, home to 750 inmates. My breathing accelerates as I hold the steering wheel. I forget what I am saying.

Chuck notices. "Are you okay? Are you sure you want to do this? Gary really would like to meet you."

"I'm fine. Really. I just didn't think I would feel this way. It's just so weird being back here. At a prison. It's been a while."

This looks a little bit like Texas' Death Row without the high-powered rifles. The first entrance, a chain-linked fence surrounded by steel, is locked. After a minute we are buzzed into a small outside holding area, with another steel door. Then another buzz. Up some stairs and into the prison waiting room to fill out the paperwork.

Two hours later, I am back in the reception area. Chuck has been patiently waiting, reading a new book of poetry, stepping out a couple of times to smoke. He's not allowed inside. Visiting Gary would be a parole violation. Chuck is banned from associating with convicted criminals.

"So, how's he doing? Is he okay? Are you okay?" Chuck asks, whispering as we walk out of the prison.

"I hate this damn place. I got in trouble in there. Can you believe that?"

I am madder than hell. It's bad enough that I have to take off my shoes, glasses, earrings, and half my clothes to get in.

Once inside the visiting room, I sit sideways at a small table talking to Gary. I'm one of the few women in the visiting room wearing a dress. I cross my legs, very lady-like, and discreetly pull my dress down past my knees.

Gary is telling me about his time back in. How he cooks in his cell on a hot plate; he knows I love to cook and wants to swap recipes. Out of the corner of my eye, I see that our visit has been interrupted. Standing at my side, a tall guard lightly taps my foot. He barks: "Lady, keep two feet on the floor at all times. Those are the rules."

The last time I'd been warned about the "two feet on the floor rule," I was a senior in high school. My father was checking up on my boyfriend and me watching television in the family room.

"Excuse me?" I ask.

"You heard me. On the floor. Both of them."

He leaves and Gary bursts out laughing. I am mortified.

"Listen, Cheever. Quit fooling around. Now get those feet on the floor," Gary whispers, shaking his finger. I am 17 again.

Gary keeps talking, but I'm not listening. I'm embarrassed and angry.

I look around the visiting room and see at least a dozen couples making out, their hands groping breasts and buttocks. I stare at the guards sitting in the front of the room; I catch one guard's eye and he quickly looks away.

I am a newbie. A virgin. It must be obvious. If I had shown my Texas bar card at the front desk, I know I would have been treated differently. With respect. Gary and I would have been given a private room to talk, without guards. I could've put my feet up on the table, for Christ's sake.

During the nine years I visited Walter on Death Row, I gained entry with my lawyer card, was given a private cubicle and allowed to bring just about anything inside, with the exception of drugs, alcohol, or a gun, of course.

In this New York prison if you're not a lawyer or journalist, you're treated as though you are a criminal, too – guilt by association. I feel sorry for the families, for the wives, mothers, and girlfriends who dutifully visit every week.

It's hard to interview Gary without a pen or pad of paper. But those are considered contraband. No purse or briefcase either. I am allowed only my driver's license, as identification, and some coins for the vending machines – machines Gary isn't even allowed to touch. Prisoners have to ask their guests for coffee or snacks.

When the visiting hour ends, I practically run out the door. Chuck is outside, smoking.

"I can't believe I was so intimidated in there," I complain.

"Yeah, it sucks," he laughs. "But I think everyone feels exactly the same way."

It's not a big deal to Chuck – I have to remember that he went through much, much worse, on a daily basis, for more than 26 years.

While I've been inside visiting Gary, Chuck has been busy. He's taken the wife of an inmate clothes shopping. The woman, who traveled 12 hours by bus from New York City with a cranky two-year-old for the Sunday visiting day, was told she could not go into the prison because she was dressed "inappropriately." I saw the heavy-set black woman before I went in. She was wearing a long, tailored, button-down dress shirt over black leggings. The guards decide the leggings are too revealing. Hours ago, before I passed through the gate to visit Gary, I overheard the woman pleading with the guards.

I quickly make a mental inventory as to what I had in my suitcase; I whisper to Chuck that I have nothing in my car that will fit this woman. Now she is crying. So is her child. He's hungry and tired. She's exhausted. Visiting time will end in two hours and the guards aren't going to let her in.

It doesn't seem fair. I am visiting a man I don't even know, yet her man is the father of her child. We have both started our journey from New York City. But that's where the similarities end. It takes me only one hour to get to Buffalo, flying in a comfortable, empty 727 jet. She has been awake for 12 hours on a crowded Greyhound bus, a sleepless drive with a wiggly toddler. Her leggings and the jumper I'm wearing, that I find on the $21.99 sale rack at the Gap, probably cost the same. But I'm being allowed inside the prison and she isn't. I wish I could have traded places.

It turns out that I don't need to. Chuck, the eternal optimist and diehard activist, has a plan. He asks for my car keys and I quickly hand them over before I pass through the metal detector. Once inside, I'm hoping that Chuck has a driver's license and won't wreck the car. I'm wondering how I will explain to the manager of Enterprise that I had lent his car to an ex-con I barely know who has no license.

While I was visiting with Gary, Chuck drove the woman and her son to a nearby Walmart where she bought black slacks with an elastic waist. When I find him, Chuck hands me the car keys, smiling.

"She found the pants on sale for $19.99," he laughs.

I didn't ask who paid. I knew.

It is a little victory for Chuck but it means a lot to him – just another struggle with "an unnecessary and oppressive government." Chuck seems to fight others' battles better than his own. Visiting Gary would violate parole, as would (until recently) driving a car. I'm not sure of the underlying reasons for either rule. His parole officer lifted the four-year driving ban but I'm not sure Chuck has bothered to get a license. He's prohibited from drinking alcohol and can't make any public statements about the death penalty. The latter is blatantly illegal and Chuck violates it with regularity. It's hard to be an abolitionist and keep quiet.

After his release from prison in 1992, Chuck returned to college for his Master's, taking several courses in psychology at SUNY Buffalo. He completed the coursework for his degree, but he doesn't have the $2,200 for tuition.

He regularly attends a church that is known for its long history of social activism. He makes the 25-mile journey to Riverside Salem from his home on Buffalo's East Side whenever he can get a ride.

And he's faithful about visiting Herbert X. Blyden, his friend and fellow prison activist, who is in a hospice, dying of cancer. Today I am Chuck's driver. But he says we can't show up without a copy of the Sunday *New York Times* which Chuck has promised. By now it is late afternoon and the convenience stores are sold out. By the time we get to the hospice, we've already been to six stores. Chuck walks in empty-handed and incurs a good-natured tongue-lashing from Herb, a Black Panther and one of the leaders of the bloody 1971 Attica prison uprising. In a September 15, 1971, article in *The New York Times*, Herb, then 34, was called "one of the most eloquent spokesmen for the prisoner revolt."

Herb is now 59, bedridden, and hooked up to oxygen. But he is still articulate and full of energy, even though it's obvious he's losing the battle to cancer. He's full of questions for Chuck – about the comings and goings of various NAACP leaders and recent speeches made by local community activists. In particular, he wants to know the gossip about those involved in a recent Attica commemorative 25th-anniversary event. [10]

This animated conversation between the ex-cons is momentarily interrupted by the television set. Clint Eastwood is in a shoot 'em up scene in the movie, *Dirty Harry*.

"Go on, Harry. Now get the hell out of there," Herb says, laughing. Without missing a beat, he turns to Chuck and they get back to the first item on Herb's agenda – raising college scholarship money for poor black kids. They both agree that education is the ticket out of the ghetto and to stay out of prison. [11]

Like almost every former Death Row inmate I've interviewed, Chuck is struggling financially. It isn't easy getting a job when you are a parolee – and very few employers want to hire a convicted killer. Most of the ex-cons admit they don't tell their employers about their past, at least not the specifics.

But Chuck is different. He just doesn't seem to care that others know. He figures many people already do. Gary and Chuck's case, and their eventual release from prison, received a lot of media attention as the artistic community worked tirelessly to get them out of prison.

They were close to winning their freedom in 1985 when Mario Cuomo granted clemency to Gary, the first time the New York Governor had done so in a murder case. But the clemency was subject to the parole board's approval and they turned Gary down repeatedly, after angry protests by groups of police officers and prosecutors. Finally, in March 1989, the board relented. Three years later, Chuck followed Gary.

When Chuck was paroled in 1992, his parole officer ordered him to sell his car and barred Chuck from driving. Without a car it's difficult to get to a job, especially if you're relying on public transportation in the harsh winters of Buffalo. Chuck takes the bus and sometimes walks the five miles to the campus.

He does odd jobs for friends and church members, and he's paid $100 a week to teach the class at the college. He stays at the Peace Center for free, in exchange for being its handyman. He also counsels young addicts, for free, at a youth center around the corner from the Peace Center.

He eats very little and, after being in prison for 26 years, hasn't acquired many material possessions. "Not having a lot is not bad. I have freedom. And that's pretty wonderful."

One of those freedoms was being able to attend a death penalty awards presentation at the New York City Bar Association in midtown Manhattan.

A few months after I watched Chuck teach the death penalty class, I invited him to the Thurgood Marshall Awards ceremony when I found out that Anthony Amsterdam, the man who argued *Furman*, would be the guest speaker.

I had envisioned a perfect moment when the two men would finally meet, more than 25 years after that historic Supreme Court decision. Both men are very shy and it is painful watching them talk; like trying to get two wallflowers to slow dance at a high school party. I take my "Kodak moment" picture, but it certainly isn't the kind of precious scene advertised on TV. I should have left it alone. I didn't know it, but Chuck and Amsterdam have written each other over the years; Chuck, I find out later, has thanked the lawyer repeatedly for saving his life.

It is a life that has undergone an incredible transformation. While incarcerated, Chuck took university classes and worked on his poetry. He became a nationally recognized, prize-winning poet, winning first place in 1989 from PEN, the international writer's group, for his poem "Of Cold Days." In 1988 Chuck won PEN's second place prize for "Last Christmas For Death Row" and dedicated the poem to then-California Supreme Court Chief Justice Rose Bird, an anti-death penalty advocate.

In the poem he spoke of those men who were also sentenced to die – "his brothers on the Row" – Gary (McGivern), "Raheem" (Butler), "Bubba" (Hayes), and Fitz (Fitzpatrick).

... I give praise to the passing of death row,
Last Christmas for the electric chair –
It was nothing but a mistake, the mystique of death is gone.
600 lives later, I give praise to the whitewashed room above,
Wherein sits a wooden lifeless tree of civilized insanity –
And it shall take no more life in New York.
Give praise to the demise of mindless and spiritless power,
Give praise to the death of legalized murder. [12]

Chuck's poetry has been published in *Candles Burn in Memory Town: Poems From Both Sides of the Wall*; in 1997; more of his poetry, along with that of writer Jack London, was published in an anthology, *Prison Writings in The 20th Century*. In 1999, more was published in a PEN American Center Prize Anthology called *Doing Time: 25 Years of Prison Writing*.[13]

He's also won two PEN awards for his one-act plays. *A Passage* is about a man on Florida's Death Row in a case in which the prosecutor suppressed evidence; the other play, *Cape Man – Salvador Agron* is based on a true story about a Puerto Rican teenager who stabbed two people to death in 1959 in a fight in Manhattan's Hell's Kitchen. Described by witnesses as wearing a black cape with red lining, the 16-year-old was nicknamed the "Cape Man" and was the youngest person ever sentenced to death in New York state; his sentence was commuted by Governor Nelson Rockefeller after prominent citizens, including Eleanor Roosevelt, intervened.[14]

Chuck collaborated on the play with singer/song-writer Paul Simon of Simon and Garfunkel. On January 26, 1998, Simon's musical, *The Capeman*, opened on Broadway. Six weeks later it closed, but Chuck managed to see a performance.

On my next visit with Chuck, a year later, he seems depressed. He broke some ribs during a recent fall and doesn't have enough money to go to the doctor. But most importantly, he complains that he can't find time to write. In prison, time was never lacking, nor was material. Not that he wants to trade places.

In the Free World, Chuck is busy working, trying to come up with enough money every month to buy food and pay his bills. He has the material to write, but no time; probably because he also spends many hours giving it away – as a political activist.

He smiles as he rattles off his resume: He's the Buffalo, New York, contact for the death penalty committee of Amnesty International, an active member of the Buffalo Chapter of the Free Mumia movement, a founder of the Woodstock Committee to Abolish the Death Penalty, and an active member in New Yorkers Against the Death Penalty. He's appeared on death penalty panels both in New York City and Washington, D.C. He protests regularly against capital punishment in front of government office buildings and courthouses. Often times I have to remind him to shield his face from newspaper photographers. Chuck needs a permission slip from his parole officer before he can attend any of these protests, much less speak.

But he manages to work behind the scenes. He has become friends with Bud Welch, the father of Julie Welch, the 23-year-old college graduate and Spanish interpreter for the Social Security Administration who was killed along with 167 others in the April 19, 1995 bombing of the federal building in Oklahoma City.

Welch says his daughter had been a member of Amnesty International since age 16 and had strongly opposed the death penalty. He felt differently. In the first month after the bombings, Welch didn't even want trials for Timothy McVeigh or Terry Nichols. "I just wanted them fried." [15] By the end of the year, he changed his mind. "I realized executing them wasn't going to bring her back," says 66-year-old Welch, a Catholic who serves as present of Murder Victims' Families for Human Rights.

In November 1999, Welch was honored at the annual convention of the National Coalition to Abolish the Death Penalty and Chuck wrote a poem in his honor, "April 19, 1995." [16] Sister Roslyn – the chaplain of Attica who had been at the death penalty class at the college – and Chuck orchestrated a meeting between Welch and Tim McVeigh's father, Bill. The two men talked for more than two hours on September 5, 1999, and they still keep in touch regularly.

Chuck also kept in close contact with Gary; Chuck was Gary's link to the Free World. He often called collect from prison asking Chuck to check up on his lawyers and on the appeal and to deliver messages to mutual friends. Despite his limited income, Chuck always finds some money to deposit into Gary's prison account.

"He's always been there for me," Chuck says.

And Chuck is always there for Mary, an 83-year-old, housebound, arthritic widow who lives across the street from the Peace Center. She's been in the same house for 58 years and

Chuck visits her daily. On Palm Sunday, he delivers palms to her door. On Valentines' Day, Chuck surprises her with a bouquet of red carnations. In March he takes Mary to an Ice Capades production of *The Wizard of Oz*. During the harsh winters in Buffalo, Chuck shovels Mary's steps regularly (for free) and goes to the pharmacy to pick up her medicine. He takes her shopping and cooks her dinner.

Mary has no idea that Chuck has spent 26 years behind bars. It's not a subject that has come up, he explains. He says he can't find the right words or the right time to tell her.

"I think she'd be shocked. I don't know why I haven't told her. I just haven't."

Perhaps he's afraid he'll lose a friend. There's no easy way to tell someone about your past, one that includes armed robberies and a murder.

Mary sits in front of her television spending endless hours watching talk shows and the news. She worries about crime – crime in the neighborhood and crime in general. But when Chuck, a career criminal, comes calling, Mary quickly unlatches the deadbolts, locks, and chains on her front door and welcomes him with open arms. "He's such a nice young man," she tells me. "A good friend and a good neighbor." She rattles off the news of the day and the two interact more like mother and son. They argue about the politicians in Washington or down at City Hall, articles in the newspaper, and gossip in the neighborhood.

Chuck has kept the promise he made to himself back in 1972, to dedicate his life to fighting against the death penalty. He no longer lives in a cell but makes his home in a cramped apartment littered with cat toys, poems, books, and newspaper clippings on recent executions, press releases, and newsletters from abolitionist organizations.

The anti-death penalty movement is an uphill battle and, at the moment and especially after his Monday night class, Chuck believes it's probably a losing one. Yet he remains undeterred. And somewhat optimistic.

Unlike lightning, Chuck believes luck can strike twice. In 1972, he held a winning "lottery" ticket. He won his freedom and a second chance at life. He thinks it may happen again.

———

One former Death Row inmate in Texas would have preferred to have been struck by lightning. He remembers the day the death penalty was abolished as the worst day of his life.

CHAPTER SIX

FROM A CELL OF LAW BOOKS TO A LIBRARY OF ONE

There were four armed robbers on Death Row in 1972. Three were in Texas, one was in Georgia. Texan Calvin Sellars is the only one still alive.

Calvin Sellars jumps up for what is the hundredth time this afternoon, and I know it will be some time before he sits down.

"A chair is not just a chair. It could be wired with electricity! Like 'Ol Sparky," he screeches, laughing at his own joke. Pushing the tape recorder closer to the edge of the table, I decide that I, too, can do this interview standing up. I've borrowed the conference room at this downtown law firm in Houston from a former co-worker at the Texas Court of Criminal Appeals. When Mike's secretary walks in to ask if we want coffee, Calvin declines.

"Oh, no thank you, Ma'am. I've had my coffee quota today. You wouldn't believe how many cups I've already had."

I can just imagine, but I don't think it's just the caffeine that makes Calvin excitable. Every time I've talked to him in the past two years over the phone – at all times of the day and night – the 56-year-old convicted armed robber sounds the same. He's small in stature and he talks fast. He thinks faster than he can talk and, for a native Texan, he talks incredibly fast. He's high-energy. Calvin makes me tired.

Earlier this morning, when I flew into Houston from New York City, Calvin calls my cell phone to tell me his "stakeout" in

Calvin Sellars

Oklahoma has been postponed. Hired as a private investigator for a Houston-based law firm, Calvin this morning was to either catch an adulterous husband "in the act" or return a wayward teenage girl who had been "kidnapped by a cult" to her distraught parents. Calvin talks so fast I can't figure out which stakeout had been put on hold but, he says, he now has time.

"Where do you want to meet, Miz Cheever? I'm ready. Just tell me where. Got all my documents here with me."

"Give me 15 minutes and I'll let you know," I say. I'm thankful my friend Mike isn't in court when I call asking "to borrow" the conference room.

"It's all yours. I'll let my secretary know." Little does Mike know that Calvin and I will be "conferencing" for more than five hours.

Calvin was only one of four armed robbers sitting on Death Row in 1972; he had been on Death Row for 10 years and inside for 23. He was sent to Death Row when he was 21 with only an 8th-grade education.

It was late Friday morning on a hot steamy day in June when the news of the *Furman* decision reached Calvin Sellars, Elmer Branch, and the other 45 men on Texas' Death Row. That day was just like all the other days Calvin had spent in the last seven and a half years in his 5′ × 9′ cell.

The schedule differed little. Guards served breakfast at 5:30 a.m. Radios were turned on at 6. Lunch at 11. Dinner at 5 and lights out at 10. And if it was their lucky day, an inmate might get 15 minutes out in the yard, closely monitored by the guards. Calvin could exercise, smoke a cigarette, breathe in fresh air, or just do "plain nuthin" for 15 minutes outside.

But he didn't feel much like "recreating" on that day or any of the other 3,359 days he had spent on Death Row. Calvin had work to do. And he didn't have time to read the Bible. Calvin got permission from the warden to read law books, as long as his family paid for them. Every inch in his small, cramped cell was filled with legal papers and law books, stacked so high you could barely see the diminutive 31-year-old man, one of six children whose mother was a housewife and whose father sold vacuum cleaners. In his earlier days, Calvin looked a bit like James Dean.

For 18 hours a day, Calvin studied the law: "I woke up each morning with the law on my mind. And when I went to sleep at night, I dreamed about the law."

Time went by slowly for those on Death Row. Especially for those men who had no current execution dates. Calvin, white with Death Row Number 472 stencilled on the back of his prison uniform, had already gone through five dates.

He came to the Death House a year after 30-year-old Joseph Johnson, a black man, also from Houston, was electrocuted on July 30, 1964, for killing a Chinese storeowner during the course of an armed robbery.[1] Between 1924 and 1964, 361 men had died in the execution chamber at the Walls Unit in downtown Huntsville, the same place I had witnessed Walter's death.[2] After

Johnson there had been no executions, but Calvin and several others came close.

Calvin received a death sentence for a robbery even though the victims didn't die. Although the assault was vicious, I was surprised to find that you could end up on Death Row in a case in which no one died.

But then I had to remember where I was – Texas. I had grown up hearing the story about my grandfather and his brush with armed robbers and I knew that the law of the frontier, not of man, prevailed. In cases of armed robbery, the law of man and the law of the frontier are one. I knew the story about Grandpa and Pancho Villa – and remember a photograph of the two of them sitting at a banquet table at the Tecalonas Club in Chihuahua, Mexico, where the mining company executives were entertaining Villa after he signed a peace treaty with the Mexican government.

Grandpa was in Mexico working as an accountant for an American-based mining company. The pay was good, but it was hard work. It was during the Mexican Revolution and Pancho Villa's men roamed the countryside on a murder-robbery spree.

One evening Grandpa, his friend Henry, the mining company doctor, and several co-workers had just left the town of Parral where they had dinner, when their car was stopped by a cable placed across the road. Suddenly they were surrounded by shotgun-wielding men on horseback. With guns pointed at their heads, they put their hands up, but Henry grabbed a diamond engagement ring he had bought for his fiancée and stuck it under his tongue.

Grandpa and his group struck a deal with the bandits – the ransom was 10,000 pesos, about $5,000 U.S. dollars in 1920. They sent one member of the group back to the mine to get the money; they were told that if he didn't return, the bandits would kill their hostages.

The Americans waited all night and most of the early morning in the mountains for their friend's return. It was cold in the mountains and the bandits wouldn't light a fire for fear they would be spotted; one of them took Grandpa's new leather coat.

Sometime during the night, Henry spit the ring out over the side of the mountain.

When the mining company employee returned with the pesos, the bandits left with their bags of money and Grandpa's coat. He was happy they didn't take more – like his life. [3]

A few days later, the Mexican police asked Grandpa to go to the local jail to view a lineup. A few of Pancho Villa's men had been captured by the Federales (police) and they needed Grandpa to make a positive I.D. He looked directly into the eyes of his kidnappers and armed robbers, and shrugged: "Never seen any of 'em."

He didn't believe in the death penalty for armed robbers.

"If I had said yes, they'd have taken those Mexicans and marched them outside to the back of the jailhouse and executed them right then. They told me that's what they were going to do. I didn't think a man should get the death penalty for stealing a coat, even though it was expensive."

In Calvin Sellars' case, the armed robbery involved more than a coat – $3,900 in cash, a man's 4.8-carat diamond ring, and a 2.7-carat diamond necklace. No one died, but it didn't matter. This was Texas.

While on Death Row, the 9th-grade dropout didn't spend much time socializing. While his fellow inmates usually spent their hours sleeping, watching television, or listening to the radio, Calvin went to "law school." He spent every nickel he had, not on cigarettes, candy, or ice cream at the prison commissary, but on law books. Calvin figures he invested $4,000 in books and untold hours in his legal education.

Calvin devised a study schedule and created his own curriculum. He specialized in four subjects: criminal law, criminal procedure, federal courts, and constitutional law. This morning in the law firm's conference room, Calvin rattles off sections of the Texas Penal Code – verbatim and with section numbers – like he's giving directions to Houston Intercontinental Airport.

His federal writ of habeas corpus, *Calvin Sellars versus The State of Texas*, was pending in 1972 at the same time *Furman* was before the U.S. Supreme Court. Calvin's federal writ would be his final exam. If he passed, he was out and off Death Row. If he failed, the next stop would be the electric chair. Calvin never imagined a different scenario: that his writ would be returned – without a grade.

But that's what happened on June 29, 1972. He didn't hear the news about the Supreme Court at first. He was deep in thought writing yet another brief or writ and trying to figure out who to sue and for what. Calvin started hearing whoops and hollers and comments like "Right on" and "Thank you, Jesus" reverberate up and down the Row.

Unlike the other 46 men, when Calvin heard the news he was furious. Angry. He felt as though he'd been kicked in the stomach. He couldn't breathe. He was devastated that the Supreme Court never even looked at his writ. His application for a federal writ had been in Washington, D.C. for 23 months. Now it was moot and his day at the nation's highest court – to argue the evidence in his case – was postponed, forever.

"My issues concerned guilt or innocence. Not cruel and unusual. I was mad. Very mad. Very," Calvin says.

Those seven years of 18-hour days studying the Texas Penal Code, the Texas Code of Criminal Procedure, memorizing the U.S. Constitution, reading opinions, writing briefs and letters to lawyers and law professors all over the U.S. were wasted.

His case would never go back to the Supreme Court. He'd lost his chance to tell a panel of judges – any panel, anywhere – about what really happened on March 11, 1964, when three hooded gunmen armed with double-barreled shotguns forced their way into the Memorial Drive home of Bertha and Mair Schepps, heir to a candy and tobacco fortune, in the exclusive River Oaks suburb of Houston. The same neighborhood where I slept, or tried to, just hours after Walter was executed.

In 1964 the word on the street was that Schepps supplemented his income as a bookmaker; he was to have recently returned from making a lot of money in Las Vegas. The gunmen were looking for the $300,000 in cash they believed was hidden in the mansion. Mair Schepps told the men that he didn't keep that kind of money in the house. One of the gunmen answered: "Our information never lets us down."[4]

They then put the barrel of a shotgun in Mrs. Schepps' mouth and hit Mr. Schepps in the face with the butt of the gun, giving him a gash near the eye that took 34 stitches to close. The couple survived; the robbers took off with $3,900 in cash and diamonds.

Six days after the robbery, Police Officers J.E. Hodges and Robert Shallert followed Calvin in his car and pulled him over on Highway 59. One officer then got into Calvin's car and drove it to the Cedar Lounge, a beer joint, and put Calvin in the patrol car. It was then they began their eight-hour interrogation about the Schepps robbery.

At first, Calvin denied that he'd been there. But several hours later he pointed the finger at three other men – John Oscar Young, Sam Spivey, and astonishingly, famed criminal defense attorney Sam Hoover, a former mayor of nearby Pasadena, Texas.

Spivey "turned," agreeing to testify against Calvin, Hoover, and Young. After a brief trial, both Young and Calvin were convicted of armed robbery and given the death penalty.[5] Attorney Hoover had been tried earlier – within four months of being charged. Even though he was represented by the famed criminal defense duo of Richard "Race Horse" Haynes and Percy Foreman, the 62-year-old Hoover was convicted of being the mastermind behind the robbery and sentenced to 60 years.[6]

The conviction shocked many in the legal community. Hoover was a giant – a dazzling trial lawyer who was in the same league as his lawyers, Haynes and Foreman. He had a keen legal mind and a record-setting acquittal rate that will probably never be matched by any Texas attorney. Of the 1,250 felony cases he defended, he got 1,236 acquittals.[7]

Six months after Hoover's conviction, Calvin went to trial, maintaining his innocence and that his confession was the product of threats by the police. Calvin and the officers drove around

Houston for eight hours, during which time he was told he would die unless he "cooperated." Calvin "confessed" and pointed the finger at Hoover, Spivey, and Young.

His confession was the most crucial evidence against him. Without one, the police didn't have much of a case. The Schepps weren't able to identify Calvin and although a car similar to Calvin's was seen in the neighborhood shortly before the robbery, there was very little physical evidence to put him in the Schepps house that night. The only link came through the testimony of a police chemist who said one strand of hair found in a black hood used by the gunmen, retrieved from a nearby trash can, was the same as a human hair taken from Calvin's head after his arrest. But on cross-examination the chemist admitted that it was rare to make a positive identification based only on a single strand.

On parole for a 1961 burglary, Calvin had an alibi: his mother, wife, brother, and a neighbor testified that he was with them at his own home during the time of the robbery. Nevertheless, a jury took just four hours to find him guilty of armed robbery and sentenced him to die in the electric chair.

Throughout the years, Calvin has always maintained his innocence.[8] He filed a flurry of writs, wrote a carton-full of letters to lawyers asking for help.

So when the *Furman* ruling came down in 1972, it's easy to see why it was such a dark day for Calvin Sellars. The darkest came just two months later when the governor of Texas commuted the death sentences of the men on Death Row. Most received a sentence of life but Calvin and the other men who had been convicted of either rape or robbery, crimes not involving murder, received 99-year terms. It didn't make any sense.

Those murderers would be eligible for parole in less than 20 years, maybe even 10 if they accumulated "good time" based on their "good" behavior while inside. If he had gotten a life term, Calvin would have been eligible for parole in 10 years or less – which by now was only two and a half years away. With a 99-year term, Calvin Sellars was facing a minimum of 17 years of hard time.

"What really did it, what really made me mad came 67 days later, when I was re-sentenced. They graciously granted mass commutations. But not for me," Calvin says. "They told me there's three sentences: death, life, and 99 years. And that I had no life sentence to commute. I was doing 99 years. And that was that."

The ever-litigious Calvin took that issue up to the 5th U.S. Circuit Court of Appeals. With Calvin on the brief were an impressive list of high-powered appellate attorneys that included the prominent Charles Alan Wright, the University of Texas law professor who, just four years earlier, had been Calvin's adversary as the lawyer arguing in favor of the death penalty.

Despite the impressive group of litigators, Calvin lost again.[9] He was back doing 99 years for a crime he says he did not commit.

It was a setback, but the legal pit bull remained optimistic. "Just to show you how naive I was, I really believed in the U.S. Constitution. The law would set me free. I always believed that."

He went back to the law books and kept reading.

One of Calvin's "clients" was his brother Wesley, who was sentenced to a 99-year term in 1965 for stealing $25,000 in furs, jewels, and cash in a burglary. In 1968, a federal court overturned Wesley's conviction and he was released from prison. The charges were eventually dismissed.

But four years later, Wesley was arrested again – this time for a much more serious offense. He was convicted in the shooting death of Officer Kenneth Wayne Moody in a botched burglary attempt at a school in Houston. The jury gave him life, instead of death.[10]

Calvin worked on Wesley's appeal and got it reversed on the ground that police officers had suppressed the confession of another man, who had admitted to the shooting. The charges were dismissed.

With that big win under his belt, Calvin wasn't too upset in 1976 when the 5th Circuit upheld his 99-year term. It just made him more determined. He knew that eventually he would get his day in court; he just didn't know when. He remained upbeat, deciding it was just a minor setback.

There must be a way to reopen this case. I've just got to figure out how, Calvin told himself.

And in June 1977, he did. That's when he first read the transcripts from the case of Attorney Sam Hoover who was the first of the three defendants to go to trial – a time when recollections and the resulting testimony are "still fresh."

At Hoover's trial, the two police officers testified that Calvin was at the Houston police station at 8 p.m. when he signed his confession. But a year later, during Calvin's testimony, the officers put the hour at 2:15 a.m. – the following morning. [11]

The discrepancy was an important factor in the appeal, because of what transpired, Calvin says, during the hours when he was first picked up by police at 4 p.m. Hours later he confessed, both verbally and in writing. At his trial, Calvin argued that the confession could not be evidence since it was the product of death threats. The officers vehemently denied they had threatened Calvin; the confession, they said, was one of free will.

What transpired on December 7, 1977, in the courtroom of U.S. District Judge Finis Cowan, even surprised Calvin. As usual, Calvin was acting as his own lawyer during the hearing. He had subpoenaed Robert Shallert, who had retired from the police force after 20 years and was then selling real estate in Houston.

When Calvin tells the story, he becomes even more animated and excitable. He's jumping around like a man who's walking on hot sand in August on the Texas Gulf Coast. Occasionally he sits back down and pulls out a file from his battered brown leather briefcase; its contents, photographs, newspaper clippings, copies of appeals and writs, and photocopies of old appellate opinions, take up half of the long mahogany conference table. He pulls out dates or quotes from his seemingly endless memory. Sometimes he gets off track, interrupting his story with what sounds like even more "tall Texas tales," but they aren't. They are all true. He has documentation. Affidavits.

I find the whole scenario unbelievable. But that is probably because we share a common bond: both Calvin and I are incredibly naive about the criminal justice system. Or, at least we *were*.

In Walter's case, I believed that the state of Texas wouldn't execute him because he did not have a prior record. The prosecutors agreed and that's why they pushed so hard for a plea bargain. Walter's trial lawyer believed it too, telling him the case would certainly be reversed on appeal. We were all wrong. Dead wrong.

Calvin Sellars never envisioned his own death because, he says, the U.S. Constitution "prohibits the execution of an innocent man." And that's why he decided one afternoon to sit in the electric chair – voluntarily.

"I just wanted to see how it felt," Calvin laughed mischievously, explaining why he sat in the electric chair. He says the warden considered sending him to the mental hospital for evaluation.

"He didn't know whether to send me to the 'nut house' or keep me right there on Death Row," Calvin quips. "He 'bout had a heart attack. He was sayin: 'Calvin, boy, have you lost your mind? What if they were testing it to see if it worked and flipped the switch right now? Lord have mercy. You'd be one fried son of a bitch.' "

But the story illustrates the real Calvin Sellars – this cocky, fearless, God-fearing, swashbuckling man. Calvin prefers to call it simple naiveté.

"I *never*, not once," Calvin squeals, slamming the table and then jumping up, "*ever* thought I'd be executed. Because, you see, I truly, truly with all my heart, believed in the United States Constitution. That it would save my life. Can you believe that? But that's what I thought. I was that naive. Lord have mercy!"

Calvin is both naive and fearless: only one of those traits will keep you alive on Death Row. The other will kill you.

It was probably that naiveté that made him a successful jailhouse lawyer. He was so successful that the State of Texas tried to shut down what they called "Calvin's legal practice." In his 15 years of filing lawsuits on behalf of himself and his friends, Calvin had an impressive record.

"The absolutely most interesting case I ever argued was my own." Naturally, I think, as we go back in time to Huntsville, Texas.

It's December 7, 1977 and the most incredible story is unfolding in U.S. District Judge Finis Cowan's courtroom. So incredible that the judge said: "I can't believe what I'm hearing."

What Judge Cowan heard was Officer Shallert admitting that he and Officer Hodges had used threats and intimidation during a six-hour ride around Houston to get Calvin Sellars to confess to the Schepps robbery. [12]

Judge Cowan was startled. It's one of those "Perry Mason moments" that happen only on television or in the daydreams of those men in prison for crimes they did not commit. He could not believe the turn of events. He decided that, despite his legal brilliance, Calvin needed to be represented by a licensed attorney. He kept Calvin in the courtroom and sent the van back to the prison. The judge then roamed the hallways looking for a lawyer. He found Larry Watts in the hallway, outside another judge's courtroom. Dragging him into his, the judge made the introductions.

"Larry Watts. Meet Calvin Sellars. Mr. Watts, you're Mr. Sellars' new attorney. I'm appointing you. Today. Right now. Mr. Sellars will fill you in."

The legal team of Watts and Sellars had eight days to prove that the 1965 confession was involuntary and that the charges against Calvin should be thrown out. They had one week to prepare to cross-examine the other police officer, Hodges. They knew that officer would not contradict his earlier testimony.

When Hodges entered the courtroom, Calvin knew what his side of the story would be. Calvin was just surprised that Hodges would accuse his former partner of lying.

Hodges, now a pipe fitter in Craig, Colorado, denied that either he or his partner ever threatened Calvin.

"Who is the liar? You or Shallert?" Attorney Watts asked the former police officer.

"I'm not a liar. He [Shallert] is a liar."

When asked to explain the conflicting testimony, Hodges blurted: "He [Shallert] must have lost his mind. It [threatening Sellars] didn't happen."[13]

But, in his opinion, Judge Cowan said he believed Shallert. He ruled that Calvin had been illegally detained by the State of Texas for 14 years. Immediately, the state appealed the ruling to the federal appeals court; Texas would have 45 days to retry Calvin Sellars for armed robbery.

On January 27, two days before the 45-day period was to expire, Calvin was filling out paperwork for his release. Prison Superintendent E.J. Estelle, the named defendant in all of Calvin's prison lawsuits and those filed on behalf of his fellow inmates, stopped by to wish Calvin well. Estelle had called the Attorney General's office to tell them he was releasing Calvin at 4 p.m. Friday, because the 45th day of the federal court order fell on a Sunday and inmates were generally released on a weekday. The state didn't budge.

And then the call came in at 2 p.m.

"Mr. Estelle came to see me. I could tell by his expression, something was terribly wrong. I sensed he had something painful to tell me. I believed it hurt him more than it hurt me," Calvin told a reporter at the time.

The state had gotten a federal judge to stop Calvin's release.[14]

There would be no homecoming celebration that day. It would have to be postponed another two months. Calvin had already waited 4,772 days. He could wait 100 more. It was rough – emotionally. Calvin had been so close.

On May 5, 1978, Judge Finis Cowan had had about enough. Ever mindful that his earlier order for release was still on appeal, he went ahead and released Calvin from prison – without setting bail.[15]

Calvin Sellars, a man who'd spent eight years on Texas' Death Row with three execution dates, and who had come within 18 hours of execution, spent his first hours of freedom with his family: his brother Lucky, sister Linda, and daughter Kay who was only one year old when her father was arrested. Calvin's wife, Micki, died in a car accident in 1976.

From 1978 to 1986, Calvin worked as a paralegal and private investigator for Houston attorney Jay Burnett. For eight years he stayed out of trouble. But then he stumbled. In July 1986, Calvin was arrested for threatening three customers at a bar with a pistol.

Calvin is not surprised that he got in trouble then. He says he started drinking again when he found out his brother Wesley, once his cellmate in K1 at the Texas Department of Corrections' Loveland Unit, was arrested for yet another burglary. While both men were inside for capital murder, Calvin had worked hard to get his brother's case not only reversed by the 5th Circuit Court of Appeals, but to get him released from prison. [16]

"It took me almost four years to walk him out on the last one – a classic suppression of the evidence motion. This next one [burglary] was really minor. And in a nutshell, well, I thought we'd work it out," Sellars said. "But my brother already had his mind made up. He was not going back to the penitentiary again." While out on $140,000 bail, Wesley skipped his July 7 court date on the burglary charge and skipped town.

"That really did something to me. Because I knew my brother. I knew he wasn't coming back." He had a premonition that the only way Wesley would return to Houston was in a pine box.

With his brother a fugitive, Calvin's life unraveled. He began drinking and using cocaine. On August 20, Calvin went to a bar, picked up a woman, and they started drinking whiskey. At the next bar, a very drunk Calvin got into a fight with the bartender and pointed his pistol at him and two other customers. Calvin was back in jail.

Meanwhile, Wesley was laying low – until mid-November when he surfaced in Phoenix. Within an hour, he stole five cars at gunpoint, abandoning them in succession. The last one led to a high-speed chase in Tempe, Arizona, where he kidnapped a six-year-old boy as he walked home from school and held him hostage.

After a four-hour standoff, Wesley came out of the house and began shooting members of the SWAT team. One police officer was shot in the eye when he went into the house to get the child out safely. Another officer fatally wounded Sellars with a shotgun blast to the chest.

On November 21, 1986, the manhunt was over and Wesley was dead.[17] Calvin's prediction had come true.

In July 1987, Calvin was back in court to answer to the aggravated assault charges against him. Now the most successful jailhouse lawyer in Texas prison history had to decide whether to fight or give up.

Five months earlier, Calvin traded all his law books for the one book he said he'd never read on Death Row but has ended up saving his life – the Bible.

On February 9, 1987, Sellars became a Christian. "Before this went down, before I pulled that pistol, never have I been religious. I never got down on my knees on Death Row." He said a book called *The Invisible War* by Donald G. Barnhouse jump-started his journey. "There was no conversion like Paul [St. Paul the Apostle]. I didn't see a bright light. It doesn't work that way," Sellars said. "And I don't call it religion. Mine is a way of life. I put God into everything." Calvin says he feels lucky to have been sentenced by another born-again. Judge Charles Hearn is known to go into his chambers before sentencing and pray.

Calvin turned down a plea bargain of two years and, against the advice of his attorneys for the first time in his life, he pleaded guilty to the charges.

Calvin said the judge was confused. "He said: 'I want to know why. I got to know why. With your record [as a jailhouse lawyer] it [pleading guilty] doesn't make any sense.' Calvin quoted Hearn as saying: 'Mr. Sellars, you believe what I believe. But you gotta grow, boy. And I gotta do what's right.' " He then sentenced Calvin to the maximum – 10 years.

"He could've given me two years, but the Holy Spirit led him," Calvin said. For the next 26 months, Calvin didn't pick up a law book.

"I never thought I'd be able to talk about God. I am a super-duper writ writer; I've done at least 20 successful writs," Calvin said. "But during those 26 months, I had the time. To read the Bible. I just grew stronger."

Once he was released, he returned to Houston and paralegal–private detective business. He lives with his second wife in a house on five acres and earns $75 to $125 an hour, "depending on the case." He makes his money the old-fashioned way: hard work.

A year after our visit, I see Calvin again; we meet at his gray and white ranch-style house just 40 minutes outside of Houston. The one-level home is filled with mementos of the Lone Star state – longhorn skulls, candlesticks made from branding irons – and Calvin has a collection of American Indian art. He is most proud of a vintage jukebox of 45s of Elvis, which sits prominently in the center of his sun-filled living room.

It's an August afternoon and the temperatures are in the low 100s. A neighbor knocks on the front door and asks if Calvin can help his "out-of-town" brother-in-law get his station wagon, buried deep in three inches of Texas mud. The neighbor raises his eyebrow and carefully enunciates nouns that have turned into adjectives – "out-of-towner" and "brother-in-law" – as he describes "the nincompoop" who's stuck in the mud. I can tell he wants to say more, but he stops. Calvin gives him a look and it is only then that he realizes that Calvin's guest is also an "out-of-towner."

"No problem!" screeches Calvin, and he races to his mini-pickup truck and stops briefly to make sure I'm following. Excited, the chivalrous Calvin runs to the passenger door and opens it for me, and then jumps in the driver's seat and we barrel down his long unpaved driveway to the muddy dirt road.

Before entering the muddy zone, Calvin stops the car and gets out. He bends down and touches the ground, like he is tracking a bear that has gone into the woods.

"It don't make sense for both of us to get stuck." He turns around and takes off running. Like a puppy dog, I run after him.

Immediately I am covered with mosquitoes. He hears me slapping my arms and quietly cussing. The long-sleeved and blue-jeaned Calvin reaches in his pocket and tosses me a bottle of "Off." After spraying every uncovered portion of my body – which is a lot considering I am dressed for the 102 degree heat in a skirt and sleeveless blouse and not for the mosquito-filled jungle I am about to enter – Calvin issues a warning that sends my pulse racing.

"Now, I don't have anything for rattlesnakes. Except some good common sense. Be careful. There's snake in dem hills," he says laughing, jogging to meet the other stranded out-of-towner. I don't see any snakes out in the brush and after an hour and a half, and many mosquito bites later, we manage to pull the out-of-towner out of the mud.

Calvin is eager to get back to work – he's talking to lawyers and clients on each one of his phones and is faxing documents while reviewing legal papers.

Getting Calvin to talk was easy. Getting him to stop is a lot harder. Unlike another former death row inmate, Calvin never once asked me about my faith or subjected me to the "born again" Christian test.

But William "Rusty" Holland, on Death Row in South Carolina for two brutal murders, said he wouldn't talk to me unless I assured him that the message in *Back from the Dead* would focus on Jesus Christ.

That was going to be a challenge.

CHAPTER SEVEN

ONCE A CON, ALWAYS?

Of the 589 members of the Class of '72, 322 have been released from prison.

"N-31. N-32. I-16. N-39. N-43. N-45. N-35. G-54. G-57. I-20, I-19." Some are working four cards at a time. Others focus on the one in front of them.

"Hey, y'all. Do we have a winnah yet?" the gravelly throated bingo caller shouts through the microphone as I look out from the snack bar into the bright, fluorescent-lit room where clouds of smoke hang from the ceilings undisturbed. Bingo Heaven[1] – once a sporting goods store – in a strip mall in Spartanburg, South Carolina, is now just a large, bare room filled with dozens of bingo enthusiasts. Rows of oblong Formica tables where polyester-shirted and blue-jean-clad men and women are slumped in uncomfortable metal folding chairs have replaced the racks of Day-Glo orange hunting jackets, leather boots, duck callers, and rifle scopes. Everyone's eyes are peeled on their cards. It seems that I am the only one bothered by breathing in everyone else's poison – tonight I wonder why I have been so careful never to pick up a cigarette. My lungs start to fill with nicotine from the cartons this crowd is devouring.

There is nothing in this sparsely decorated hall to muffle the sounds from the many animated conversations that surround me. Both the smoke and the barking of the Bingo caller, in between drags on his cigarette, have given me an excruciating headache. I am relieved to find that the snack bar sells aspirin – Advil and Anacin for 75 cents – in addition to pork rinds, three kinds of potato chips, kosher dill pickles, and 11 different types of sandwiches. Usually, I would have bolted from a room like this, but I am here tonight to watch a convicted killer from Aiken, South Carolina, in action – at his job as food manager in the snack bar at Bingo Heaven.

Everyone is focused on the $500 jackpot riding on the 7:30 p.m. game, and for those who can't hear the call, the numbers are prominently displayed on eight television monitors mounted throughout the large room.

The $500 game gives Lynn and Anne, the 40-something tall blonde sisters who are working behind the food counter, a brief respite. They sit down only for a moment but jump up once they see their boss, William "Rusty" Holland, walk from the kitchen to the snack bar. In the crook of one arm, decorated with a crude U.S. Marine tattoo, he holds a plastic bowl of hard-boiled eggs to replenish the dwindling egg salad supply. In the other is a cardboard box with the name "Moores" on its side; it is a case of pork rinds and potato chips. There is no sitting down on the stools hidden behind the peacock blue Formica counter at the Bingo Heaven snack bar.

At 49 years old, Rusty Holland looks his age. And a bit more. He's in pretty good shape, strong and muscular. The redheaded ex-con has a well-groomed mustache and a receding hairline; his arms are sprinkled with freckles. Rusty was hired by Marcie, the girlfriend of Larry, Rusty's former cellmate.[2] Larry served 10 years for first-degree murder and then went back in for another 10 for a parole violation: he was caught carrying a gun while drunk. That combination might have been lethal for an ex-con with a drinking problem; Larry really got 10 years for being incredibly stupid.

Rusty was in prison for 11 years – three and a half were spent on South Carolina's Death Row where he and 11 other members of the Class of '72 sat waiting to die. Rusty had company; four members of his motorcycle gang, a group called the "Tribulators," later renamed the South Carolina chapter of Hell's Angels, were sentenced to death for the murders of two members of a rival gang, the "Dixie Dragons," and the attempted murder of two of the Dragons' girlfriends. They left the Dragons' clubhouse certain that the four were dead; all had been hogtied with their throats slashed. Both women miraculously survived.[3]

I know the snack-bar sisters have no idea who their boss is or was; I'm certain they would've found another summer job to help pay for their daughters' band and cheerleader expenses. I wonder if I would be here tonight if I had seen the grisly autopsy photographs that were introduced at Rusty's trial.

Marcie, the owner of several "gaming establishments" as Rusty calls them, doesn't seem to care.

On the drive from the airport earlier this morning, I can't help but notice how many places there are to feed this addiction. I'm surprised, not only at the number, but at how many are open before noon. Marcie's gaming rooms are filled with "Pot-O-Golds" and "Shamrock Sevens," video-gambling machines that seem to make it all too easy for a customer to lose his or her paycheck without realizing it. Marcie's "Town Bingo" is just one of the more than 7,000 places in South Carolina you can go to lose your shirt, about three times as many as in the gambling Mecca of Nevada – Las Vegas.

When I visited, gambling was big business in the Palmetto state and there was no official oversight. The industry was virtually unregulated: the state collected no taxes, imposed no real regulations, didn't restrict those who could own machines, didn't require that the machines be honest, and didn't forbid children from playing. So, it's little wonder that this "convenience gambling," as it is called, grossed $2.5 billion annually and netted $728 million, owners paid no taxes, and profits climbed 20 percent a year.[4]

Marcie seems a little unnerved at my presence and I don't blame her. While it may be "legal" to have two convicted murderers on her payroll, I'm not so sure it is smart. And knowing the severe restrictions imposed on parolees, I am confident that having Larry and Rusty work there might be a parole violation and could send both men back to the Big House.

After lunch at Fatz Cafe, well-named for the platters of calabash chicken (fried chicken) and an entire Vidalia onion dipped in some sort of spicy batter, washed down with about a gallon of sweet tea and lime, Rusty and I take a tour of Marcie's video empire. She hired Rusty because of his experience in the food business – Rusty left prison in 1981 and bought three Subway Sandwich franchises.

Rusty jumped at Marcie's offer. He left his job as a supervisor in the seasonal fruit packing business of Vero Beach, Florida, to escape the Florida summer heat and make some quick money. Legally.

And Marcie needed the help. She'd been "robbed blind" in the past few months, Rusty's wife confided, so she really needed a former junkie, professional thief, and ex-con to watch her back. I guess if you look at it that way, it makes perfect sense to hire a convicted killer to keep a close eye on the cash box.

During our brief tour, I learned more about video gambling than I ever wanted to know. The rooms are dark and smell of stale cigarettes. There are middle-aged white women, with cigarettes hanging out of their mouths, perched on stools in front of the "Pot-O-Gold" machines, their eyes are glued to the screen.

I'd never been around gambling growing up, with the exception of those wildcatter friends of my father's who struck it big in the Texas oil boom of the 1960s and 1970s. Gambling was forbidden in our home – all kinds, legal and not. In fact, on a family trip to the West Coast in 1970 we stopped in Las Vegas, not to take in the shows or sights of the Strip, but for a quick lesson on the evils of gambling.

We were excited about seeing comedian Carol Burnett in the elevator at Caesar's Palace, but even more so at the thought that within minutes we would be watching our mother confront the "one-armed bandit" while she gave us a "good, hard lesson" about the dangers of gambling.

We followed Mom as she marched passed the nickel slots. And those that took dimes. She turned her head slightly to make sure that her "little Army" was following. She walked right up to a quarter slot. We stopped breathing. A quarter was a lot of money. You could buy a burger for 19 cents at Jim's Frontier. And a nickel Coke. To see my mother part with 25 cents was nothing short of a miracle. It was going to be some lesson.

She took a quarter out of her coin purse and held it in the slot. She didn't let it fall until she was sure she had her five children's individualized attention. Then, in a very dramatic gesture, she let it drop. We were stunned.

She pulled the lever down and started her "Baptist-like" sermon about how people just throw their money away with these "damn machines," spend their paychecks in an hour, leave their families poor and hungry, can't pay their bills, and, in the end, Sally Cheever preached, they all end up on welfare.

We weren't really listening; we were mesmerized as the apples and pears and black bars that screamed "Jackpot" quickly spun on the reels, around and around. She turned her back on "the bandit." She wasn't even paying attention, but we were. She began rattling off a whole list of forbidden items she said you could buy with the "government gift" of food stamps.

She was so into her lecture that she didn't notice the red light blinking. She didn't hear the sound of the quarters as they crashed into the coin box and spilled onto the floor. She was in a trance. Our screams brought her back to reality.

"Oh, my Gawd, in merciful heavens," she said loudly, and soon, my very petite mother, all of 5 feet and 100 pounds, was down on the whiskey-stained and cigarette-butt littered carpet along with the rest of us, grabbing the quarters from the $25 jackpot and quickly stuffing them into both her pockets and ours. While crawling around looking for quarters that had rolled under the other "bandits" in the smoke-filled room, Mom came across a pair of polished black, military-style boots. They were attached to a pair of creased, dark blue trousers. A police officer loomed over her. Jumping up, she smoothed down her sleeveless, empire-waisted shift dress, and before she could get a word in edgewise, the policeman gave her a little lecture of his own.

"Ma'am, do you realize you are in violation of the law by bringing these minor children into this gaming room?" he barked, wagging his finger in her face. "You need to leave immediately or I'm going to have you arrested!"

"But, officer, I was just giving them a lesson about the evils of gambling and these one-armed bandits. And I had no idea it was against the law. With the kids and all. I mean, sir, I was just trying to make my point and –"

He held up his hand for silence and she stopped talking. He looked at Mom and then at us, our pockets spilling with quarters, the fruits of her passionate lesson. And then he started laughing.

"Well, Ma'am, I'm not sure your kids here get your point, if you know what I mean. Now, get out of here. Oh, and good luck with your *lessons*," he said, before walking away.

Tonight, Bingo Heaven's jackpot is worth a lot more than 100 quarters. We are making a lot of money at the little snack bar, too. It is so busy that I begin jumping up to work, side by side, with Rusty and the sisters, filling orders from hungry gamblers and working the cash register. I am supposed to just be observing.

I am trying hard to breathe and concentrate on memorizing the price list – Moore's pork rinds are 70 cents, Super Nachos with chili and cheddar cheese is $2.50. The 11 different sandwiches all have different prices, but it's not more than $2. That's because, Rusty says, our customers are on a tight budget and are really only here tonight for the game and the chitchat.

Mrs. Rodgers, an elderly woman in green polyester pants and a pastel-flowered long-sleeved shirt, is one of those customers whose only means of income is her Social Security check. I can tell she is one of Rusty's favorites because when he sees her sitting outside in her car, waiting for the doors to open at 4:30 p.m., he goes outside to walk her in. I tell Rusty she looks familiar, but I know that is impossible since I have never been to Spartanburg.

"Oh, you've seen her all right. She was at Town Bingo on the Asheville Highway when we were there earlier this afternoon."

Tonight Mrs. Rodgers is short on cash. Rusty gives her a $15 "advance" until she can cash her check.

"Are you sure that's $15?" she asks, winking.

"Just barely."

"Well, you know that I'm good for it."

"I know, Ma'am. If not, I'll just keep chasing you," Rusty says, smiling, trying not to show his teeth, a testament to the lack of dental care in prison. I wonder if Mrs. Rodgers would be laughing so heartily if she knew that her "banker" is a convicted killer.

At 11:30 p.m., in the last game of the night, there is a $2,000 winner. The real winner tonight is Bingo Heaven's owner, Marcie. The customers are quickly ushered out and the doors are locked exactly at midnight, one of the few rules that this state, full of conservative church-going Christians, imposes. I have no idea just how much cash Marcie has but I've got a pretty good picture when she, Rusty, and Larry go into a back office to count it. I hear the door lock.

I am now on my own, but there is nowhere to go. I spend an awkward 30 minutes sitting at one of the long metal tables in the bingo room, looking down at the cigarette butts scattered on the cement floor. A few times I look up and through the plate glass windows. There is nothing to protect me except sheets of glass, and I wonder, as I look out into the parking lot, if someone is going to make an unwelcome entrance with a shotgun blast.

A half hour later, the money is counted and the three return. I walk to the back door and am about to make my exit when Rusty grabs my wrist and tells me to "stay put" with Marcie. I can tell she is annoyed having to "baby-sit."

Rusty and Larry then engage in their nightly post Bingo Heaven ritual. They lock Marcie and me inside Bingo Heaven and then scour the parking lot looking for prospective armed robbers.

I see Rusty approach one car, its lights off and its engine idling. Within seconds the car leaves. Rusty has told the lovers – probably adulterers, he says forcefully – to move their "make-out session" down the road.

When the key turns in the lock, I know it is safe to leave. And I can't wait. This whole ritual is unnerving. I've read enough cases to know that the hour between closing and locking up is the most dangerous – when employees, or in my case, a naive journalist who looks like an employee, get herded into a back office by an accomplice while his partner is looting the safe, or in this case, a briefcase full of cash.

Once the door opens Marcie walks out into the parking lot and, in her left hand, holds the briefcase tightly, keeping it right by her side. My gut tells me to stay close because I am sure that in her right hand, which has now disappeared and is inside her shoulder purse, she's holding a gun. Marcie is just the kind of woman who will use it if she is interrupted in her walk to her new Ford pickup truck, which will soon be loaded down with tonight's winnings. I figure she is probably a good shot.

I am relieved to bid Marcie and Larry goodbye; we exchange quick and strained pleasantries. I make a mad dash for my car and I don't care how I look. I am scared silly. I jump in the car, lock my doors and turn on the ignition. Rusty is still talking to the two. I wait for him to get into his car and then follow him into Sunglo, an all-night gas station, another dangerous spot for a woman traveling alone.

He needs gas and a soda pop, he says, and I wonder why he didn't get the soda while he was at Bingo Heaven.

Rusty returns to his truck and I follow him to the Marriott Extended Stay, the same place where he's been living for the past five weeks.

It is 1 a.m. by the time I get to my room, and Rusty walks me to the door. My path is momentarily blocked by the guest next door, a young kid in cutoffs with shoulder-length brown hair who's probably about 17.

Six empty cans of malt liquor lay at his bare feet; his attention is centered on a joint in his mouth. He is having difficulty lighting it, made even harder by the fact that he's drunk. I immediately freeze, wondering if it is smart to continue to my room and let him see that I am alone. I wonder if I should turn around and get back into the car.

Instantly Rusty senses my discomfort, grabs the room key out of my hand and puts his arm around mine. He starts calling me "Darlin," as though we are a couple. He opens my motel room door, and once inside, closes the curtains, locks the door, along with the deadbolt, and puts on the chain. My discomfort level soars. But Rusty seems to think it is still centered on the beer-drinking, dope-smoking teenager next door.

I am safe from him, but now I'm locked, dead bolted, and chained inside a room with a convicted killer. Minutes later, my next-door neighbor leaves his perch on the sidewalk and returns to his room. The sound of his deadbolt assures me he is in for the night.

"Are you sure you're gonna be okay? Do you want me to stay for a bit?" Rusty asks, oblivious to my anxiety.

"I'm fine. Really. Thanks so much for walking me in. I'll see you tomorrow," I say as I escort him to the door.

Once I hear his truck leave the parking lot, I then relock all three locks. For good measure, I drag a reading chair from the corner of the room and prop it against the door handle. I grab my black suitcase with wheels, which now seems heavier, and sandwich it between the door and the chair. I call the front desk for a wakeup call, take a Tylenol P.M., leave the bathroom light on and pray.

I decide then that when I relay the highlights of my Bingo Heaven trip to family and friends upon my return home, some things are better left unsaid. This is one of them.

Six months later, I am back in South Carolina. Back with Rusty. In a motel. But we aren't alone. Rusty's wife, Vicki, and their daughters Jeannie and Karen,[5] have joined us in what is to be the Hollands' annual trip to Columbia, South Carolina – an appearance before the South Carolina Board of Pardons and Parole.

I don't know why I am so nervous when I walk into the small room where the pardon board is meeting. I am dressed appropriately, in a blue business suit, and I look more like a lawyer than a reporter. But I don't feel like one. With the exception of the infrequent court appearances for Walter, I'd always been at hearings and at trials as a reporter – busily taking notes of others' quotes, not being the one quoted.

I had been trained to be impartial, to not get involved, and to write with a clear and objective eye. But for some unknown reason, that all changed a couple of months earlier when I wrote a letter on behalf of Rusty. His wife, a good-looking blonde who reminds me of either a former high school cheerleader or a small town, West Texas beauty queen, asked me, in a series of very long emails, if I would write the parole board on Rusty's behalf.

I must have been flattered when Vicki told me I was really in a "unique position" to assess whether a man like her husband was truly rehabilitated since I'd spent so much time with so many other former Death Row inmates.

"Rusty *is* a star, isn't he?" she asked.

I'd already interviewed more than 100 men just like Rusty who had been paroled from Death Row. But very few were just like Rusty.

He earns a good salary as a supervisor for the fruit packing company. He works nights and weekends in the ministry program at his church, the Central Assembly of God. And unlike most of the others, Rusty isn't ashamed of telling anyone and everyone that he is a former convicted killer. In fact, he seems to delight in the details about his time on South Carolina's Death Row.

It was there, he said, while serving three years in solitary confinement, that he found Jesus, on Christmas Day in 1971. Shortly after we met, Rusty sent me a 90-minute tape recording of a speech he made to the members of his congregation, where he was introduced by the Rev. Buddy Tipton, an evangelical minister who, like Rusty, frequently made appearances on Jim and Tammy Faye Bakker's 700 Club.

Rusty didn't go looking for me. I found him and convinced him to talk to me, against his better judgment. In fact, it was Vicki who initially called and left a whispered message on my answering machine very early one morning in December. She gave me her home telephone number and suggested a time when I should call back. She also told me that Rusty didn't want to be interviewed, but that she felt it was important.

My letter was on his desk, under a stack of bills, and that's where it was going to stay, Rusty told me when we first spoke. He wanted no part of a book about ex-Death Row inmates unless the book's focus was Jesus and the role He played in his Death Row conversion. When I called later that week, Rusty was adamant that he wasn't going to agree to an interview until I was able to convince him that every former Death Row inmate's story was unique; if Rusty wanted to attribute his success to Jesus and that was *his* story, I'd include it.

I had spent a lot of time talking to Rusty on the phone and through emails, and finally I flew to Vero Beach. I spent several days with Rusty and his family, friends, and fellow churchgoers. When I returned home, I "observed" him, without his knowledge, through his postings in anti-death penalty chat rooms, and his letters were full of what I'd expect from a "born again." He was very consistent about the role Jesus played in his life.

I tell myself that I have spent enough time with him and his family to feel comfortable saying, publicly, that Rusty is the real thing. He is different from most of the others.

I am convinced that Rusty is rehabilitated and deserves a pardon from the South Carolina Parole Board. I don't think my request to the South Carolina board is unusual. There are many members of the Class of '72 who are no longer on parole only because the laws in the states in which they were sentenced to die have made them eligible for a discharge from parole, merely by the passage of time. But South Carolina is different. As a former Death Row inmate, Rusty Holland's parole can end in only one of two ways: at his death or by a pardon. To Rusty and Vicki, a pardon means everything.

When he was first paroled in 1981, Rusty, who had just married the widow of a local doctor in Spartanburg, South Carolina, lived with her and her two children. He walked out of prison and walked head first into a ministry where he "took the message of Jesus and the Gospel" to all 50 states. He told me he was a frequent guest on a Christian television program, *The 700 Club* with his "good friends," TV evangelists Jim and Tammy Faye Bakker; he said he preached the Gospel many times at the Bakkers" Heritage Park. Rusty says he's gone to Rio de Janeiro, Puerto Rico, and Spain on missionary work and ministered with another evangelist, Barry Mayson, a former vice president of the state chapter of Hell's Angels and author of *Fallen Angel: From Hell's Angels to Heaven's Saints*.[6]

The amount of time he spent in the ministry was taking a toll on his new marriage. Rusty decided to cut back because he needed a good-paying job to support his new family. He invested in the Subway Sandwich Shop franchise and within five years he ended up owning all three in Spartanburg.

"I became so involved in my business that my ministry began suffering and soon neither one was succeeding, or my marriage," Rusty said.

But it was the sudden death in 1986 of his mentor and very close friend, Bill Howell, that sent Rusty spiraling downhill fast. Howell, 64, took a nap after a church service and never woke up – dying of a massive heart attack.

"I loved my family and they were a tremendous comfort to me but Bill Howell had a special place in my heart," Rusty said. "He loved me when I wasn't loveable, and when he died, I really got disillusioned with God. I was angry at Him. I was mad that Bill had left and that he had been taken away from me."

At the same time, evangelists Jim and Tammy Bakker fell from grace, and Rusty says he was so disenchanted with the church that he decided to rebel. He "walked away from God, my wife, and family" and divorced in 1986. A short time later he met Vicki, also a recent divorcée in Spartanburg who had a two-year-old daughter. Within a year they married and moved to Vero Beach, to be closer to his aging and ailing mother. But the travel restrictions for a parolee were much stricter in Florida and Rusty was required to apply for a permit to travel, even from county to county.

Without a pardon, Rusty will be a parolee for the rest of his life. With a pardon he would regain rights we all take for granted: the right to vote and the right to own and carry a gun.

But the most important right, he says, is the freedom to go across the country, and the world, to continue preaching the message of Jesus.

Two months ago, it was only a letter. But that all changed less than 12 hours before the hearing. My involvement was about to turn much more personal.

When I fly into Columbia earlier this evening and meet Rusty and Vicki at the motel, I am surprised to find that he has already checked me in. The thought bothers me during dinner at the Cracker Barrel where we meet a friend of Rusty's from the penitentiary days, a former bank robber who had been, until he was caught in the mid-70s, very successful. He knows Rusty from their years together in prison in South Carolina where they both were involved in prison ministry. Before meeting Rusty, this 60-ish ex-con did time in the federal system, serving several years in Leavenworth Penitentiary.

We are sitting in the middle of the restaurant, and before eating, Rusty asks his friend, seated next to me, "to thank the Good Lord for our bounty." First, Rusty insists we all hold hands while asking for God's blessing. It is not the choice of dinner companions that unnerves me; by this time, I am used to having dinner with men who have spent most of their adult lives behind bars. It is about taking religion, or in this case a simple prayer that turns into a miniature sermon, so public.

When dinner ends, we bid farewell to Rusty's friend who assures us he'll be at the hearing tomorrow morning. In addition to Rusty, he has a couple of other friends who are up for parole.

When we return to the Day's Inn, I pull Rusty aside, insisting that I pay for my room. It is against journalistic ethics for my interview subject to pick up the tab, but I tell him I appreciate the offer. Rusty reluctantly agrees, and after I return to the registration desk and fill out the paperwork and hand over my credit card, the clerk asks if I need *another* key. For a moment I am taken aback. I've never gotten the first one.

It all makes sense when I check into Room 304. The Holland family is settled into the room next door and the door between the two has been left open. Soon, their daughters are in my room, sitting on the other double bed making polite small talk. Rusty and Vicki are in the next room whispering.

Then Vicki enters my room and tells the girls it is time for bed. They both scurry off to the bathroom to get dressed. Vicki invites me to join her and Rusty in their room so we can talk about the hearing and what time we need to leave the motel.

That's when Vicki asks if I would speak before the pardon board.

My letter is good, Vicki says, but a plea in person will be so much more powerful. I look over at Rusty, sprawled out on the double bed, his right leg in a bright blue soft spandex leg brace, the result of a recent dirt bike accident. "It would really mean a lot to me, Joan, if you'd talk to the board tomorrow," he pleads.

I surprise myself by agreeing. This promise is so out of character and breaks all the rules of objective reporting. But I do feel as though I have a message and it is one worth delivering.

After two years of interviewing Rusty, his friends, and family members, I am confident that I know enough to tell the seven-member board, honestly, that Rusty Holland is the "Poster Boy for Death Row Rehabilitation."

When the girls emerge from the bathroom, dressed for bed, I say goodnight and walk out through the door that connects our rooms, convinced that in a few minutes it will close.

I get ready for bed, brush my teeth, check the deadbolt and put on the chain. The adjoining door is still open. I pull down the covers, crawl in, and close my eyes, wondering how long I should wait before getting up to close it.

Within minutes, Vicki is in my room. In her pajamas. "You don't mind if I sleep in here with you, do you?" she asks. "You do have an extra bed."

Again, it is hard to say no. The door stays open all night.

The next morning, I follow the Hollands in my car to a nearby Hardees for breakfast. I spend some time sitting by myself at this fast-food chain, trying to write some notes about what I am going to say.

I look outside. It is pouring rain. Thunder and lightning. An old wives tale says it's good luck if it rains on your wedding day. I wonder if the same could be said on the day you ask the state of South Carolina for forgiveness.

Because of the rain and the hour, we are practically crawling through rush-hour traffic to the parole and pardon building. I am in no hurry. My breakfast of biscuits and gravy is churning. We take the elevator to the pardon board office and walk into the waiting room and sign in.

A heavy-set older man, a board bureaucrat, politely asks me if I am an attorney and if I am representing Mr. Holland, because, he says, that would move us to the front of the line. Attorneys, he says, winking, are "very busy and important people."

My answer – "I am one, but I'm here as a family friend" – keeps our place secure at Number Six.

As we stand waiting, during which time I am pacing, I watch the faces of the families of other parolees – usually the wife or mother – as they walk out of the room. I'm looking for clues. No one is smiling but that's just because, I think, *their* parolee isn't like *my* parolee.

When we walk into the stark, sterile hearing room, I stand before the seven-member board, convinced that Rusty is a perfect example of the reality of rehabilitation.

I feel honored at being given a chance to speak on behalf of a pardon applicant, something I hadn't been able to do with Walter. When I wrote Walter's clemency application to the Texas Parole

Board, just days before his scheduled execution, I was frantic. I knew the odds were against him because then-Governor Anne Richards had granted hearings only twice during her entire tenure – one time for Gary Graham and the other for Robert Black.

I had written hundreds of pages of motions, memorandums of law, and legal briefs during the nine years as Walter's attorney, but on that Thursday night when he asked me to file a clemency application, the huge box filled with all those files and briefs in his case were 2,000 miles away, in the Galveston law office of Robert Hirschhorn – and my co-counsel was 2,000 miles away from Galveston, somewhere in Idaho.

When I decided to leave my box in his law office a year earlier, it seemed like a logical plan. I had been lugging it back and forth from New York City to Texas for the past eight years. On my last trip, I was traveling with an impossible two-year-old on two flights (a total of eight hours) and carrying a stroller, a laptop computer, a diaper bag with several leaky juice boxes. I was seven months pregnant and tired, and it was 102 degrees – in the shade. The box stayed in Texas.

A year later, I was desperate. The clemency application had to be in Texas by 9 a.m. Monday.

On Friday afternoon, Robert's secretary in Galveston dropped the crucial documents in a FedEx box so that I would receive them by noon Saturday. Friday night I pounded out a rough draft and went to bed. Awakened at 6 a.m. by the cries of my hungry nine-month-old, I waited for the FedEx delivery. By the time it arrived, I had cooked 12 quarts of three different kinds of soup. Some people exercise to alleviate stress; I cook.

The application for clemency, with 20 copies to members of the parole board, had to be in the FedEx office before it closed at 5 p.m. Saturday. The nearest office was a good 25-minute drive away. At 4:30 p.m. my husband and I packed the kids in the car (it was too late to find a babysitter) for the drive. We arrived at 4:57 p.m. – at the wrong FedEx store. The other one was 15 minutes away. Racing through red lights, we arrived at 5:04 p.m. The FedEx clerk shook his head when I showed him my 11 packets.

"Lady, you're too late. We've got a shipment to get out."

"Please, this is a matter of life and death," I pleaded.

When he saw the address, he quickly escorted every other customer out of the store and then he helped me fill out the paperwork. He stopped to make a quick call to let the FedEx pilot know the shipment would be a little bit late.

But we are right on time this morning, in Columbia, South Carolina, as I stand before an almost all white, almost all male and definitely all older Board of Pardons and Parole. And I know exactly what my message is: Rusty Holland is an example that rehabilitation is possible.

In my remarks, I add what I think is a brilliant twist – if I can make his success their success too, the board will be hard-pressed to turn him down. How can they rebuff this compliment? I know how to characterize the argument: if they reject Rusty's pardon then they are, in effect, rejecting the hope, dreams, and efforts of every hard-working and dedicated corrections employee in the entire state. How can they turn him down?

I am confident it is a winning argument but, still, I'm anxious as I begin my statement. I apologize for my obvious nervousness. "Rusty Holland is the success story of South Carolina's correction system. His success is your success," I tell the board members, adding that in my many conversations with Rusty over the years he has always been quick to give credit to those many prison employees who, early on in his incarceration, saw something in him that he did not see. And they never gave up on him.

"The success of William Holland represents a successful partnership between those people working in South Carolina's prisons and Mr. Holland." I tell them that the pardon application "means something more than a well-deserved congratulations to South Carolina for a job well done."

"It is that thing that gets people out of bed in the morning and to work. It is that thing that gets you to burn the midnight oil, reading the files, and getting here this morning to give careful consideration to this case," I say. "It's what motivates all of us to do our very best – whether it is in our professional lives or private ones. It is a thing called hope," I say, making sure I emphasize the word "hope." I speak slowly.

"William Holland represents hope – to many people, but most importantly to those in corrections. Hope that he would make it. Hope that your decision 17 years ago [in granting him parole] was the right one. And it was. He represents hope to all of those in corrections who went the extra mile in encouraging him; who stayed on their shift just a little bit longer to talk to him, to work with him."

I end by pleading with the board, not to give up on ex-cons like Rusty or the thousands of men and women in law enforcement and corrections.

"They, those prison guards, wardens, and all of those hard-working people in corrections had hope that Rusty Holland would turn out well. And he has. Please send a message to all involved in his case – Don't give up. Have hope. Your efforts, hard work, and faith will pay off."

When I finish, Board Chairman Smithers thanks me for my time. He adds: "Miss Cheevah, if you'd ever like to come down here and practice law, we'd love to have ya. We could use an attractive and well-spoken young lady like yourself down here in South Carolina."

I should have known then, with that patronizing tone, that they hadn't taken me seriously. At all. They were probably pinching themselves to keep from laughing.

Fifteen minutes later, the board's secretary walks into the waiting room to deliver the news.

"I'm sorry. Pardon denied."

Vicki bursts into tears. Her daughters join her.

Rusty asks: "What was the vote?"

"Six to one," the woman says before quickly disappearing back into the boardroom.

———

Back in the 1960s, two men who sat only a few feet away from the electric chair also had faith. But of a different kind. Freddie Pitts and Wilbert Lee didn't believe the State of Florida would execute them – because they were innocent.

CHAPTER EIGHT

THE INNOCENTS: PITTS AND LEE

To date, seven members of the Class of '72 have been found to be innocent: four from the State of Florida and three from Massachusetts.

Since 1973, 123 inmates have been freed from Death Row; there were 15 cases in which DNA evidence played a substantial factor in establishing innocence, according to the Death Penalty Information Center.

To date there is no scientific proof that an innocent person has been executed in the United States. Results of a January 13, 2006 post-execution DNA analysis in the closely watched case of Roger Coleman proved he was guilty of the 1982 murder that sent him to Virginia's Death Row. In 1992, Coleman went to the electric chair proclaiming his innocence.

Caught in a rainstorm and Friday rush hour weekend traffic, I am more than an hour late to meet Freddie Pitts and Wilbert Lee – two men who have spent almost a lifetime waiting to be vindicated of the crime that sent them to Florida's Death Row. They spent nine years in cells next to each other, down the hall from the electric chair. They were inside another three years before being released. When I meet them in Miami, the two have been waiting for 35 years for the state of Florida to admit they are innocent and to pay them for the 12 years they were illegally imprisoned.

Freddie and Betty Pitts

Wilbert Lee

It is daylight when I leave my motel for Pitts' home where I am to have dinner with him and his wife, Betty, and Wilbert. Even though Betty has given me good directions, I didn't take into account the Friday traffic on Miami's South Shore. Or a thunderstorm.

When I call this morning, Betty, the duo's press agent and social secretary for the past 20 years, answers. "Freddie is on the road. Wilbert is working and can't be reached. Why don't you come at 5:30 for a little cocktail, before dinner? Let me give you directions. I do believe you told Freddie earlier that you always get lost. He thought that was very funny."

He must have, since the 53-year-old Freddie drives an 18-wheeler for a living. His own. For him, getting lost is hazardous to his bank account. He can't afford to.

I call Betty in the middle of the thunderstorm from a pay phone in a strip mall. The battery in my cell phone is dead.

"Girl, where are you? Now don't you worry. You just come on. And drive safe," she says, with an emphasis on safe.

More than an hour later when I ring the doorbell, Betty opens the large white double doors of the small ranch house with a big smile. Then come the hugs. The bouquet of bright yellow and pink Gerber daisies I have in my arms will help ease any tension caused by my tardiness. I can see Wilbert is sitting at the table with his elbows holding up his head; he's got a scowl on his face and he isn't getting up.

"Don't mind him," Betty whispers. "He's a little cross because he had to wait a bit. We will just have a longer cocktail hour, that's all, Honey."

My late arrival has kept the man who has made a career out of waiting a bit unhappy. I apologize profusely in an overdone Texas twang.

He then starts laughing. "You look like a wet rat! And I bet you don't even have an umbrella, right? Oh, hell. It's okay. I was early."

Freddie Pitts and Wilbert Lee were on Death Row for a murder they did not commit, and when the Supreme Court ruled in the case of *Furman* in 1972, their appeals had run out. *Furman* saved them, and the 587 others, from the electric chair. But that's where the similarities end. Unlike almost all of the others, Pitts and Lee are innocent.[1]

Theirs is not a story of redemption or rehabilitation because they are innocent. They have always been law-abiding citizens, wrongfully convicted of two murders that a jury decided deserved death. They attribute their survival to an inner strength, a steely determination, and an indescribable faith. They know about forgiveness, first hand. I wonder how anyone can be so forgiving?

For 12 years Freddie and Wilbert lived next to each other, along with some of the most violent, cruel, and evil men in the state of Florida. When they were finally released in 1975, would their experience transform them into bitter men?

On the fateful night, 19-year-old Freddie had a good job and a steady paycheck as a private in the U.S. Army, stationed at Fort Rucker, close to Port St. Joe, Florida. He wonders how far he might have gone in the military had he not attended the "pay day party" at Wilbert and Ella Mae Lee's house on August 1, 1963.

The Lees were poor, paying $6.50 a week in rent for their two-room wooden shack at 215 Avenue D, on an unpaved street in the black "shantytown" of Port St. Joe, a small town on the Gulf Coast in northwestern Florida. In 1933, Alfred DuPont, a son of the powerful DuPont family of Delaware, opened the St. Joe Paper Company, after buying 240,000 acres of timberland and two railroads. Port St. Joe residents like Wilbert and Ella Mae were "dirt poor." The couple had no electricity; only a Coleman lantern for light. The gas stove worked and the furniture, just weeks away from the repo man, was almost new.[2]

Freddie really didn't know Wilbert at all – they had only recently met when Wilbert invited him to his party. Freddie knew him as "Slingshot," a nickname Wilbert earned as a young boy because his prized possession was a slingshot.

The 28-year-old laborer grew up as an orphan on his grandfather's farm outside Evergreen, Alabama. Wilbert didn't like school and he didn't much care for the five-mile walk through the swamps and past the "hanging tree," the site of numerous lynchings of young black men. He left school when he was 16, still in the 6th grade, and moved to Pensacola, Florida, where he supported himself by doing odd jobs.

In 1961 he married his girlfriend of four years, Ella Mae Purifoy, and they moved to Port St. Joe two years later because Ella Mae had relatives there and she thought Wilbert could make some money in the lumber business.

During the party, Freddie and Wilbert and three women left and drove to the nearby MoJo gas station because Wilbert had to make a phone call and Freddie wanted to buy some potato chips.

Freddie and Wilbert didn't hear the heated argument between the gas station attendants and the women who came with them about wanting to use the "Whites Only" bathroom. Freddie and Wilbert never heard the angry shouts between the white men and the black women, but Curtis "Boo" Adams did. He was hiding in the men's room next door, getting ready to rob the gas station when the argument started. Shortly after Freddie, Wilbert, and the women left the MoJo, Adams, a 23-year-old convicted armed robber, came out from his hiding place.

Moments later Jesse Burkett and Grover Floyd were robbed and then kidnapped; Adams drove them to a canal bank and shot both men in the head.

Sheriff's investigators targeted Freddie and Wilbert because they'd both been at the MoJo and witnesses had heard the argument earlier that evening. Port St. Joe police had a motive – revenge.[3] One of the women who had been with them, Willie Mae Lee (no relation to Wilbert), told police that the two men killed the attendants, but her "confession" came only after police officers told Willie Mae they'd take away her young daughter and put her in the electric chair.

The two men were questioned – at one point for more than 17 hours. They were beaten and told to confess or face a lynch mob. Freddie and Wilbert confessed.

After pleading guilty before an all-white and all-male jury on August 28, 1963, the attorney for the two men, W. Fred Turner, asked jurors to spare their lives because they would make "good prison laborers." He described them as "an asset to the prison chain gang." Twenty minutes later, the jury returned with a verdict of death.[4]

When the judge pronounced their sentence, he ordered courtroom spectators to remain seated for 10 minutes. The judge said he wanted to give Freddie and Wilbert enough of a head start to Raiford – Florida's Death Row 240 miles away – without being lynched by an angry mob.

Six hours later, Freddie and Wilbert arrived at the Death House and for the next 10 years they would be known simply by their Inmate Numbers, 009491 and 009492.

Even though the "killers" were safely behind bars, the murders didn't stop. Five hundred miles and two weeks later in Fort Lauderdale, Florida, a Shamrock Oil gas station employee was killed in almost the same way as the men at the MoJo. Four months later, in December 1963, the law caught up with Curtis "Boo" Adams, the white man who hid in the bathroom at the MoJo, after he was arrested for robbing a loan company in Key West. He was sentenced to 20 years.

But Adams wasn't quite ready to go back to prison, writes *Miami Herald* reporter Gene Miller in *Invitation to a Lynching*, a book based on reporting that resulted in freedom for Wilbert and Freddie and a Pulitzer Prize for Miller in 1976.[5]

Adams first wanted to go home, to Port St. Joe, to visit his dying mother. He told a Key West detective that he had information for the Port St. Joe sheriff about the MoJo murders; he thought that would be enough to earn him a ride home.

But he underestimated Sheriff Byrd E. Parker's search for the truth. In a telephone conversation, Parker told the detective: "I already got two niggers waiting for the chair in Raiford for those murders."[6]

The months of "waiting for the chair" were excruciating for Freddie and Wilbert; they knew they were about to be executed for a crime they didn't commit. Each man spent his "last months" in very different ways.

Freddie, a native of Mobile, Alabama, worked nonstop on his appeal, writing the sentencing judge and the FBI. The Bureau sent two agents to Raiford to interview Freddie and Wilbert, investigating Freddie's claims of civil rights violations arising from the beatings that elicited the confessions. Since Freddie had been in the Army at the time of the murders, an Army investigator from the military's Judge Advocate General's office was sent to Raiford. Freddie also wrote to lawyers at the American Civil Liberties Union and the NAACP Legal Defense Fund.

Meanwhile Wilbert, who could not read or write, spent his time listening to prison guards describe how a man dies in the electric chair. They spared no detail. A month earlier, 33-year-old Charles H. Lee, a white man who killed his estranged wife and father-in-law, was executed.[7] The guards crowded outside his cell, entertained by Wilbert's escalating fear. They told him to listen for the generator, a signal that an execution was imminent.

Even though it's been 34 years since he first heard the hum of the generator, Wilbert says he will never forget it. "It was just a horrible sound. The sound of death."

The memories are painful. Wilbert rubs his forehead and wipes his eyes several times, and I'm not sure if he will continue. Finally, he looks up. "How can you make up for all that lost time? It's like ripping pages out of a book. But this isn't a book. This is my life. I can't get that time back. I lost my whole family while I was inside."

Betty pops her head out of the kitchen. "Something should be done. This is just the worst thing that could ever happen to a person – being on Death Row for 12 years for a crime they didn't commit."

The back door closes.

"No, you're wrong. The worst thing is being executed. Hell, we're alive." It's Freddie. He's home and he's exhausted; he's been up since 4 a.m. driving all over Florida, picking up and delivering his loads. Dressed in his dark blue trucker uniform, with the logo Penn Tank Lines Inc., Freddie sits down; he can barely keep his eyes open.

Betty has made one of Wilbert's favorites – her version of Chinese food. It smells "divine," I tell her, but I've never seen okra in Chinese vegetables.

Betty has an infectious laugh. "Oh, Honey. Don't ya know where you are? The South, darling!"

She jumps up a couple of times and dishes out second and third helpings. Soon she is standing beside me with a cup of coffee. I don't have the heart to tell her I don't drink anything with caffeine after 4 p.m. So I drink it.

The conversation moves from Death Row to the Clinton White House to the "hazards" of female drivers. Freddie is at the head of the table, with his eyes closed. I think he's snoring. Wilbert talks about how women are dangerous behind the wheel and about how they are always getting lost – a not-so-subtle reminder that I had kept him waiting for almost an hour.

"They're a hell of a lot better than most of the men out there," Freddie barks, slowly opening one eye. "I feel safer with them on the road, believe me. You ought to see it out there. These guys in their little BMWs whipping around."

Then his eye closes. No one speaks. We just look at each other.

And start laughing. The "Great Oz" has spoken.

We start talking about the case that sent Freddie and Wilbert to Death Row. I probably should have left after coffee and dessert. While Freddie was still sleeping. Then I never would have asked "the question."

In journalism school, they teach you there's no such thing as a stupid question. As soon as it came out of my mouth, I knew my professors had lied. "What I don't understand is, well, hmm," I stammer, not really sure if I should continue. But I do. "How can *anyone* confess to a crime he didn't commit?"

Wilbert doesn't respond. Freddie looks at me. Silence. I wonder if the interview has just ended.

"Miss Cheever, how old were you in 1963? Do you know exactly what was going on in this country?"

Quickly, I answer. "Mr. Pitts, sir. I was six. I know that my Mom and Dad didn't like draft dodgers or hippies or people who smoked dope. I remember exactly where I was when I found out President Kennedy had been shot. I even remember where I was when I heard about the assassination of Martin Luther King and Bobby Kennedy."

I stop and look into Freddie's eyes, bloodshot from the 12 hours he has spent driving up and down IH-95. They are warm and forgiving. It is true. Freddie's eyes mirror his soul.

He reaches across the large, heavy mahogany table and pats my hand. His question about where I was in 1963 was purely rhetorical; he didn't expect an answer. "I'm sure it's hard for you to put yourself in our shoes. But we were so happy that after they beat us up for the confession, they didn't kill us, too. We figured that the Army, the court system, the justice system – someone – would just sort this mess out sooner than later," Freddie says.

We both share a belief, however, that in the end justice will prevail. That's what kept him going for so many years: his unwavering faith that the criminal justice system wouldn't allow an innocent man to die in the electric chair. His faith was tested daily as he sat in his cell on Death Row, especially on those days in the early 1960s when other men were led to the execution chamber.

Before tonight's interview, I reread Gene Miller's *Invitation to a Lynching*, which provides a detailed account of the trials of Freddie and Wilbert, the ensuing cover-up, and what transpired, legally, during those 12 years in prison. I also reviewed a folder filled with newspaper articles about the two.

It's still hard for me to understand how an innocent person can plead guilty, but Freddie and Wilbert aren't the only ones. According to the Death Penalty Information Center, of the 122 men and one woman who have been released from Death Row based on innocence, 15 "confessed" to murders they did not commit and another 54 were sent to Death Row on the basis of perjured testimony from "witnesses," many of whom were jailhouse informants who testified for the government in exchange for leniency in their own cases. [8]

Freddie and Wilbert are 2 of the 22 men from Florida that have been wrongfully convicted and sentenced to die; the state of Illinois has sentenced 18 innocent men to death. Of the 123 exonerees, 74 are black or Hispanic and the group spent an average of 9 years in prison before being released. [9]

Freddie and I both know that I'll never really be able to understand how an innocent man can confess to a crime. But what's even harder is trying to understand how Freddie and Wilbert can forgive those who put – and kept – them on Death Row.

I am about to apologize for "the how can you plead guilty" question, when I see Freddie wink. He starts laughing, a slow, guttural guffaw. It's contagious; I start laughing, too. And then Betty giggles. Finally the somber Wilbert joins in.

Tonight we are to talk about the future. The past is just that and Freddie doesn't want to walk down that road again. He hasn't forgotten; he just doesn't want to talk about it. Besides, it feels better to laugh.

I should take lessons; I need to laugh more.

Unlike Freddie, Wilbert is pretty serious. Behind his dark brown eyes, I get a sense of a deep loneliness. During dinner he jokes endlessly about "finding a good woman like Betty" to share his life. "And one who can cook, too."

Freddie also likes to eat but he said when he was first released from prison he had to relearn the basics of using a knife and fork. Prisoners are allowed only a spoon, Freddie says. Tonight, I look down at the knife and fork in my own hands.

Freddie watches me.

In 1972, when the *Furman* ruling moved Freddie and Wilbert, and 97 other men and one woman, off Death Row in Florida, Freddie wasn't happy. Years earlier, when the ACLU filed a class action on behalf of all of the Death Row inmates in the state, Freddie told the lawyers he didn't want to be involved.

Freddie didn't want to be part of a class. He was innocent and that put him in a class all by himself. Or at least, only with Wilbert.

"I was only interested in proving my innocence. I know that ruffled some feathers, but I didn't care."

In 1970, their case was reversed and the two were retried – by an all-white jury, again in the Panhandle area of Florida. The judge refused to allow jurors to hear the taped confession of the real killer, Curtis "Boo" Adams. And Adams refused to testify without immunity. The judge also would not let Mary Jean Akins, Adams' girlfriend, testify that he told her of the murders.

Again, the case was based solely on Willie Mae Lee, who this time went under hypnosis in the courtroom, recanted, and stuck to her original story.

"The jury had no other choice than to convict us. I didn't fault them," Freddie says. Then Freddie and Wilbert's lawyers found out that the prosecutor had withheld evidence at the first trial – that Willie Mae had withdrawn her confession. Freddie and Wilbert were then offered a deal: if they pleaded guilty, and with the amount of time they had already served, they'd be free in less than three years.

"But we weren't guilty, so we didn't go for that."

The two might still be in prison if not for Warren Holmes, a polygraph examiner who told his good friend, *Miami Herald* reporter Gene Miller, that he had uncovered an investigator's memo about Willie Mae's confession. [10]

In 1975, Florida Governor Ruben Askew issued a pardon, saying: "I am sufficiently convinced of their innocence." [11]

Once released, Freddie got a job as a guard for a Miami security company and was given a gun. He worked his way up to patrol supervisor but then left that job, deciding he could earn more money in the trucking business. He drove trucks long distances and sometimes drove tour buses before saving enough money to open up his own business as an independent trucker. He and Betty have been married for 20 years, and they live in a middle-class neighborhood in the Miami Shore suburb. Freddie dotes on Betty's grandchild and he proudly shows me pictures. Freddie also has two daughters with whom he's lost touch.

Wilbert lives close by. The three get together often, especially when a journalist or film crew is in town. When they were released in 1975, the two bachelors lived three doors away. Two years later, Freddie met Betty.

Wilbert never remarried; he received divorce papers from Ella Mae in 1973 while he was still in prison. He says he got one letter a year from his wife during the entire time he was on Death Row. And exactly one Christmas card. And then the divorce papers.

Even though it has been 34 years since he was sent to Death Row, it is very hard for Wilbert to talk about it. The pain is raw; the wound is open. I've been there a while, and Wilbert still has not taken off his jacket or loosened his tie. He's a serious man. His work, the case of *State versus Pitts and Lee* and a $1.5 million claim which has been pending for the past 22 years against the State of Florida for wrongful imprisonment, fills up his life.

Wilbert grabs the stem of his wine glass so tight I think it might break. Peering into his glass of rosé, Wilbert gathers his thoughts, bracing himself for what he's about to say.

He knows when he tells me the story about the generator, he will relive the horror and those ugly memories will flood back in. I can tell he has worked hard to keep it in. But I have asked, and Wilbert is a man who likes to please.

"They say if you hear that generator crank up and your door opens, that means that you're gonna be executed. And about five days later, my door opened and that generator was running. And I heard someone shouting, 'Hey, Wilbert Lee'," he says, taking both hands off the wine glass, cupping it close to his mouth like a human bullhorn, mimicking the guards and their accents. "But I didn't say nuthin'. I was thinking, Oh, Lordy. I've been here jus' five days and now they gonna execute me."

Wilbert ran to the corner of his 6' × 9' cell and cowered.

"I thought I was going to be executed then and they opened the door and I was shakin' so bad. And the guard says: 'Boy. Why you shakin'? Hell, I'm just taking you up to the classification office.' " And then the guards started laughing.

But Wilbert had good reason to be fearful. On May 12, 1964, everyone heard the generator hum and the doors opened on the cellblock twice that day. The men, those in their cell and the two who were taking their last walk, began to cry.

Emmett Clark Blake, a white man, walked down the corridor of Death Row. Blake "volunteered" to be executed; he had written Florida Governor Farris Bryant asking him to speed up his execution. Blake wanted to die for the murder of a Panama City man two years earlier. [12] Unlike the others, Blake didn't struggle with the guards. He sat in the electric chair and told the executioners: "Well, I'm not mad with anybody. I hope none of you are mad with me." [13]

But the scene was different hours later. When Sie Dawson, a 54-year-old black man with an IQ of 64, was taken from his cell and strapped into the electric chair, he kept telling the guards that he didn't do it. [14] The one-legged killer told police officers he saw his boss murder the boss' wife and the couple's two-year-old child with a hammer. [15]

But the police officers didn't want to hear it. They told Dawson if he didn't confess they'd turn him over to a mob to be lynched. At trial, Dawson recanted his confession, but the all-white male jury convicted him anyway – without a recommendation of mercy. That meant death.

Wilbert says he will never forget the smell.

"That was a hell of day. I tell you. I never smelled anything like smelling a human being. The worst smells. And the sun don't shine right that day."

Since he couldn't read, the prison-issued Bible and daily delivery of *The Miami Herald* didn't help pass the time.

But in another cellblock, convicted murderer Jesse Pait read the newspaper every day, carefully rereading the story about the $15,000 reward for information leading to the killer of the Shamrock gas station attendant in Fort Lauderdale. That murder sounded familiar; his ex-cellmate, Curtis "Boo" Adams, had told him about it. Adams also bragged about the cold-blooded execution style murder of the MoJo employees.

Hoping for the reward, Pait wrote Broward County detectives; they drove to the prison to question him. After talking to Pait, the detectives knew that two innocent men were in Raiford waiting to die. They took the new evidence to the prosecutor in Freddie and Wilbert's case. But Prosecutor J. Frank Adams told the detectives he wasn't interested.

"His statement to me was that the two fellows had admitted the crime in open court and there was no reason to open the case at all," said Broward County Detective Quentin Long.[16]

When police confronted Curtis "Boo" Adams about the Shamrock murder, he confessed and pleaded guilty on December 16, 1966. He was spared the electric chair.

Freddie and Wilbert were released in 1975, and job offers poured in to the new Death Row celebrities. For the amount of time he spent behind bars, I thought Wilbert's choice of careers was unusual.

Wilbert went back to prison to counsel young offenders; in 1985, the 62-year-old Miami-Dade County corrections counselor was named "Counselor of the Year." But then, a few months later, he was removed from his position because of a new law barring felons from working with children. Attorneys from the state told Wilbert his pardon didn't exempt him from the law and he was transferred to the Health Department to work as a file clerk.

Wilbert sued, but a Dade Circuit judge ruled against him in 1986. The ACLU appealed on his behalf, and in 1987, a state appeals court sided with Wilbert, ruling that the new law unjustly pushed Wilbert out of his job working with juveniles.[17] Even though he won, Wilbert continues to work with adult inmates in the Dade County Jail, which he says he prefers. He describes the suit as another "nightmare," adding, "It caused me a lot of heartaches and pains. And it put me through a lot of stress."

The other nightmare is a "claims bill" that has languished for 21 years. In 1976, Freddie and Wilbert asked the Florida Legislature to compensate them for wrongful imprisonment. They have been vigorously lobbying legislators for $3 million in compensation for losing 12 years of their life.

When we met, there was no news.

A year later, in a small room at a black-owned radio station, Freddie and Wilbert were each handed a check for $500,000, drawn on the Florida State Treasury. [18]

A *Miami Herald* reporter described their reactions as identical. Each scanned his check for a few moments, then carefully folded the paper and tucked it in a breast pocket. There were no shouts, no cries of joy, and no fits of elation. [19]

Since then, the two have again hit the lecture circuit to speak out against the death penalty. Sitting with 27 men and one woman on stage at the National Conference on Wrongful Convictions and the Death Penalty at Chicago's Northwestern University Law School in 1998, Wilbert told the 1,200 in the audience how helpless he felt on Death Row as he watched others walk to the Death House.

"You know you are capable of going, too. You don't want to die for a crime you didn't commit." [20]

Many in the audience wept and gave the innocent ex-Death Row inmates a five-minute standing ovation. There were 29 who came to Chicago, but across the country there were 46 more who were unable to make the trip. Since 1973, 123 people have been released from Death Row with evidence of their innocence. [21]

As they walked to a podium to the heartbeat-like sound of an African drum, each former Death-Row inmate recited what sounded like a prayer. "The State of Florida sought to kill me for a murder I did not commit," Freddie Pitts told the group. "I was sentenced to death in 1963 and finally released in 1975. Had the State of Florida gotten its way, I would be dead today."

One by one, each man picked up a sunflower and placed it in a crystal vase.

"I dare anyone to look at those flowers that they wanted to extinguish and tell us that their death penalty works," said Lawrence Marshall, a Northwestern University law professor and organizer of the meeting. [22]

One of those sunflowers, representing, at the time, one of the 75 former Death Row inmates whose lives were saved, sits on top of my computer screen, fastened by bits of packing tape. It arrived several weeks after the conference in a large box; the return address was Attica State Prison. It's from Sister Roslyn, Chuck Culhane's friend and Attica's chaplain, who was at the conference. Like me, the sunflower also has aged. It's no longer bright yellow. There are only four petals attached, barely clinging to the calyx.

Like the flower with its few intact petals, there are also only a handful of states without the death penalty: Alaska, Hawaii, Iowa, Maine, Massachusetts, Michigan, Minnesota, North Dakota, Rhode Island, Vermont, West Virginia, Wisconsin, and the District of Columbia. [23]

At dinner tonight, William Furman's name comes up. Even though he wanted nothing to do with Furman back in 1968 as part of the ACLU's class action, Freddie asks how Furman is doing.

"I wish I knew. I can't find him anywhere and, believe me, I've tried."

Freddie folds his arms and leans back in his chair, a habit that catches Betty's disapproving eye. Quickly he puts all four legs back on the ground. "Don't sweat it. He's probably dead. Death Row wasn't very good for your health."

But I am focused on finding Furman. Like Earnest Miranda whose case required police officers to read a suspect a list of their rights, Furman's name is synonymous with the death penalty. Caught unwillingly in the national spotlight on the debate about capital punishment, William Henry Furman is famous.

That night at Freddie's house, I had no leads.

———

Seven months later, I received a telephone call – Furman had surfaced. But he might go back into hiding.

Time was running out.

CHAPTER NINE

"POPS": THE OLDEST MEMBER OF THE CLASS

The average age of the Class of '72 in June 1972 was 31;[1] in June 2005 the average age is 63 – for both those who are incarcerated and those who have discharged their sentences or are on parole.

There is no national statistic on the average age of the more than 3,300 currently on Death Row in the U.S. In Florida, where there are 385 inmates awaiting execution, the average age is 44.[2]

Currently the oldest Death Row inmate in the U.S. is 90; the youngest is 21 years old. Before the U.S. Supreme Court abolished the death penalty for juveniles in March 2005, there were 72 juvenile offenders in 12 states.

In the Class of '72, the oldest member is 88-year-old Moreese Bickham of Louisiana. The youngest, Joe Newton Kagebein, was 15 years old when he was indicted for capital murder in Arkansas. Kagebein was paroled in 1974; 6 years later, the 25-year-old was killed in a motorcycle accident.

Moreese "Pops" Bickham is the oldest of the Class of '72. For the better part of four decades, from 1958 to 1996, he was incarcerated in Louisiana's infamous Angola prison, one of the most dangerous penitentiaries in the country. And 14 of those

Moreese "Pops" Bickham

38 years were spent living in a 6′ × 8′ cell, just down the hall from the electric chair.

I know that an interview with Moreese isn't going to be easy to get; he's a busy man. After *The New York Times* published a story about him in January 1996,[3] Moreese is inundated with requests for interviews, speeches, and appearances at anti-death penalty seminars and rallies.

I write him anyway and a short time later I receive a telephone call, not from Moreese but from the man he credits with getting him out of prison – New York attorney Michael Alcamo. The lawyer took on his case as a favor to David Isay, a radio producer-friend who met Moreese in 1990 while recording *Tossing Away the Keys*,[4] a half-hour radio documentary about men serving life without the possibility of parole. Isay begged Alcamo to "find a way to get Moreese out of prison."

Alcamo gives me Moreese's telephone number and after talking several times I know I have to meet him, if only to make sure I am quoting him correctly. He has quite a story to tell and he sounds utterly charming, but I am having difficulty understanding him because of his thick Louisiana accent.

I know a trip to Oakland, California, where he was living at the time, will be worth it, even though my funds are being stretched pretty thin. I call around and find that Tower Air (now out of business) is the cheapest way I can fly to the West Coast; my brother-in-law Jack offers me a place to stay at his apartment in downtown San Francisco.

I have only four and a half hours to find Moreese's house, interview him, then drive back across the Golden Gate Bridge, another bridge, another white-knuckled trip, where I am to meet Jack at the classy St. Francis Yacht Club. The clubhouse has breathtaking views of San Francisco Bay, including Alcatraz, the former maximum security prison which closed its doors in 1963 and is now one of the most popular, National Park Service sites in the country.

Fortunately, I don't have much trouble finding Moreese's house, nestled in a crime-ridden Oakland neighborhood. I park the car in front, and when I knock on the door of the modest stucco ranch home, I am immediately engulfed by a group of giggling children, all of whom seem to be greatly amused by my garish hot-pink rental car.

A moment later, Moreese pushes through the crowd and comes to my rescue. "This young lady traveled half-way across the country to see me, not a bunch of little kids. Now, go on! Git!"

As he ushers me inside, I'm immediately struck by the fact that it's filled with even more people. Sensing my dismay, Moreese quickly explains that not all of them actually live with him. He introduces me to each one – great-great-grandchildren, great-grandchildren and grandchildren. Family is an integral part of Moreese's life and this small house is bursting with relatives. The eldest of five siblings and the only one surviving, Moreese says he's making up for lost time.

After he walked out of Angola prison at 12:01 a.m. January 10, 1996, he kissed the dirt, and said: "This is the ground I longed to get on." He then asked his lawyers to drive him to Tylertown, Mississippi, two hours away, where he grew up. He spent the night at the home of a local preacher and the next morning was reunited with family and friends.[5] He then flew to Oakland.

Moreese and his wife, 76-year-old Ernestine, pay $800 a month in rent from their meager savings, a Social Security check and a World War II veteran's pension. His only child, Vivian Jefferson, also contributes to the rent, but I can't tell if she lives here, too. The house is always full, too full, Moreese says, half joking, as Vivian's 6 children and his 25 great grandchildren often drop in, unannounced, for dinner.

"Like last night's that didn't start until 10 p.m., five hours later than when we ate in the pen," grumbles Moreese, goodnaturedly. As I examine his scowling face, noticeable for the well-trimmed graying mustache and goatee, I see that Moreese looks worn out. But I don't know if he's tired because he was up late or because he's gearing up for our interview. His life on Death Row. A life spent locked up.

"They eat late, they stay up late and they sleep all morning long," Moreese says, loud enough to be overheard, in a half-complaining, half-teasing manner, still smiling at several of the great-granddaughters sitting in the living room braiding each other's hair.

"Family has always been very important to me," he says; his dark-brown eyes begin to tear. "That's what kept me alive while I was sitting on Death Row," he adds, as he grabs my hand and leads me to the burgundy-colored corduroy sofa where he begins to tell me the story of what happened in the early morning hours of July 12, 1958, a day that changed his life forever.

"I can't figure out how it happened. I go over it and over it and it seems like such a nightmare. But it's real. It happened. And I can't change things. If I could, I would," Moreese says, his voice faltering. I look up from my notepad and see his eyes are filled with tears. I look for an escape; a quick way to change the subject. I am so uncomfortable. I don't want to cause this old man any more pain, but it is too late. Sensing my discomfort, Moreese reaches out for my hand and I drop my pen. The tears begin to drip down his weathered face as he squeezes my hand, telling me how sorry he is for the shootings that caused the death of two police officers.

"I pray. Lord, I pray all the time for forgiveness. I remember it like it was yesterday. It always weighs heavy on my mind. I didn't feel like I had a choice that night. It was me or them."

The great-grandchildren, all teenage girls, sitting on the floor in front of us, seem oblivious to the conversation behind them. All but one continues braiding hair. The 18-year-old turns around and stares at me, in an effort, I think, to gauge my reaction. I am embarrassed; I feel as though I've forced Moreese into a full confessional in front of his family and I want to change the subject or figure out a way to ask the girls to leave the room. But soon I see that talking about it seems to help Moreese, even as the tears continue to fall. With my free hand, and my eyes fixed on him, I grab my purse sitting on the floor by my feet and try, discreetly, to find a tissue. But I can't find one. He wipes his eyes on his short-sleeved white shirt and Ernestine makes a clucking sound as if to say, "Don't make me launder that shirt again, old man." She hands him a handkerchief that she has been safe-guarding in the pocket of her long pleated orange skirt. I look up, relieved, and she returns my look with a smile. It is then that I notice what is written on her white-cotton T-shirt. Under two large brown hands, folded in prayer, are the words "Jesus Saves" in bright yellow letters. She returns to her knitting. Her eyes stay down, and I can't tell if she is monitoring our conversation or praying.

Ernestine knows all too well where the conversation is headed; the next part is probably more painful – for her. She wasn't with her husband the night of the murders.[6] He was out with his girlfriend, Florence Spencer, on July 12, 1958, at Buck's Bar in Mandeville, a small town founded in 1840 on the shore of Lake Ponchartrain that was first inhabited by wealthy families of New Orleans who came for the summer to escape the heat of the city and the threat of malaria. Mandeville, now with a population of less than 10,000, is an area where Jim Crow segregation prevailed in the 1950s and had an active chapter of the Ku Klux Klan called the "White Camellias of the Ku Klux Klan." It is the hometown of former KKK leader David Duke and serves as the world headquarters of Duke's National Organization For European-American Rights (NOFEAR), described as an anti-black and anti-Semitic hate group.[7]

On that night in Mandeville, Moreese and Spencer were in the "colored-only" segregated bar called Buck's when the couple began fighting. "The next thing I knowed, she hit me over the head with a bottle," Moreese recalls. "Then the deputy come over and took her away and told her he was taking her home. And I said, 'Not without me. You want to arrest me, go ahead.' " Moreese pauses, looks up at Ernestine and continues. "The deputy said, 'If you get into this car, nigger, I'm gonna kill you.' And then I said: 'When?' And he said: 'Tonight.'

"So, I walked to my uncle's house, about five or six blocks away, to get a gun. But when I come home, I didn't see nobody. When I went back outside, those deputies were there. One said: 'Hey, he's gotta gun' and the other one said, 'Good. He'd better have one.'

"But I told them, 'It ain't loaded' and then I put my hands up and got shot in the chest. I fell down and then loaded my gun and when he came up to get me again, I shot him. Then when the other one run around and grabbed his shotgun, I shot him too. And they both got killed." Moreese claims he only shot in self-defense: "It was me or them."

After being shot, Moreese was taken to Baton Rouge Hospital and within a few days, he was sitting in a jail cell.

At the trial, Florence Spencer testified that Police Officer Gus Gill told Moreese that he would "take care of you [Bickham] later on."[8] But Moreese's brother-in-law, Gene Dyson, told the jury that Bickham was just out to settle an old score and had told him that he was going to "kill Gus Gill – he had messed with me one time too many." Moreese denies ever saying that and maintains that Dyson was intimidated by the KKK into testifying against him.

Prosecutors maintained that Moreese returned to his house and waited to ambush Officer Gill and another policeman, Jake Galloway, when they arrived to confront him.

Today, Moreese says that he was more surprised that he was still alive on the day his trial began than when the all-white male jury took only two hours to find him guilty and give him the death sentence.

"In those days a black man didn't hardly get to the courthouse. They got killed," Moreese explains.

This wasn't the first time I'd heard that. Even Moreese's lawyer, who refused to put his client on the stand, called him "a darky on a Saturday night."[9] Moreese, a World War II veteran who had no prior record,[10] says he survived because he knew how to live with whites. "I was living in a mixed neighborhood. I grew up with white folk. We all got along just fine."

Just days after his cell door shut behind him, Moreese says his mother appeared in a dream and told him that neither he nor any of the other men with him on Death Row would ever see the electric chair.

Moreese claims he was never afraid that he would be executed because "the Lord had told me" otherwise. "Well, I got in on a Saturday morning and I asked the Lord about getting out and He showed me by Monday night that I was going to get out. When they set them dates on me, the Lord showed me I'm going to California. I'm not going to die. And in all of them 37 years, I looked forward to that."

When Moreese entered prison at 41, he had a good job, working for the town of Mandeville as a utility meter reader. He owned his own home and lived in a white community.

Moreese does have some regrets – the 38 years he lost while in prison, the time away from his brothers and sisters, from his mother, and the time away from Ernestine and their daughter Vivian. His mother visited him every week while he was on Death Row and she eventually sold the family farm to pay for Moreese's legal fees.

During his 14 years and 10 months on Death Row, Moreese had seven execution dates. During one four-month stretch, he had a date with death every month. He clearly remembers the day when he came within 14 hours of execution. From 9 a.m. to just before midnight, he sat in his small cell waiting to be taken to the electric chair. "Everyone in there swore they were gonna get me, but I just kept prayin' and the good Lord listened."

Weekdays were the worst on Death Row because from Monday to Friday "you'd expect those death warrants to be coming any time." But from Friday evening to Monday morning, a collective sigh of relief could be heard in Angola, since death warrants weren't signed over the weekend.

Death penalty lawyers had a strategy to keep the executioner at bay and, for a while, it worked. During the mid-1960s, judges were setting execution dates on inmates, two at a time.

"Two days a week, you know they set mine and they set yours," recalls Moreese. "The next month, they set his and his. So as fast as they were setting them, we were going to Jackson. That's what they called the nut house."

At the time, Louisiana law banned the execution of any inmate who was declared insane. "So, that was what those lawyers were aiming to do. Get everybody declared insane. So if you're declared insane then you had to be insane. Or something bad would happen to you. I stayed there for two years and eight months."

On Death Row, Moreese was Number 10. When he left the mental hospital, there were 33 on Death Row. When I ask him whether he really was insane, Moreese pauses a moment before answering. "I do think I was. I asked the Lord to move all my understanding and everything and make me a vegetable or something outta me if that was going to cause me to live."

While on Death Row, Moreese grew close to many fellow inmates. One was David, a white man who had murdered a gas station attendant during an armed robbery. Moreese describes his friend as "the kind of fellow that always liked anybody. One time, this fellow had asked him for a stick of butter to make a candle or something, and David refused. He said, 'Look. I'm going to save what little money I have.' And the next thing I know he was going in to take a shower and he was stabbed in the back."

After the Furman ruling in June 1972, Moreese's sentence was changed to life which, for a brief time, meant a maximum of

10 years and 6 months. It looked as though Moreese was going home. But to avoid a mass exodus by the old-timers on Death Row, Louisiana legislators quickly changed its life sentence statute to mean exactly that – a life sentence. The only way to leave was either by a pardon, a sentence commutation by the governor, or death and that's the only way Moreese's family believed he would get out: dying in prison of old age or of murder.

Once off Death Row, Moreese spent another 23 years on "the farm," the nickname for Angola, a sprawling 28-square-mile plantation, bordered by the Mississippi River on three sides and snake-infested hills on the fourth. Also called the bloodiest prison in the nation, 40 prisoners were stabbed to death and 350 more were seriously injured by knife wounds from 1972 to 1975.[11]

When he was finally released into the general prison population, Moreese lived in fear. He was terrified that he would die in a prison brawl. The then 59-year-old Moreese spent many sleepless nights with a JC Penney catalogue strapped to his chest as his suit of armor.

He focused, briefly, on educating himself and brought his reading scores up from the 6th-grade level to almost the 11th grade. He didn't seek out his G.E.D. immediately because he wanted to work in a job that gave him the freedom of going fishing and hunting.

For all his good work in prison, Moreese and two of his friends – Orly and Danny – were even given "appreciation points" by some prison officers. "They put up $500 out of their salary to give us an appreciation party. When the party was over they said, 'We got $50 apiece left over. What do y'all want?' Well, Orly asked for a robe and sneakers and cigarettes and Danny asked for blue jeans and a shirt and cigarettes. And then they say: 'Bickham, what do you want?'

"I say I knowed what I want, but I doubt I can git it. I want new shirts I can wear for visitors or if I go out in the streets or wherever I go. He [the prison officer] says, 'Give me three days.' On the third day, he comes back. 'What is your shirt size?' I say, 15½. He says 'Okay.' Two days later, he give me three shirts from

J.C. Penney. A blue one, long sleeve; a yellow, long sleeve; and a knitted green one, short sleeve. He said anywhere you want to go, you wear these. And I wore them another year on the farm and in the streets and on speaking trips.

"One day I was at the work camp and I got a visitor and I put on a yellow shirt. And the captain, a new fella, said: 'Hey, boy. You run this camp? Why you wearing this shirt?' He didn't like it none. And he didn't want to hear about how or why I got them. I told him I'd like to keep the shirts, at least the green shirt because one day I might go free and I'd like to wear it. That was in 1977. And you know what? I still got that green shirt."

Moreese wore those shirts while he was a "trusty," an honor he received nine months after he left Death Row. It meant he was free to move throughout the prison and even off prison grounds. Sometimes he left Angola to go on speaking trips and most of the time he was left unsupervised.

"Sometimes they'd take me to a place and leave me, but they'd come back and get me that evening."

"Didn't you ever think of escaping?" I ask incredulously. "Man, I would have!"

Moreese looks hurt at my overly enthusiastic reaction and says simply: "No. No way." He thinks about the question again and then offers, what is to him, a very simple explanation: "I had something to live for. I knew I was getting out."

Moreese worked diligently toward the day he would get out. He worked in the kitchen for 2 cents an hour, while his better-educated friends such as Wilbert Rideau, editor of *The Angolite*, earned 50 cents an hour working on the prison newspaper.[12] When Ross Maggio became warden he instituted a savings plan, requiring inmates to put 2 cents of their increased 4 cent an hour pay into a savings account, accessible only when they were released from prison. By the time he left Angola, Moreese had $864.10 in his prison savings account.

During those prison years, Moreese kept his head down and tried to focus on his freedom. At age 64, when most men his age are ready to pick up their Social Security checks, "Pops" Bickham finally went back to school and earned his G.E.D. Two years later, he received a certificate from an auto mechanics school and then went into the ministry.

Moreese also credits his survival in prison to his religious faith. While inside, he became an ordained Methodist minister and the prison church's pastor and president for nine years.

"I'd been churching for the Lord, been baptized, and in the church all my life from 13 years old up. I was brought up in the church and knowed where my health comes from and my strength."

He needed that strength after the Board of Pardons, in large part because of opposition from many residents in Mandeville, rejected his application for clemency three times in the 1970s and once in 1981. But a year later, after 500 Mandeville residents signed a petition on Moreese's behalf, and with strong support from the religious community, the Pardon Board recommended that his sentence be reduced to 40 years.[13] That recommendation remained on Governor Edwin Edwards' desk his entire second gubernatorial term, from 1984 to 1988, and during most of Edwards' third term, from 1992 to 1996.

In 1988, the new governor Buddy Roemer sent the application back and told Bickham to reapply. Moreese did, and it was denied again. The Parole Board then closed the case.

But Moreese wasn't deterred.

"I know that as long as there's life, there's hope. I knew how to be patient." But the legal setback took its toll on his health. That's when he had his first heart attack, which frightened him. After all, in Louisiana not many lifers walk out of the prison gates. Most leave in a pine box.

Moreese was the caretaker for two years at Point Look-Out, also called Boot Hill, and he had helped bury many of them. He says the hardest funeral he went to was in 1980 for his best friend, James Edward Cripps, who had been with him on Death Row in 1968.

Cripps murdered a tourist during Mardi Gras after he and an accomplice, Larry Joe Purkey, befriended the victim, Taylor

McLaurin Jr., in a bar in the French Quarter. Purkey broke McLaurin's neck, and Cripps took $40 out of his pocket and then threw his body in a lagoon. They fled in the victim's car.[14]

Moreese and Cripps had struggled many years for a freedom that neither had realized. They had been through a lot of good and bad experiences, had slept only a few beds away from each other, and now Moreese stood over the grave of his best friend.[15]

Moreese remembers thinking that Cripps was too young to die the way he did. He was athletic, a white man who played on the all-black softball team and was nicknamed the "White Shadow." For several years Cripps was a bull rider at the annual prison rodeo. But several months before his death, he started feeling sick and he couldn't figure out why. He had recently been transferred to the main prison's maintenance crew, but he began to lose weight fast. Cripps was admitted to the prison infirmary in February and then sent to hospitals in Baton Rouge and New Orleans. In 1980, at age 37, Cripps died of heart disease, chained to his bed in the Charity Hospital in New Orleans.

At Cripps' funeral, Moreese stood next to Prison Chaplain Gary Penton and Prison Warden Ross Maggio, and read the 23rd Psalm. He picked that passage for Cripps, an only child who was raised in rural Michigan, because "that's what James' Mama wanted." On the day of the funeral, Cripps' mother was thousands of miles away in a nursing home in Michigan. She was too poor and too ill to come to Angola to bury her son and bring him back home.

Moreese moved slowly that morning as he began reciting the Psalm – "The Lord is my shepherd; I shall not want. He maketh me to lie down..." According to Wilbert Rideau and Ron Wikberg in their book, *Life Sentences*, Moreese, then 67, faltered as he read the passage from the Bible. The words soon blurred from the tears that filled his eyes. He continued to recite from memory, fighting the anguish that stirred in his gut.[16]

Cripps' funeral resulted in "some tall thinking," Moreese told radio producer David Isay. More than anything else, he wanted to avoid a funeral at Point Look-Out.

"The next year I paid for me to be buried in the cemetery alongside my Mamma. Won't be buried at Point Look-Out. See, if you buried out there, you really forgotten. Nobody come out to visit, nobody even passes by Boot Hill," Moreese told Isay. "Old-timers think about that a right good deal, but they don't like to talk about it much. Because they 'fraid they might end up out there." [17]

In 1993, Moreese's sentence was commuted and, because of the time served and credit for good behavior, the then 78-year-old prisoner immediately became eligible for release. Even though it had been more than 35 years after the murders, the Gill and Galloway families of Mandeville weren't able to forgive Moreese Bickham. The board denied Bickham's application because the families opposed it.

On January 10, 1996, Moreese had accumulated so much in "good time credit" from his 13,695 days behind bars that his sentence automatically expired. Earlier that day, Moreese went to the funeral of his friend, Edward R. Gleim, a convicted murderer. As he peered into Gleim's grave, Moreese realized how lucky he had been not to have died in Angola and been buried in the prison cemetery where the dead are identified by name and prison number. [18]

Before leaving Angola that day, Moreese knelt by the grave of James Cripps and prayed. "It was real tough. Not only his funeral but going to pay him a visit on that last day before I left prison. For good. It was very hard to say goodbye. It bring back a lot of old memories."

Shortly before midnight, Moreese took a few things out of his green metal trunk, including his Bible and a few toiletries, said his goodbyes and gave his locker key to one of the residents of the prison dormitory.

"I told him, 'You go back there and get whatever you want out of them boxes and give the rest to whoever you want to have it,' " Moreese remembers saying. "And then I watched. They all went over and sat on the bed. The key unlocked the box and then nobody taked nothing; they all just set there with the box like it was a dead bird."

He then walked to the front gate with Burl Cain, the warden of Angola prison. "I went to sign my name on that sheet. Now that's when I knowed I was getting free," Moreese said. "I'd promised the Lord if I got free, I was going to kiss the ground outside. And I did. I got down on my knees and got a handful of it and did it."

Moreese can't help but smile as he remembers the night he was released. There were a lot of firsts: a ride in a limousine, an airplane trip to California, and a conversation on "one of those cell phones – can you believe that?" Moreese says, laughing. He also talks about stopping at a convenience store to buy root beer on his way home to Tylertown. "I get up to the cashier and put down 25 cents. She looks at me like I'm crazy. She says, 'Sir, that would be a dollar.' Lord have mercy, was I surprised. When I went in, it was a nickel. I figured 25 cents was enough. Can you believe a whole dollar for a little bitty root beer?" Moreese laughs, holding the sides of his stomach.

We are both laughing until I hear it; the sound of either a gunshot or car backfire. I flinch, unable to tell the difference. But Moreese can.

"You thought that was a car, right?" he asks, smiling. "No, young lady. You'd be better off movin' away from the window."

I jump up and quickly move to the corner of the couch.

Moreese's granddaughters stop talking and braiding, and look at me hopping around like a Mexican Jumping Bean. Then they start to whisper and the giggles follow.

"Jesus H. Christ," I mumble, silently, thinking I am going to get killed here in Oakland, California, 3,000 miles from home, in a drive-by shooting between rival gang members.

I start to fiddle with my tape-recorder, pretending that the only reason I got up was to get another micro-cassette tape from my briefcase. Part of me wishes this interview was over. I am wiggling around, moving to the far end of Moreese's dark-brown, well-worn tweed couch to get out of the firing line in case of a stray bullet. But I am determined not to leave this house without getting the whole story. After playing musical couches, I get back to the interview and Moreese continues.

He complains very little and says while he loves his life in the Free World, he admits it's taking "a little getting use to." Living without a set schedule is tough and so is the lack of privacy as his grandchildren and great-grandchildren traipse through the bedroom he shares with his wife of 58 years.

"They're here all the time. All of 'em. Can you believe I have so many kids? The door open and shut; open and shut. All day long."

I'm surprised when he tells me that he has installed a padlock on his bedroom door and it's always locked. He says his most prized possession is in that room.

"Mr. Bickham, you have lived almost your entire adult life in prison and you have a room with a lock? I don't understand that. Really. I'd think you'd want to get rid of those locks!"

He looks me square in the eye and then raises his index finger to give me a lecture. "You don't understand, because you don't know anything about maintaining credit, now do ya? See, I got me a telephone line. And that is the only way this old boy is gonna get credit so I can get me a loan so I can buy me a house. We clear, now?"

Since Moreese has spent most of his adult life in prison, he has no income or pension, only a few thousand dollars in savings and no credit cards. Without any credit history, no bank would loan him money. Steady and on-time payments of a telephone bill taken out in his name would, however, establish a credit history. Grandpa's unlocked phone with "free" long distance would be too tempting to his grandchildren, Moreese says, and would jeopardize his credit rating and dream of home ownership.

Moreese says his dream is to own a home where he and Ernestine can live out their remaining years. He wants a house with a garden and lots of rose bushes like the ones he tended for so many years at Point Look-Out and in his cellblock courtyard. They were big and round and he named them all, affectionately, "Ernestine." He calls the rosebushes his "company keepers."

I leave the Bickhams as the sun begins to set and drive to the St. Francis Yacht Club – a few miles but a world apart from Moreese's ranch house in nearby Oakland. But I have more questions. I ask if I can return tomorrow.

When I come back at noon, Moreese meets me at the door. We need to hurry and sneak out for lunch before the rest of the group will ask to tag along, he whispers.

"Where do you want to go?" I ask, not sure what kind of restaurants there are in this run-down neighborhood. We drive by a diner, across the street from a church shelter, where there's already a line of homeless men, young and old, down the block.

"We could eat over there and it'd be for free," Moreese says, grinning, and I can't decide whether he's serious.

The restaurant we finally choose has usual diner fare spiced with some Mexican dishes; it's owned by a Chinese couple who can barely speak English. For just $4.99, Moreese and I each order a stack of meaty fried pork chops, a heaping bowl full of lettuce and tomatoes, a pile of French fries, and a large plate of refried beans, served with coffee or sweet tea. I notice that Moreese puts eight packets of sugar in his coffee – a habit shared by almost all of the members of the Class of '72, which leads me to believe that there must have been something inherently vile about prison coffee.

An hour later we are ready to leave, and I get up from the table to pay the check. "He you grandpa?" the waitress/owner/cook, asks. "He very nice old man."

I can't help but laugh and share this tidbit with Moreese.

"I'm not yo Grandpa, but will you be my driver? Mind if we take a little drive around the neighborhood? I want to show you something."

He asks if I will take him to a house he has set his sights on. He doesn't want his daughter, grandchildren, or great-grandchildren to know. It will be our secret.

"Just you, me, and Ernestine knows about this. I don't want all those kids at this house. You know what I mean?"

"Sure. Hop in."

Moreese has decided that since I have a car, am white, and look like a real estate agent, no one will worry if we are seen peeking in the windows. And since I'm a lawyer, Moreese adds with a wink, I can keep him out of trouble if we are charged with trespassing, a thought that never even occurs to me.

We drive to the house and look around. It is *perfect*. The backyard is filled with lemon, lime, and peach trees. He picks up a lime that has fallen off a tree and shoves it into his pocket. It's for Ernestine.

"If I take this, they can't get me for theft, can they?"

I am surprised at the question. "No. It fell off the tree. And besides, you're a potential buyer, aren't you?"

It's obvious to me that Moreese doesn't take anything for granted. Not the prospect of one day buying a house and certainly not his freedom.

When we return to the ranch house, Moreese surreptitiously passes the lime to Mrs. Bickham; she returns the handoff with a smile.

She whispers: "Right nice, isn't it? We just prayin to the good Lord, all the time. You never know."

We sit on the sofa and I take out my notepad where I've scribbled a few follow-up questions. One in particular, which has been on my mind all day, centers on Moreese's brief incarceration in the 1960s at Jackson, the state's mental hospital.

I've been with Moreese for almost two full days now and he doesn't seem the least bit crazy. I have to ask: "Was it a legal ruse? Were you really crazy?"

"Well, let me just tell you. Between the two of us, I think maybe *you* are the one who is a little bit off in the head."

He starts laughing, a low chuckle. The giggling turns into a loud guffaw. Finally, he sputters: "I don't know what a nice, young lady with two little kids at home is doin' driving around in this neighborhood. It's dangerous. Didn't you hear that gunfire yesterday? And you thought it was a car, didn't you?" he says, laughing so hard he wipes away tears. He turns to look at Ernestine.

He stops smiling. Her glare is piercing.

163

She whispers: "Jus' hush ya mouth." With tight lips, Ernestine scolds him, telling him that I didn't travel 3,000 miles for a "lecture."

"Don't you be poking fun, old man."

I start laughing. Because it does seem ludicrous. Of the two of us, I probably am a little bit nuts. Ernestine turns to me and smiles. If I can laugh at myself then she can, too. But she's also ready to keep the interview moving. She looks back down at her knitting, chuckling.

I spend many hours with the Bickhams and when I return a year later on other business, I call. They insist that I meet them the next day – Sunday – at their church.

While getting dressed in what will have to pass as my churching clothes, I wonder if I shouldn't have tried harder to get out of it. I haven't been to church in a long time. I can justify my return today, only because I know that I won't be exposed to the long-suffering, guilt-ridden Catholic church of my childhood where it seemed I was constantly forced to listen to an old, uninspired, and recycled lecture, rarely a thought-provoking sermon. I always felt worse at the end of Mass.

I know that where there are black people there will be gospel music, and that kind of music always puts me in a good mood. Their church is so much more alive. And happy. Maybe it's because they move around and dance and sometimes, just for no reason at all, shout "Amen."

Besides, maybe I need to follow Moreese's advice. Countless times during our hours together, he's told me I need to pray.

"Now, I don't know if you are into church or anything, but you should be. All you have to do, Miss Cheever, is ask the good Lord and he will provide. If you don't have goals or dreams, then you're dead while you live. You've just got to have dreams. Like that house on the corner that we looked at last year."

On that bright Sunday morning in May, when I open the door of the Riley Chapel Christian Methodist Episcopal Church on 80th Avenue in Oakland, the sunlight seeps into the tiny white clapboard church. It takes me a moment to adjust my eyes to the darkened room. I can see that the pews aren't full, but the church is somehow filled with the soulful sounds of music. I look to see where the organ and choir are located, but I can find neither.

The music is coming from the handful of women, scattered throughout the church. Mrs. Bickham sits on the front row, right in the middle, and leads the others in song. I don't see any men. Just a handful of women and children, yet it sounds as if there is a full church choir.

Fifteen minutes later, the pastor, Rev. Frederick R. Taylor, and Moreese walk to the altar and the service begins. When Taylor asks all the mothers in the church to stand, the pews give a collective sigh. I am puzzled at his request. He then asks for a round of applause and since there is no one left in the audience but the little children, we clap for ourselves. I glance down at the two-page church bulletin. It is only then that I realize it is Mother's Day. I wonder if my own children remember and if so, whether they are celebrating the day for Mom, in absentia.

At the end of the service, during the "announcements" segment, Reverend Taylor looks at me and asks if there are any visitors. All eyes turn as I meekly raise my hand.

"Stand up, sister. And tell us who you are and why you're here."

I say only that I am a guest of the Reverend and Mrs. Bickham.

Do I need to say more, I wonder? Do they all need to know the details about this former Death Row inmate – that their associate pastor is a convicted murderer from Louisiana and was behind bars for almost 38 years?

I am sure they already know because, as far as I can tell, there is not much that the Bickhams hide.

After church, there is a brief social period, where all the members stop and wish Mrs. Bickham a Happy Mother's Day and warmly greet Rev. Bickham with bear hugs and kisses. They also shake my hand or give me a hug, too, welcoming me to the Riley Chapel. Everyone wishes me a Happy Mother's Day.

I'm feeling guilty that I've missed it; I didn't even know it was today until Reverend Taylor made the announcement. How many other family holidays would I miss in the future, intentionally or not?

We leave church and drive to the same diner where Moreese and I had gone a year ago, to celebrate Mother's Day. It's not a long lunch – Moreese and Ernestine are ready to get out of their "churchin clothes." And I'm eager to see the Bickham's new home.

"See, Joan. The Lord did hear us and He answered our prayers," Moreese says, on the drive over.

Soon we arrive at that same gray, three-bedroom California-style stucco house I'd seen a year ago. It's 10 blocks from the crime-ridden area where they once lived; it has wall-to-wall carpet, built-in bookshelves, and a fireplace.

As we sit outside, surrounded by the lime and peach trees, drinking iced tea in tall glasses, trying to cool off, Moreese tells me he doesn't have one minute of regret of his 37 years in Angola. When he calls the experience "glorious," I almost spit out my tea.

How could that be? And yet this is the same description that I have been getting from many ex-Death Row inmates. No one has gone so far as to call it "glorious" but they do credit it with a "rebirth."

Of the many men I've interviewed, Moreese is the most upbeat and positive about his years on Death Row. Because of his age, he is also the closest to dying. He admits that he was a "little wild" during his youth and probably drank and partied much more than he should have. But he says that Death Row kept him alive and out of trouble.

These days he worries more about the health of Ernestine. In a recent Christmas card, Moreese wrote: "How is my good friend Joan?" and then continued letting me know the latest Bickham family news. He closed by noting, "Ernestine had a bad fall a couple of days ago and is laid up in the hospital. Please keep her in your prayers. Love, Moreese Bickham."

I tape Moreese's card next to a photograph I have of him that hangs on my office wall. I took it the afternoon of our Mother's

Day lunch, when I visited his new home. He's sitting on a white, wrought-iron chaise lounge with a blue and green floral cushion. The lime tree in his garden provides shade from the hot Oakland sun. Moreese is staring directly at the camera, with a close-mouthed grin because he is embarrassed of his teeth. The prison sugar and lack of adequate dental care during those years behind bars have taken their toll. But only physically. Mentally, Moreese is alert and in great spirits. I wish his enthusiasm was infectious.

Moreese Bickham is a survivor. He's survived a bullet fired by one of the police officers he shot, three heart attacks, and prostate cancer.

He gives credit to a positive outlook on life and to the help he's received from others.

"I knowed that I'm in a bad situation, but I'm gonna make the most out of it. And it looked like everyone who was trying to make it better, well, they was right there helping me. If I had just set down and looked at my condition, one thing and another, the weight of the world would have just pushed me down into the earth."

———

Across the country, another convicted murderer attributes his success to the support of his brothers and sisters. Still another points to a band of "brothers" – his Death Row family – as the reason he won't be going back to prison.

CHAPTER TEN

A PROMISE TO KEEP

There were 69 men in the Class of '72 who killed a police officer, and 37 have been paroled. Most of those men have never been in trouble again. But prison is still home to 32 former Death Row inmates in this group who killed law enforcement officers, and, most all of those will probably die there.

I am sitting in my office trying to coordinate the kids' camp schedules when the phone rings. I let the answering machine get it.

"Joan, this is Bill from your mailbox."

Quickly I lunge toward the phone. "Hey, sorry. I'm here. What's up?"

"Well, I just wanted to let you know that this guy named Carl Russell [not his real name] called about five minutes ago. He said he knows you, but he asked a lot of questions. Like where you live and what's your telephone number. What you look like. Are you married? Do you have kids? Weird questions. I'm just calling to give you the heads-up. He sounded pretty angry."

My hand squeezes the phone receiver so tightly I can't feel it. I try to respond, but all I can say is "Ahhhhh..."

"Don't worry, Joan. I told him we don't give out that kind of information. It's company policy and all that. I don't know what he's going to do. I just thought I should let you know that he called."

"I really appreciate it and sorry to have bothered you," I half-whisper into the phone.

"No problem at all. Take care and, oh, have a good day," he says, before hanging up.

My day goes from okay to disaster. I know I am just minutes away from a telephone call from Russell, so I quickly scoot over to the file boxes to find out what little information I have on him. When the phone rings, I realize my lead time has been reduced to seconds.

"Joan, this is Carl Russell," the voice on the answering machine says, before I quickly pick up.

"Oh, hello Mr. Russell. How are you?"

"Not happy. In fact, I'm downright pissed off. I got your letter and I don't appreciate it one little bit. I know you have a phony address. I know so much about you, you haven't a clue. You think you're so smart, don't you?" he barks.

I start to respond and he snaps: "Don't interrupt me." He continues his tirade.

Quietly, I move a few steps from my desk with the phone in my ear, stretching the cord as far as it can go. I need to know what sent him to Death Row in the first place before I know how to respond. Quickly I thumb through my files, organized by state and color-coded for those who are still in prison, those who have died, and those on parole. I scan the court's opinion, *Russell v. State*, and the words "cold-blooded" and "shot six times" jump out.

"Sir, I'm really sorry to have upset you. Just ignore my letter. Your name won't be used. Let's just pretend I never wrote to you and you never called me. I've forgotten your name already. I'm very sorry to have bothered you."

"Not so fast. You're gonna listen to what I have to say." He then tells me he's innocent of the conviction that sent him to Death Row. Back then he was a "semi-professional weightlifter" who could bench press 650 lbs at least seven times, Russell says, so he wouldn't have needed a gun to kill the store clerk. "I could've snapped his neck like a twig," he brags.

He says it was "pure hate" that kept him going during the 19 years he was incarcerated, three of which were in the Death

House. "Believe me, there have been a few times that I've wanted to pull the trigger."

Russell says he lives on Social Security benefits and food stamps, and earns about $125 a month doing "odd jobs." He also volunteers for a non-profit group and is given $7 per day for meals and reimbursed 10 cents a mile for gas.

For a man who called me only because he was angry that I knew his whereabouts but not much more, Carl Russell sure talks a lot. During our one-sided conversation, my call waiting beeps. As usual, I ignore it, but the caller is insistent. Whoever it is keeps hitting redial, a signal it is a family emergency or a pesky friend who wants me off the other line. This is not a good time for either.

I have to put an angry killer on hold. "Mr. Russell, can you wait just a minute? I'll be back in a second. Sorry, gotta take this call," and I hit the button before he can answer.

It's Antoinette, my children's babysitter. She's out of breath and seems upset.

"What's the matter? Are the kids okay?"

"Oh, Mrs. Cheever, I have Luke and you were supposed to pick up Lily from camp about 15 minutes ago," she says in her lilting Haitian accent. "I'm about 30 minutes away. Can you get her? You said this morning you'd pick her up. Or do you want me? But it'll be 30 minutes. Traffic is bad."

"No, okay. Don't worry. I'll get her. I just forgot. But I've got it under control."

But my life is out of control and it doesn't help that Carl Russell is waiting on the other line. Reluctantly, I push the "flash" button to continue our conversation.

"Sorry about that, Mr. Russell. And you were saying?"

Fifteen pages of notes later, Russell finally tells me the reason for his call – he wants to let me know what happened to that last reporter who made inquiries about him. He assures me the journalist is still alive but has moved several states away. I get goose bumps on this hot July afternoon when Russell snickers: "Let's just say he won't be asking any more questions about me. I make him nervous, you understand?"

"Absolutely. Completely. I am sooooooooooooooo sorry to have bothered you," I answer, speaking slowly and deliberately in my best Texas drawl. "You won't hear from me again, I assure you. I've even forgotten your name," I say, laughing nervously.

He starts laughing, too. "That's exactly what I wanted to hear." Click.

The call is over but my blood pressure soars. I sit back and take deep breaths. My five seconds of "yoga" is interrupted by the thought of little Lily sitting alone, waiting for her ride.

On the drive to camp, I pray that I'll see a familiar face, a friend I can talk into going with me and our little campers to a nearby restaurant, within walking distance from my home. The kids can have ice cream sundaes; I'd like a glass of wine. As I drive into the parking lot, looking for some mother I know well enough to ask, I realize I don't know any of these women. The seven years I spent commuting to New York City had sharply curtailed my suburban social life. Very few mothers here work "outside of the home' and today I don't recognize a soul in the sea of Lacoste tennis skirts or in the groups of pink and lime sundresses that Lily Pulitzer made famous.

Most of the mothers are young, quite young, and almost all are in the "summer uniform" of this little town – tennis dresses. They are either on their way to or from the country club.

My six-year-old daughter stands waiting, her eyes focused on every car that comes into the driveway; her arms are folded tightly across her small chest.

"Oh, Sugar," I yell, calling her by her nickname, waving my hands so she can see me. "I'm so sorry I'm late, honey," I say, while I'm crossing my heart and holding up my three fingers in the Girl Scout promise. "No excuses. I promise it won't happen again." I look over at Lily's college-age counselor who seems overly annoyed.

"Mom, you're late. Real late."

"I know, I'll make it up to you. How about if we go downtown for an ice cream? And Mom can get a dessert, too."

"I just want to go home, Mother," she says, exaggerating the word "Mother" as though today, once again, I have not earned the title. "Luke and me are going to the park. Antoinette's waiting for me. I wanna go home – now!" she barks, turning "now" into a two-syllable word.

But I don't want to leave her. It means that I will have to go back to my office and figure out how to deal with Carl Russell's phone call. My zone of privacy has just been shattered and I am a nervous wreck. Will he call again? Will he visit me? What exactly is he planning to do?

I don't have long to linger over this scary ex-Death Row inmate; within a couple of hours I am back on the phone with another. And he is happy to hear from me.

Michael Turczi, a truck driver in Gary, Indiana, lives with his sister Sue Ann[1] and works with his brother; another sister lives next door and a third sister is only 10 minutes away. At 46, Mike is the youngest of 12 siblings.

He went to Indiana's Death Row in 1971 after being convicted of the 1970 murder of a business partner – the two men owned land together. Mike and two friends[2] had arranged to meet the victim at a gas station and the four then drove, in two cars, to a secluded area. One of Mike's friends turned off the car and lights and ran. He then heard gunshots. The victim was shot three times in the head.[3]

Mike says he couldn't have survived prison without his family – they visited faithfully and have stuck by him on the outside. One of his older brothers, a truck driver, helped Mike get a job driving. They pass each other frequently on the interstate.

He says he turned his life around inside prison.

"Prison was a total culture shock. I came out with a totally different attitude. I stayed away from drugs, girls, and homos. I decided to get out and buckle down."

Paroled in 1991, Mike got married a year later to a woman he'd met in prison, the widow of a corrections officer. With a new wife and her three children to support, Mike knew he had to find a job that paid a decent salary, a difficult task for an ex-con, especially one who had been on Death Row. He went from mowing lawns to pumping gas at a truck stop to driving 18-wheelers – the job that he loves. But the love in the marriage didn't last. In 1997, he and his wife divorced; he stays in touch with her children, even though they live in another state. He says he doesn't mind the drive.

It's hard for him to describe what his freedom means.

"When you're looking at a forty-foot wall from the inside all the time – this is heaven. I feel like a bird flying over. I sit here, at home, at the kitchen table and look out the back door, I see a beautiful scene. Even the weeds in the backyard are beautiful. This is what people take for granted."

Looking out onto his backyard driveway, Mike's eyes rest on his new light-blue fishing boat.

"I can't wait for spring. You like to go fishing? One day maybe you'll go fishing with me?" he asks. Before I can answer, Mike points to his Ford pickup truck. "I'd love to show you around. Let's take a ride." His sister is sitting in the other room, playing a game of solitaire on the computer. She stops and turns around, curious as to how I will answer.

"Sure, I'd love to. And when we come back, I'd like to take y'all out to dinner. You pick. My treat. How does that sound?"

"That's very nice. We'd love to, wouldn't we, Mike?"

I began to relax, a bit. I hadn't planned on dinner in Indiana , especially since my sister is waiting for me about an hour away in Chicago; we are going to have dinner together at her hotel, a definite upgrade from the motel rooms I have been accustomed to. Jean is in Chicago on business, and she has a room with two double beds. I am her guest and for the first time, in a very long time, I know that once I put my head down on the pillow tonight, I will sleep. I won't be propping the furniture up against the door.

I don't know why I asked them out for dinner; perhaps out of politeness for taking up so much of Mike's time on a Sunday afternoon. More probably, it is an unconscious thought verbalized. Sue Ann is in the room when the offer is made. Perhaps it is my way of taking out a little "personal insurance," knowing that if we do not return soon for dinner, Mike will have to answer to his sister, and then maybe to the police.

I climb into Mike's truck and we tour downtown Gary, recently named the "crime capital of the world." Ten minutes later, Mike asks if I would like to see his truck. The big one. The 18-wheeler.

Sure, I answer, and we drive a little farther, to the outskirts of town where there are empty warehouses and shuttered factories. It's desolate. Then I get nervous. I am driving with a convicted murderer who, 25 years earlier, took an unsuspecting friend on a drive down a dead-end dirt road.

I am being stupid, I think. My sister is expecting me back in Chicago. Mike's sister is waiting for us to return for dinner. My rental car is parked in front of her house. I have the keys. I am perfectly safe.

We drive to the black-paved lot where Mike parks his truck. I have a camera in my pocket and ask if he will pose for a picture.

"Go ahead and take a couple. Will you send me one? How'd you like to see the inside of the cab?" Turczi asks, but before I can answer, he remembers that he's left the keys to the big rig at home.

I look at my watch and remind him that his sister is waiting. Sue Ann greets us at the door and I feel silly for having worried. I get in my car and they in theirs, but first Mike wants to stop at another sister's house. Mike proudly introduces me to his sister and his nieces and nephews, who are racing in and out of the kitchen, stopping briefly to wave and say "Hi" before continuing their game of tag.

We have dinner at the Old Country Store and an hour later, after I say my goodbyes and promise to write and send the pictures, Mike asks if I know how to get back to Chicago.

"Sure. I've got a map and you gave me directions to get to your house, so I'll back track. No problem."

I get on the Interstate and glance at my watch, realizing that I am running late. I've been gone since noon and have told Jean if she doesn't hear from me before 8 p.m. then she should get worried. It's 7:45 p.m. and my cell phone doesn't work. The battery is dead.

By the time I drive to the outskirts of Chicago, it is late. And dark. I exit the highway and find a Dunkin Donuts with a pay phone outside. I picked the wrong exit. This neighborhood looks tough. Groups of teenage boys and girls are walking up and down the street; they hang outside several convenience stores, and the donut store is packed with teens. I'm starting to get a little scared. I'm lost.

I park my car right next to the pay phone and call Jean at her hotel.

She's not in her room, so I leave a message.

"I'm running a little late. I'm okay. I'm somewhere in Chicago. Kinda lost. But I'll find my way." While I am talking, I observe a four-door navy-blue sedan stop and park right next to me, blocking my car. I wonder how I am going to ask him to move. The balding, 50-ish white man gives me the same kind of look a father gives his teenage daughter after finding her sneaking back into her room after missing curfew. He stares at me, shaking his head. He's frowning. Immediately I know who he is.

I mouth, "I'm lost. Where's downtown?"

I see a smile creep onto his face and then he nods; his eyes point in the direction of my car. I jump in and lock the doors. He inches his car forward so I can back out and follow him. I notice he has an "exempt" license plate; I look closer and think I spot a small siren light sitting on the dashboard. He glances frequently in his rear view mirror, slowing down through green lights and stopping at yellows. He wants to make sure I am right on his tail.

Fifteen minutes later, I am at the hotel, enthusiastically waiving goodbye and mouthing an overemphasized and much appreciated "thank you very much" to the undercover police officer who has safely escorted me out of one of the worst neighborhoods of Chicago right into the hands of valet parking.

When I walk into her hotel room, my sister is stretched out on the bed, watching a movie. "So, how was the interview?" she asks, never taking her eyes off the TV.

"Jesus, Jean. Didn't you get my message? I am three hours late. Remember this morning I told you to call the police if I didn't get back by 6 p.m.! I thought you'd be freaked out!"

"Oh God, Joan. I knew you'd find this place. After all, it is the nicest hotel you've stayed in a long, long time, isn't it?"

She doesn't have to rub it in. I vowed that night not to put myself into any more potentially dangerous situations. No driving at dusk in big cities, without better directions.

But I have a short memory. A few months later when Leroy Johnson called,[4] I agreed to meet him even though I didn't know the details of his crime.

Leroy just wanted anonymity and, after that threatening telephone call from Carl Russell, I decided that I wanted some too.

Leroy was on his state's Death Row for the same crime as Chuck Culhane of New York: but he says he pulled the trigger in self-defense and to save someone else's life. On that summer night in 1971, two police officers were killed. That's the only thing Chuck and Leroy have in common: a police officer was killed. Unlike Chuck, Leroy is fiercely protective of his privacy and he insists his real name not be used.

When he called that morning, I was barely awake. But after he identified himself I raced up the stairs to my attic office to grab his file buried among the other 588 stacked in boxes, separated by those who are on parole, those still incarcerated and those who have died. They aren't filed alphabetically, but rather by state; there were 31 states and the District of Columbia that had active Death Rows in June 1972.

While searching, I make small talk to keep Leroy on the phone; I can tell he is nervous and I am worried he will hang up. But his name doesn't ring a bell and I need to know where he is from. Inadvertently he then tells me the name of a city in the state where he was convicted and I grab that box and rummage through the files. On the outside of Leroy Johnson's file, I'd scribbled P.O. (police officer) murder.

I don't have time to read the facts of the case in the court's opinion that upheld his death sentence. I only have time to focus on the man on the phone.

Leroy is guarded and offers little information. He says he really doesn't know why he is calling because the "Death Row Five" – five men who sat together in the Death House in a Southern state – have decided they are going to ignore me, hoping that I will just go away. While on Death Row, they made a pact that if they ever got off "The Row" and, eventually, out of prison, they'd stick together on the outside. And they have. The group has gone through divorces, financial stress, and clinical depression. But they've all made it. That's because a call for help from anyone in this group means it's time to hit the road – by plane, train, or automobile. Leroy Johnson has kept my letter on his kitchen table; he says he looks at it almost every day.

He wants to see me. He has something to tell me. And Leroy says I need to hear it. I need to see it.

I agree to meet him even though I don't have a clue as to the nature of his crime or the gory details I will soon read in his file. But he has said "Yes" to an interview so how can I decline?

I used to think I was afraid only of flying. But it's not enough to keep me from traveling. I just put in my drink order before anyone else, sometimes before I buckle my seat belt. It's always the same – a Bloody Mary with limes. Then when I moved from Texas to New York City, I discovered a new fear. It's not what one might expect.

It happened one morning when I was driving a friend's rather large 1974 Buick Skylark, and I came face to face with the Lincoln Tunnel. I'd never driven through a tunnel before; we don't have them in Texas. That morning, a new phobia was discovered: tunnels. Ten years later, I added bridges to the list.

So when Leroy Johnson calls and tells me to rent a car with 4-wheel drive and then describes the icy road conditions and gives directions that include driving over several bridges and through one long, dark tunnel, I panic.

"Isn't there another way to get to your town without going through a tunnel?"

Leroy laughs: "No. That's the only way. Don't worry, though. I'm sure the state highway patrol won't close it. It has to get really icy. Just make sure you get 4-wheel drive because I wouldn't want you to skate off the side of that mountain. You do know how to drive in the ice and snow, right?"

That's when I tell him the first lie.

My nerves are frayed when I check into the Best Western several days later; I'd just survived a one-hour flight in a 20-seat Brazilian commuter plane that took off in a blinding snowstorm through the mountains. By tomorrow morning, I'm sure the troopers will close the tunnel; I'll have to cancel the interview and then I'll get to go home.

Before I climb into bed, I engage in the same nighttime ritual I've been doing for the past couple of years.

I drag what furniture I can move and push it up against the door. I lock the door and turn the deadbolt. I fasten the chain. Sometimes I wad up pages of newspaper – a makeshift "alarm" – and scatter them around the door. It's a trick I learned from a friend who does it even when she stays in an upscale hotel with her husband. "The noise of the newspaper will wake you up before you're attacked," she says, excitedly.

I do wake the next morning to find that it has stopped snowing. The roads are bad, but not bad enough to close.

With the 4-wheel drive engaged, I conquer the first bridge. No problem. I peer over the side of the mountain and continue driving two more hours. The roads are slick and I hope that the state police have enough good sense to close the tunnel to keep motorists like me off this road.

As I approach it, I see that it is open. I take deep breaths and start the rosary. I am on the fifth decade before I see daylight. I've made it.

Now it's time to find Leroy. Considering what I've been through, this will be easy. He's told me to look for the gray house with the boat parked in the driveway. When I drive up, Leroy is standing at the door.

He quickly ushers me in, away from the view of any nosy

neighbors. The rules have been established earlier by phone. No photographs; no tape recorder. Only notes. Hidden in my purse is my cellular phone. I keep it turned on. Back home, I left my itinerary, complete with Leroy's address and phone number, on my refrigerator door. Just in case.

Any fear I had about the meeting is gone, minutes after I meet this small, slightly built man with piercing green eyes, handsome in a rugged, outdoorsy way. He is more nervous about meeting me. He lives in a small town of 8,000 and "everybody knows everybody's business." But at the same time he says that's what makes living in this small town so appealing.

"You don't get that in the bigger cities. Here everyone is extremely friendly. I have not had one argument; not heard one bad word. I have excellent neighbors," he says, leaving me to wonder why I am quickly being pushed inside the front door.

"I mean police wave and stop and speak to me. At first it freaked me out. It was one of the first things I noticed." When in prison he was afraid he would be killed by a prison guard to exact revenge for the murder of a police officer.

"The biggest shock I had was when I was qualified for minimum security. One day they [prison guards] said, 'You're going to the farm.' I thought that meant they were going to take me out and kill me."

Leroy is 48 and was on Death Row for two years and inside for 18.

"I know nothing is promised to me. I lost 18 years and they were very important."

He's been out of prison for eight years and has no intention of going back. "I'd lose everything if I go back to crime. My mind is set. I'm not going to do anything that would cause me to go back."

As I look around his light-blue painted living room, over-flowing with two couches, an aquarium and a large Magnavox TV, and notice the boat and the light-blue convertible parked next to a pickup truck outside, I see what he means.

"I've worked hard during the time I've been out. Two hundred and fifty dollars a month, that's okay. No complaints. I got paid $3 or $4 an hour and I saved my money. I've cleaned houses, been a filing clerk for a lawyer, and cut lawns."

Leroy knows he can probably earn more in a larger city, but he believes that will put his freedom in jeopardy.

"Everyone carries a gun and there's trouble in a big city. Doesn't mean something could happen. When I travel, I make sure I'm not alone. It's just better to stay away," he says, even if it means he can't see his father, his children, or a brother and sister as often as he'd like.

I ask about the crime that sent him to Death Row when he was 21 years old. Leroy admits he was no stranger to the criminal justice system, spending most of his youth in juvenile detention centers for theft. An 8th-grade dropout, he just about lived on the streets, stealing to survive.

He shifts uneasily on the couch as he recalls the night the police officer was murdered. He pauses and then says he'd do it again because it was self-defense. And he was protecting someone he loves. [5]

"He [the officer] didn't deserve to die. We were black and they were white. We had a keg of beer in the car and we were high. I knew he was going to shoot me. I had no choice. And I have to live with that for the rest of my life. It bothers me," Leroy says, stopping before saying more.

The story of that night is not one of which he is proud. Twice he leaves the room to cry, alone. But the house is not big enough for privacy. He knows that I know where he is going and why. With a handkerchief in one hand, and the other rubbing swollen eyes, Leroy returns to the living room and finishes his story.

"I didn't feel like I could do 18 years. I wasn't strong enough to endure 10. I really thought they would kill me because I killed a police officer."

When Leroy was released from prison in 1988, he was employed as a paralegal and a file clerk. The jobs paid well, but he felt confined. "I don't like being around a lot of people. I don't like crowds. When I was inside, I liked to get away from everybody. I'm an outdoorsman. That's where I'm the happiest."

A year before he was released from prison, he was put in a prison program in which he worked the land – 2,700 acres, unsupervised – and counted cattle every day. It sounds incredibly boring.

"I had access to a tractor and a horse and I was totally by myself from 6 a.m. to 8 p.m.," Leroy says. "I knew it was a test. But when I was finally released, it wasn't that much of a shock. I'd been working on the outside for months. Without supervision. I was totally by myself. That was so helpful in a lot of ways."

Leroy extols the virtue of prison educational programs and said the biggest mistake the government can make is to eliminate them. He walked into prison with an 8th-grade education, barely, and walked out with a high school degree. He credits his success to going to school inside and learning a trade.

"At no time did they push it. I've always been a strong advocate that it should be mandatory. If you don't have an education, you have no job skills. And an education builds personal self-esteem."

He said algebra, trigonometry, and geometry "fueled my ego" which led him to serving as president of the prison chapter of the NAACP and the Jaycees. But he can't understand the prison system's priorities. "If you go to school, you got paid $2.50 a month. If you worked in the kitchen, you made $20 a month," he says, shaking his head incredulously. "School should be the highest paid. Anyone can get a job in a restaurant."

Still, he was smitten with the outdoors and searched for a job that allows him to be outside and to stay there – he mows lawns six days a week, sometimes seven.

After all those years of being locked up, Leroy can't get enough of the outdoors. He's gone camping in 18-degree weather with two feet of snow, testing his survival skills as a way of building self-esteem. He's flown in a small airplane "just for the experience" and has even taken a helicopter ride. "Why not? It was a blast!"

His blue convertible is parked by the side of his house, in the driveway, in front of his boat. Leroy spends a lot of time on the water.

"I love to fish. For the sport. I don't keep the fish, but I sure do love catching them." At least twice a year, the Death Row Five go on a "Boys' Weekend Out" and fish. These men are like brothers. They spent more than 15 years together locked up.

In addition to learning a job skill, Leroy attributes his success to the support he received from his "other family" – these four men who lived with him on Death Row. The Death Row Five have stayed together in the years since they were released. They've kept the pact they made when they were all facing execution dates.

"We made a promise that if we ever got out alive, we would be there for each other. For anything. Just a phone call. That's all it would take."

Last year Leroy needed help getting through a divorce, after 14 years of marriage. "My wife and I just grew apart. I felt as though we were better friends and I just decided one day it was time to get a divorce," Leroy says, his voice cracking. "I felt as though I was holding her back. She had one of the most prestigious jobs in the state and it was in the big city. Where I was from and where I couldn't return. She's been through a lot with me. When 200 police officers protested me getting parole, I just knew that tore her to pieces. She made me believe that I could achieve something with my life. She took me to a higher level."

But the stress of parole and being married to an ex-Death Row inmate took a toll on the marriage.

Leroy said he got depressed and he knew that if he didn't call the group, there was as good chance he'd end up back inside. Within hours, a member of the Death Row Five was on his doorstep.

When another member started hanging around a person of questionable character, the group convinced him that if he continued the relationship it was a one-way ticket back to the Big House. He ended it and his acquaintance was later busted for dealing cocaine.

For the past seven years, the Death Row Five have gone fishing during their twice-a-year reunions. This year, they're trying to talk Leroy into a deep-sea trip "way the hell out." But he doesn't think he'll make it. He gets seasick on the ocean.

I come up with a quick list of home remedies – the kind that combat nausea in pregnancy. I ask if he's tried the remedy advertised in the Sharper Image catalogue; he leaves the living room and returns a minute later wearing the gray bands around his wrists.

"You mean these? That's what my friends told me to do. I tried. They don't work for me."

The group is close. They have already burned up the phone lines talking about my visit. Each man received my letter – within days of each other – requesting an interview.

When Leroy first called, he said he was intrigued with my friendship with Walter. When I tried to set up a specific time to meet, face to face, he stalled. That request had to go back to "the board" – the other four. After a series of telephone calls to each other they gave Leroy permission to talk, but only if I agreed to their rules. No names. No state.

"They won't talk to you because they're doing well. I'm the least successful of all of them. We have a lot to lose by going public," Leroy says, half apologizing. "It's too bad because we also have a lot to give."

That's what he wanted to tell me on the phone, when we arranged to meet. That it is possible to change. That a life can be turned around. That he's not the same man he was at 21.

He knows many people, especially the victims' families, will never be able to forgive him. It's even harder, Leroy says, to forgive yourself. He knows that most people truly believe that the only way a killer can pay his debt to society is with his own life – execution of life in prison. He knows many people believe that killers should be left to rot and die behind bars.

He says he knows he can never give back the life he took and he says he struggles daily, trying to give something back to his community.

D.J., his parole officer, is a fishing buddy and a friend. He calls on Leroy frequently, asking him to counsel young black men who are in trouble with the law and warn them of where they are headed if they don't change. Leroy frequently gets calls from friends and neighbors for advice on how to help their own troubled sons.

He appears to be a model citizen and a good neighbor. While I'm there, his phone rings constantly. A friend needs a ride to work at the Family Dollar store; another asks to be picked up at the bus stop. He's a one-man shuttle service to church – a Pentecostal Church – although Leroy says he's "not ready to go to church, just yet."

The phone rings again and this time his voice changes. He takes the call in his kitchen, hoping that I can't hear.

He returns and tells me anyway. His ex-wife wants to come by to pick up some of her things. She also wants to tell him she's getting remarried in a month.

Four hours later, it's time to leave. Leroy and I have covered a lot of ground this morning; he now feels comfortable being seen with me in public. And he's hungry. We head to the local lunch buffet – fried catfish, ribs, okra, turnip greens, and three different kinds of beans and much more; all you can eat for $5.99.

After lunch, we drive to one of his jobs, the cemetery on the outskirts of his small town. He checks to make sure no tree branches have fallen on the graves during last night's storm. I walk through the snow, looking at names and calculating ages. I linger at a tombstone in one large family plot and fail to notice that my guide is already back in his truck, cranking up the heat.

I smile at the irony – how a man who was once so close to death returns on a daily basis to a place that symbolizes it.

But Leroy says he never believed he would die in the electric chair, even though he had two execution dates set – February 7, 1972 and April 10, 1972.

"Not knowing what is going to happen really eats at you. I had to try to prepare for it even though I couldn't believe that they would execute me."

And Leroy says he'll never be incarcerated again. He says he's not the same man, and I believe him. It looks as though he is making a good living. He has friends. He looks as though he is at peace.

We take a drive through the mountains and he shows me the striking economic disparities in this small town. We pass the homes of the rich, large houses in a manicured subdivision. We then drive by the homes of the poor, metal lean-tos with old blankets used as curtains. Rusted car parts are strewn throughout the neighborhood. I feel as though I am on the set of the 1972 movie *Deliverance*.

It is dusk by the time we return to his house. It's been a long day. I drive back to the motel and stop to pick up dinner, more fast food. Like many nights on the road, tonight the television is my dinner companion. At 10 p.m., I deadbolt the door, chain lock it and turn off the light. An hour later, I'm asleep.

But across town, sleep doesn't come easily to Leroy Johnson.

He calls the next morning, at 8 a.m. while I'm packing to drive two hours to the airport to catch a plane back home. I'm surprised that he's called because we've already said our goodbyes. He starts talking about the weather and then he stammers a bit. I wonder what he's about to say. And then he blurts it out.

"I've been tossing and turning all night long. I mean, when I first met you I was so surprised. You're not at all what I expected. You talk big and you write big, but you're a little bitty thing. And I think you are way too trusting," he lectures. "I don't want you to get hurt. But I don't know what I can do, except give you some advice. Do you have a pen and paper? Now, you never heard this from me. Okay? Write down these names. If they want to meet you, just say No. Make up an excuse. Anything. I know about them. I lived with them on Death Row. They're bad. They're dangerous. They are crazy. Don't you dare go see them. Promise?"

"Yes, don't worry. Really, don't," I say, remembering that some of the names sound familiar. I have spoken to a few of them by phone. They hadn't invited me to meet them, but if they change their minds, I have a good reason to turn them down. I have been warned. By a killer, no less.

During the two-hour drive to the airport, I keep looking at the names. I am so focused on the list and Leroy's phone call, that I don't remember driving through the tunnel. Or over the bridges.

I now have a new fear. And a new friend.

I believe it's Leroy's deep friendship with the Death Row Five, and their life-long pact to support each other, which will keep him – and them – out of trouble. He says there's no way any of them will ever risk going back. And, so far, neither he nor the other four have been reincarcerated.

Those who do return to prison, called recidivists, do so for a variety of reasons and for a variety of crimes. They either break the law again, return to a drug or alcohol addiction they had kicked while incarcerated, or fail to follow the rigorous rules of parole.

There are 111 recidivists in this group who were on Death Row in 1972; most, like Frederick Martineau, James Manier, Joseph Cerny III, and Bennett Belwood, were initially reincarcerated for "technical" or minor violations. The average length of time between parole and reincarceration for this group is approximately 4 years for "technical" parole violators, 5 years for drug offenses and 10 years for a more serious felony. For those five who killed again, while on parole, the average length of time was 2 years.

Parole officers say the rules are stringent and the parolees are very closely monitored initially because the average length of time between parole and a return to prison for inmates in the general prison population is about two years. In fact, the first few months after release are the most critical to a parolee's success on the outside.

Frederick Martineau was on Death Row in New Hampshire in 1959 for the kidnapping and murder of a man who was to testify as a witness against him in a burglary case.[6] Martineau and his accomplice were sentenced to death by hanging. After *Furman*, Martineau was released from prison in 1973 because of the length of time he had already served. But two years later Martineau returned, charged with a violation of parole – he committed "adultery." On September 5, 1975, Martineau's parole officer said that despite repeated warnings, Martineau "has continued an intimate relationship with another woman not his wife" and frequented a community club in Manchester "all in violation of Rule 5 of his Parole Agreement." The officer also noted there were allegations of an attempted burglary. [7]

In January 1979, Martineau was paroled again – out of New Hampshire to Massachusetts. Three years later, however, he was in trouble again, for not having a job and for associating with known felons. Most importantly, Martineau failed to tell his parole officer that he had been arrested in Rhode Island on federal drug charges; possession and distribution of heroin and cocaine. [8] The 80-year-old ex-Death Row inmate is currently incarcerated in a federal prison in Atlanta. He will probably die there.

At one time, James Manier of Colorado thought he'd never be paroled. The day after *Furman*, Manier told a reporter with *The Denver Post:* "When I go out of here on parole, I'll probably go out in a box." [9]

Manier was wrong. He left prison in 1981 but returned two years later – for failing to file a change of address form. He says he "forgot" to tell his parole officer that he had moved; a violation of "Rule #2–Residence." For that, he was hit with a five-year term. He was released again in January 1984 only to be revoked again in October 1985. The Parole Board says he didn't commit a new crime, but they won't give the reason for his revocation.

Manier was sent to Death Row in 1970 for murdering his wife, Josephine Manier Collins. While her husband was in prison for a previous offense, Mrs. Manier married Carl Collins even though she and Manier never divorced. Once he was paroled, Manier, in an alcohol- and drug-induced stupor, went to Collins' home and shot both Collins and Josephine Manier, who was pregnant. Collins survived.[10]

Manier says he's been turned down four times; in 1996, 1999, and 2001. His next parole hearing is scheduled for November 2006.

In Washington state, it was traffic tickets that sent Joseph Cerny III back inside.

In 1968, Cerny was sent to the Death House at Walla Walla Penitentiary, after he was convicted of being an accomplice in a robbery during which a Vietnam War hero was killed. Cerny was paroled in December 1984 and said he used his time wisely, telling me he traveled all over Europe, became a licensed real estate agent, and married a woman (whom he declined to name) who, he says, is a partner in the best criminal law firm in Seattle (they are now divorced). I am unable to verify any of Cerny's story.

But in April 1991, Cerny's life in the Free World ended when his parole was revoked for five years for what he says are "four traffic violations."

Cerny received an additional second five-year term when he came up for parole in 1998, but he declined to provide details. He was paroled in 2003.[11]

Cerny told me I could learn about his "very interesting life" for a price – if I agreed to represent him in his appeals. I declined.

Bennett Belwood of Utah says he's miserable living outside of prison and he wishes he was back on Death Row.

"Those who are executed are the luckiest. Life in the Free World is too hard," Belwood says, admitting he still craves the notoriety of an execution. A month before he was scheduled to die, Belwood told the warden that he'd prefer hanging rather than standing in front of a firing squad. Instead, the U.S. Supreme Court intervened in the *Furman* decision, and Belwood's wish "to save the state of Utah a 94-cent bullet" was never realized.

Belwood was sent to Death Row for the July 9, 1970, murder of Ronald Paul Smith, a drinking buddy. The two men went to Big Hollow Canyon near Dugway, Utah, an Army installation, to go hunting. Belwood, accompanied by his then girlfriend, now, he says, his wife, Ruby Breece, left the car with Smith and then shot him twice in the head. [12]

He confessed, boasting that he and his girlfriend were like Bonnie and Clyde, referring to his crime as a "Glory Sweep." He also testified that he drank 20 16-ounce cans of beer and took Valium shortly before the crime. He pleaded innocent by reason of insanity but was found guilty of first-degree murder. [13]

Belwood says he's sorry he wasn't executed. "I was really pissed off that Gary Gilmore beat me to the firing squad." [14]

The 60-year-old Belwood has been out of prison since March 11, 1986, and he's not happy about it. "It dawned on me that I was free and I went into kinda shock. I wasn't ready to get out." He said when he found out he was going to be released he begged prison officials to keep him in. He said he even asked them to put him back on Death Row. He didn't think he had what it took to survive on the outside. And he still doesn't.

"When I got paroled, I was freaked out. When they told me I had to get a job, I was thinking, no way! I wasn't interested. My daddy was dying of cancer of the lungs. I tried working, but now I draw Social Security checks."

He says he's tried to kill himself five times because life on the outside is so hard. I'm amazed to hear Belwood say he prefers prison, even after what he's witnessed there.

"I've seen guys set on fire in their cell. Stuck through with spears, the doors open and their throats cut. Razor blades everywhere," he says. "You don't know one minute from the next if you're gonna live or die. It was a strain on the brain. But it was home. Guys in prison are together. I felt at ease there."

In 1986, just four months after he was paroled, Belwood returned for what prison officials will describe only as "a technical violation." When I inquired further, Belwood wouldn't explain what that meant and neither would parole officials. He spent another six months inside before being released.

Belwood earns a living through a variety of odd jobs, sometimes supplementing his Social Security check with the dollars he gets by picking up soda cans on the side of the highway and turning them into cash. He says he's working hard to continue to be a law-abiding citizen.

Belwood's parole ended in 1992 and, for the most part, he has stayed out of the spotlight, except he says when he appeared on the nationally televised *Jenny Jones* talk show in 1995 to talk about killers on parole.

He was surprised by the audience's angry reaction and vows that that will be his last appearance on TV. He wants a little bit more anonymity.

"They told me I should be taken out and shot like a dog."

———

One member of the Class of '72 who had been on parole for 10 years had all the characteristics to ensure success: he learned an employable skill, despite a borderline IQ, held a steady job and was a hard worker, created a family support system outside of prison, didn't touch drugs or alcohol, and was described as a "star" by his parole officer.

His case was one of the four argued before the U.S. Supreme Court on that snowy day in Washington, D.C. My search for this former Death Row inmate ended when I was given his new address: the county jail in Wichita Falls, Texas.

CHAPTER ELEVEN

A REPORT CARD

Of the 322 men who have been paroled, 75 returned to prison briefly, for either technical parole violations or nonviolent crimes. There are 32 who committed more serious crimes such as aggravated robbery/assault, attempted murder, or involuntary manslaughter. Five parolees killed again.

I slide my Connecticut driver's license and "gold" card – the Texas Bar Card that looks like an American Express card – underneath the bulletproof glass window at the Wichita Falls, Texas county jail. I am here to see Elmer Branch, a convicted rapist who sat on Texas' Death Row and whose case was argued along with that of Furman.

This is the first county jail I've been in, other than as a reporter for *The San Antonio Light*. In the past, most of my visits were to Texas' Death Row to see Walter. During those trips, once I drive through the gates, my car and I are subjected to searches. On one occasion, in 1992, I left my daughter in San Antonio with her grandparents and flew to Houston to confer with Robert Hirschhorn, my co-counsel, about yet another appeal for Walter. I decide then that since I am so close to Huntsville, I'll go see Walter. But I don't want to go alone, so I ask a friend, who had been a briefing attorney with me on the Texas Court of Criminal Appeals. While there, Katie[1] worked for one of the most liberal judges on the bench. At the time we visited Death Row, she was an assistant district attorney whose job was to convict murderers, rapists, and robbers, and periodically she worked with other prosecutors on death penalty trials.

Years later, she would go to the other side of the bar and defend criminals. Eventually, she was elected as a district judge and she now sits in judgment.

But this afternoon as she drives to Ellis I, past the signs "No contraband, no alcohol and no firearms," I, as usual, ignore the warnings. I've never brought or even thought of bringing drugs, alcohol, or firearms to a prison. Ludicrous, I think. But on this afternoon, I ask, for safe measure: "Katie, we don't have anything that could get us in trouble, right?"

And then she starts laughing nervously: "Only my gun."

"Shit, what are you talking about? Katie, turn this car around right now. God Damnit. Why didn't you say something earlier?"

But by then it's too late. We're just 50 yards from the guard post and if we make a U-turn, we'll look very suspicious. Besides, the guard has already come out of her office to write down the number on Katie's license plate.

"Where exactly is this gun of yours that you 'forgot' to tell me about until now?" I whisper.

"In the trunk, under the spare tire. Look, I think it's legal. Hell, we're in Texas. I mean I use it when I travel and you can if you go from county to county. It's perfectly fine. You worry so much, Joan."

"It is not *perfectly* fine, sister, when you are driving into Death Row with signs all over the place that say, very clearly, 'no firearms.' "

"Be cool. They won't find it. They don't even search. Have you ever been searched on any of your visits to see Walter?"

I hadn't, I thought, as I breathed a sigh of relief. Once we reached the guard, we both dutifully handed over our driver's licenses. I also include my Texas Bar Card; Katie does not.

"Why don't you identify yourself as a lawyer? What's your problem?"

"Oh, I'll get in trouble at work [at the District Attorney's Office] for coming out here with you – a defense lawyer – to Death Row," she said making faces with her mouth as if she held a sour ball in it. "Today I'm just your driver, keeping you company. Got it?"

"You are such a coward. Jackass," I laugh, hurling as many insults as I can while the guard is gone. When she returns, she isn't smiling.

"Miz Cheever. Do you have any alcohol, contraband, or firearms on your person or inside this vehicle?"

"No, of course not," I reply. A bold-faced lie. I can't take it back. It is too late.

"Well, then would you just please step out of the car. You too, Miss," she says, pointing to Katie. "We'd like to conduct a search."

By this time I am hyperventilating while the guard and her partner, a tall, heavy-set, mid-30s white man, comb through Katie's car. But did they consider it my car because of the way I quickly answered the guard's question. Did I imply ownership? The guards look under the seats, in the glove box; in the netting on the sides of the door.

When she says, "Pop your trunk," I think I am going to have a heart attack right there on that dirt road. She then says: "Follow me back here for a moment," and I am obedient, like a sheep going to slaughter.

Until now, I never knew that I could hold my breath for as long as I did that day. The guard pushes her way through Katie's extensive CD collection, boxes strewn about; a change of clothes in case she wants to go bar-hopping with girlfriends; and some running shoes. The guard's hand rests on the spare tire.

That's when I shut my eyes, knowing the next sound will be that of handcuffs circling my wrists. Slowly, I open one eye, just in time to see the guard lift the tire, ever so slightly, and then, ever so gently, she puts it down. I don't know if she's seen Katie's "little lady's" revolver and just decided not to pursue it because of the extra burden of paperwork or because she has already had enough fun today watching this out-of-state lawyer squirm.

And I don't know if she knows that my driver works for a District Attorney who is responsible for sending hundreds of men to Death Row. All his prosecutors carry guns, legally – it's standard operating procedure. At that moment, I don't know if we are being filmed for a Candid Camera segment that's just never aired.

I do know that I will never bring Katie back to Death Row. Or I will personally search and interrogate my driver or passengers before driving into a prison.

Today, in the reception area of the Wichita Falls County Jail, I am alone. And I'm very glad.

Sitting on the hard plastic chair, along with the wives and mothers of the men temporarily housed here, I am surprised at how calm and patient everyone is, with the exception of the jail guards.

In Connecticut, the search for Elmer Branch has been frustrating. The letters I wrote kept coming back – "not at this address" or "left no forwarding address," and finally a plain "unable to forward." It was the same with William Henry Furman.

But in Branch's case, I am really confused. Officials from the Texas Department of Corrections tell me he's on parole. Parole officers tell me he isn't. For four months, Elmer Branch is lost in the system.

And then I find him – or, in this case, Elmer's employer of seven years finds *me*. Steve Smith, owner of Smith's Greenhouses Inc. of Wichita Falls, knows I have been trying to reach Elmer. But Elmer has no way of contacting me. Toll-free numbers don't work behind bars.

Elmer, whose case, along with William Henry Furman's, went to the U.S. Supreme Court in 1972, is back inside.

The penniless Elmer Branch who went to the Texas Death House in 1966 for the crime of rape is in a cell in the Wichita County Jail, charged with another sex crime – the sexual abuse of a minor.

In February 1997, Elmer's case went to trial. He was charged with exposing himself in front of a 14-year-old girl. She's the daughter of his live-in girlfriend, a parolee and mother of seven who, says Elmer, was convicted of murdering her husband. Elmer says his ex-girlfriend made up the story because she'd been smoking crack cocaine and Elmer told her to stop or he'd turn her in.

At the end of Elmer's trial, the jury believed he was innocent; they voted 11 to 1 for an acquittal. They didn't think that this quiet, 51-year-old laborer for a landscaping company could have done what prosecutors said.

Neither could his boss. Or his co-workers. Or even his parole officer.

Elmer's attorney, Bruce Martin, didn't put on any evidence at trial and did not put Elmer on the witness stand. "I'm not going to subject my client to cross-examination on a case where the state's evidence was so weak," Martin told reporters at the time.[2]

And if Elmer had taken the witness stand, the jury would have found out that he had once been on Texas' Death Row.

The jury was stuck and they weren't changing their mind. No unanimous verdict. There was only one juror who voted guilty.

Judge Keith Nelson was frustrated; he sent jurors what is known as a "dynamite charge" or by its legal name, an "Allen" charge, which is designed to help them reach a quick and unanimous verdict.[3]

The jurors responded by asking to hear the entire day's testimony again – which consisted of the victim and her mother. The judge sent them home just 90 minutes after they went into deliberations, still undecided.

When they returned the next morning, Elmer's case was featured in *The Wichita Falls Times-Record News*. The headline was hard to miss: "Jury Deliberating Former Death-row Inmate's Fate." And the vote on the jury soon changed – now it was 8 to 4, still in Elmer's favor. Over the course of the day, no one wavered. The jury foreman told the judge the panel was deadlocked and no one was changing their vote. Judge Nelson then declared a mistrial.

Two months after his near-acquittal, I am in Wichita Falls, located in the northern most part of the Lone Star state, the midway point between Oklahoma City and Dallas. In the middle of nowhere or, as we like to say in Texas, in "East Jesus."

It's a two-and-a-half-hour drive from the Dallas–Fort Worth Airport across the flat and parched fields of Clay County. In the 1900s, Wichita Falls was a bit of a boomtown, the center of the cotton industry. Ninety-seven years later, I don't see many bales of cotton or the oil wells that once dotted this North Texas landscape.

Back in the early 1900s, this small town was plagued by hot weather, dry terrain, and unpredictable rainfall. It was during those dry spells that farmers and ranchers began to try to find ways to provide water, not only for their crops but also for their cattle. They started drilling shallow wells for their livestock, and instead of finding springs of water, they found that much of the well water was contaminated with a thick and unidentifiable black liquid. The ranchers didn't know what it was that came out of the ground so they used the oil as a tick repellent. That was until the Spindletop gusher was discovered in East Texas in 1918. It was then that the Wichita Falls folks began to focus on oil exploration in their own area.[4]

The drive looks no different than those boring road trips to visit my grandparents during the hot summers of my childhood – the annual 1,128 mile round-trip trek from San Antonio to El Paso in my mother's unairconditioned 1965 Volkswagen Camper. Mom would try to break up the monotony by stopping in Fort Stockton, the halfway point and the start of the 1,100 square miles of Big Bend National Park, established in 1944 as an example of the rugged Chihuahuan Desert wilderness.[5] She'd pull up to a motel off Highway 290, now IH-10, and let us out. Since she "knew the owners," a fact I never independently verified, we had permission to jump into the motel swimming pool fully clothed and then get back into the car. We did as we were told; we were hot. Five minutes later we were back in the car – soaked. Mom was oblivious to the bickering about who got to sit where. She'd just wipe the dust from her sunglasses, adjust the scarf around her newly permed, bleached and teased small beehive hairdo, and carefully apply some bright red lipstick without even looking into a mirror to see if she got it in the lines. She drove the VW bus to the highway entrance ramp, looked in the rearview mirror, and started laughing.

"This is what I call air conditioning! Right, kiddos?" and before we had a chance to answer, she'd floor it. It was a long time before I realized not everyone crosses the Texas desert the "Sally Cheever way."

"Twister Chase" was another San Antonio to El Paso "game." If you were the first to spot the cone-shaped whirling sand kicking up on the desert horizon, you'd be rewarded with something – a window seat or a piece of gum. Sometimes she upped the ante to an ice-cold soda pop. And, on occasion, if we were making good time, Mom would point the car in the direction of the twister, floor it, and the chase began. "Go, Mom, go," we'd scream with delight, begging her to press the pedal to the metal. We never actually "caught" a twister, but it wasn't for lack of trying.

On my trip to Wichita Falls, I don't see any twisters to break the boredom, but I can't help notice the big, clear blue Texas sky and the highway blanketed in bright, beautiful colors. It's April and there's nothing prettier than Texas wildflowers; acres of blues, pinks, oranges, and yellows – bluebonnets, Indian paintbrushes, and cornflower sunflowers. Connecticut may have four distinct seasons and a beautiful autumn, but it's nothing compared to the spring in Texas.

Except for the wildflowers, the plains of North Texas look about the same as the desert drive to El Paso. Only this time, I have real air conditioning.

As I wait for Elmer's paperwork to be processed, I look around the small, cramped room and find a familiar sight. Tired women are sprawled across the straight-backed, uncomfortable, multi-colored plastic chairs crowded into an already congested room. These women are either the wives or mothers of those men who are temporarily housed in the 225-bed facility next door, which is now home to more than 400.

It is a busy day for the jailers. The waiting room is packed, the visits are taking too long, they say, and nerves are frayed. The sheriff's deputies send a handful of unruly toddlers to sit outside the waiting area and issue ultimatums to horrified mothers who are afraid if they step outside they will lose their place in line. They probably will lose their spot.

Every few minutes, someone gets up to go to the vending machine to buy peace. A bribe. Prisons always conjure up images of hot, cramped rooms filled with waiting women. They are patient. Tired.

I am momentarily lost in thought when my name's called.

"Sorry for the long wait," the guard says through the glass partition. He apologizes, explaining the jail is overcrowded and so is the waiting room and "his men" have to limit the number in the visiting area. But I didn't have to wait long – a fact that is confirmed by my watch and the momentarily puzzled look on the faces of the women who once sat beside me. But they don't complain or even look angry as I move to the front of the line and open the heavy steel gray door when I hear the buzz. With a briefcase in hand, it is obvious that I am a lawyer: "one of the good guys."

Elmer is in the middle of the room. Separated by a sheet of thick Plexiglas, I pick up the telephone on the wall to make my acquaintance. It is awkward. And Elmer Branch looks old. His large black plastic glasses look like they are from the commissary at nearby Sheppard Air Force Base. The thick lenses frame much of his long face.

I take very few notes during our talk. It centers largely on the nuances of his latest trial and the fact that his lawyer won't retry the case, even after a near-acquittal.

Like the women in the room next door, Elmer is in a legal waiting game. But unlike some of them, Elmer is a pro. He has spent almost 20 years – from 1967 to 1986 – just "waiting" in his prison cell for a chance at parole.

When I first meet him in 1997, he is waiting once again – for his retrial. Only this time, he doesn't have the high-priced legal talent of Bruce A. Martin whose fee was paid by the Steven Smith family and Elmer's co-workers.

Attorney Martin has refused to retry the case for Elmer unless he is paid – handsomely. He asks the Smith family to put up another $7,000, including a $3,000 cash retainer, immediately.

Steve Smith is upset. He too, is a businessman and he understands the lawyer's predicament. A law office, like any business, has bills to pay and payrolls to meet. Smith knows this scenario all too well. His landscaping company, a family-owned business, has fallen on some tough times recently. He has been forced to lay off many employees and ended up selling part of his business to outside parties. He knows the attorney has to be paid. But he's been paid once. And right now Smith doesn't have the money to bankroll two trials – even though he knows that Elmer is innocent. And he feels terrible about that.

Smith knows Elmer's freedom could be bought for $7,000. Smith doesn't feel as though he can go back to his staff – most all of whom are struggling themselves on a minimum wage pay – to ask for contributions to the Elmer Branch Defense Fund. They contributed to the first trial and although they continue to believe in Elmer's innocence, they just don't have enough money to prove it.

Elmer was an exemplary employee during those seven years at the greenhouse, say his supervisors and co-workers. He'd never let down Steve Smith or the Smith family. Entrusted with sets of keys to the business, the Smith family's home, their ranches, and to their cars, Elmer is an ex-officio family member.

"Steve Smith has been like a father and brother to me. He's got four boys and his sister has four boys. They [the Smiths] are all lovely and generous people," Elmer says.

And the Smiths feel the same about Elmer.

Elmer would always volunteer to work extra hours – not for the extra money but simply, Steve Smith says incredulously, just because Smith had asked. He spent his off hours driving some of the Smiths up to Oklahoma to their ranch and then back home. Elmer came to work every day with a sunny disposition and a kind word.

That probably should have been a clue that the man Smith and his co-workers knew only as "Elmer" had some sort of past life.

He was so happy, all of the time, in a job that was physically demanding and so lowly paid. At $219 a week, Elmer's paycheck barely covered the bills. But after 20 years in prison, earning 20 cents an hour, Elmer was deliriously happy just to be free.

To understand that happiness is to understand Texas' Death Row. Back in 1967.

In a prison-issued gray uniform, his wrists and ankles restricted by shackles and continuously under the watchful eyes of heavily armed prison guards, Elmer was sent to the execution wing, known as "The Walls," a unit in downtown Huntsville, the same place where Walter was executed. The unit was built in 1849 and by the 1900s it had tropical atrium gardens, turrets, porticoes, and a clock tower that the whole town told time by. But inside it was a different story.

In 1930, Texas Governor Dan Moody declared the Texas prisons were "not fit for a dog." By 1935, The Walls housed 1,000 men in 350 cells, each built to accommodate just one inmate. Warden O.B. Ellis was appointed in 1948 by the Texas legislature to oversee the construction of new prison facilities, modernize existing ones, and end the brutality of the guards and corruption in the prison system.[6]

Elmer was sent to The Walls, now a faceless brick bunker flanked by 40-foot walls topped by razor wire. From his cell, the electric chair sat just a hundred feet away.[7]

He was 24 years old when he was sentenced to die for raping a 65-year-old woman, a widow and the mother-in-law of the sheriff in the small North Texas town of Vernon, birthplace of rock-and-roll great Roy Orbison.

According to police reports, Elmer broke into her home at 2 a.m. on May 9, 1967, and raped her while pressing his arm against her throat. He was unarmed. In fact, after the rape, the woman – who had employed Elmer previously as a handyman – testified that he sat on her bed and talked to her.

Within minutes of the crime, Vernon sheriff deputies were roused from their sleep and ordered to find the rapist. Immediately they set up roadblocks and were ordered to stop any car "containing colored subjects."[8] Minutes later Elmer drove his car into a gas station. When he got out, he was suddenly surrounded by sheriff deputies. They took off his shoes, left the gas station, and went to the crime scene to see if his shoeprint matched the one found outside the victim's home. It did.[9]

But Mel Bruder, Elmer's lawyer at the U.S. Supreme Court, says the shoes were taken to the victim's house to "make the shoe print" at the scene. He says he has no doubt Elmer is innocent.

"There's too much about what he said that caused me to think it wasn't him," the lawyer says, adding that he rarely has an innocent client. TDC records showed Elmer had an IQ of 67.[10]

After a short trial Elmer was sentenced to death. In its case before the Supreme Court, the State of Texas acknowledged that Elmer's lawyer did not cross-examine the victim. The lawyer all but admitted Elmer's guilt by telling the jury he didn't cross-examine the victim because "I feel like what she said was the truth, other than possibly the identification."[11]

Elmer spent five years on Death Row and 19 in prison before being paroled in January 1986. After working for $2^1/_2$ years on an oil rig for LeBeaux Construction, outside Galveston, Texas, Elmer moved to Wichita Falls, just 50 miles northwest of Vernon, the crime scene.

Wichita Falls is the home of Sheppard Air Force Base, the city's largest employer with 3,700 workers. The name Wichita is derived from the Choctaw Indian words *wia chitoh*, which mean "big arbor," a description of the grass-thatched arbors in their village. The Indians settled near a small waterfall along the Wichita River.

Shortly after Elmer arrived, Steve Smith hired him as a landscaper and handyman. After three years at the greenhouse, Elmer approached the young owner and told him they needed to talk. Elmer is not an articulate man. He rarely makes eye contact and speaks more with his hands. This "talk" between him and the "boss man," as he called him, was excruciatingly painful for Elmer.

He had worried about it for months. But he wanted to come clean. He hadn't lied about his past. He just hadn't shared it.

Elmer began to tell Smith about his years on Death Row. That he was the Branch whose case ended up abolishing the death penalty in Texas and across the United States.

Smith was "astounded." And shocked. Within seconds of the confessional, Smith held up his hand and told Elmer to stop talking. Steve Smith didn't want to hear more. He didn't need to. The Elmer Branch he knew was a good guy – he trusted him like a brother. "Look Elmer, the past is the past. And it's behind you."

And with that, the two men never spoke of it again.

Until Elmer failed to show up for work on October 7, 1995. That's when Smith found him in the Wichita Falls County Jail.

So, when Smith visited Elmer in the reception area of the redbrick county jail, shortly after his trial ended in a hung jury, he did so with a heavy heart. He was the bearer of bad news. His employee of seven years, a friend, considered to be a member of the Smith family, had never let him down. And now Steve Smith felt as though he was letting Elmer down.

He told Elmer that his future was now in the hands of an attorney from the overworked, understaffed, and underpaid Public Defender's Office. The best he could hope for was a plea bargain. Elmer's new lawyer, Versel Rush, told him the stakes were too high to go back to trial. She told him she could "work out" a nice plea arrangement.

But there was one sticking point. Elmer insists he isn't guilty – that he'd never "exposed himself" to his girlfriend's daughter.

From March to December 1997, Elmer sat in the overcrowded county jail. He refused to plead guilty to a crime he says he didn't commit. But his lawyer refused to go to trial. And the prosecutor wanted a conviction.

Elmer was a desperate man. He was in the system and there was no way out. He couldn't believe he was going back inside. He'd worked 20 years for a chance to walk out of the Texas Department of Corrections. He had been making a decent living and even though he was living near the poverty line, Elmer felt incredibly rich. That's because he had had his freedom. But that would end as soon as he signed a plea agreement.

On January 21, 1998, Elmer could no longer keep the State of Texas waiting. He signed the plea agreement because he says he wants to get on with his life. He had already served 26 months for a crime he insists he did not commit. He refuses to plead guilty – he entered a plea of no lo contendre[12] which has the same effect of pleading guilty. It means literally "I will not contest it" and, psychologically, a no lo plea was probably easier for Elmer. But it has a negative impact on a parole board that insists inmates take responsibility for their crime and act remorseful before being granted parole. Elmer can do neither because he continues to insist that he is not guilty.

Now, the only thing standing between Elmer and his freedom is 10 years. If he earns "good time" and credit for the 26 months he served while in the county jail, his sentence could be cut to four and a half years. But nothing is certain. His chance at freedom rests with the parole board.

Elmer still wears the same prison number he did back in 1967 – Execution Number 492. His home is a small cell he shares with another inmate at the Duncan Transfer Facility, a seven-year-old prison in Diboll, Texas that currently houses 565 men in a minimum custody level.

Elmer was eligible for parole in June 1999, but two of the three board members reviewed his case and turned down his bid, telling him to return in June 2001. The board cited Elmer's "criminal record and/or nature of offense(s) and violation of previous probation, parole or mandatory supervision."[13]

In a July 12, 1999 letter, Elmer writes: "I won't be going home this year because the parole board gave me a two-year set-off ... Pray for me."

He can barely see; his eyes are diseased by glaucoma. And he has diabetes. Still, he waits patiently for the parole board to review his case. Two years later, in June 2001, he went up again for parole and, again, was turned down.

In a July 8, 2001 letter Elmer tells me he is excited to get his "piddling privileges" back for the craft shop, which had been temporarily suspended when he moved to another prison. Piddling privileges, Elmer explains, means he will soon be able to start working again on colorful purses, made from comics found in pieces of Bazooka Bubble Gum. He orders his art supplies from Dick Blick Art Materials, based somewhere in Illinois. "It will be a month before I receive this order back. So after the 15th of August, you can be looking for something in the mail from me."

At the end of his July 8 letter, Elmer writes of his recent parole hearing: "The parole board sent me a set off on the 25th of June. They set me off until 2004. Other than this, I am doing fine and hoping when you receive this letter it will find you and your family doing well."

In June 2005, the board again denied parole. He'll come up again in 2008.

Elmer waits patiently, sending me some of his handiwork – beautiful intricately carved wooden ships with hand-stitched sails, tiny lifeboats, detailed portholes, and anchors. He seems eerily resigned to his fate. Prison is not the healthiest place for someone who is already in poor health. And trying to survive in the Texas heat would be enough to kill anyone, young or old. The parole set off is tantamount to a death sentence for the 59-year-old Elmer.

He's tasted freedom – 10 precious years. Elmer considers himself a lucky man, just because he's still alive.

———

Another man sitting with Elmer on Texas' Death Row wasn't so grateful. Or patient. When Kenneth McDuff left prison in 1989, he had one thing on his mind: revenge and murder.

McDuff made his own private pact – that he would settle some scores. Once he was released, McDuff was ready to kill again. The 43-year-old former auto mechanic had been in prison for 21 years and been denied parole 14 times.

Handed $10 for bus fare, McDuff walked out of the Michael Processing Unit in Huntsville, Texas, filled with bitterness and anger.

Would he seek revenge?

Would Kenneth Allen McDuff kill again?

CHAPTER TWELVE

A PROMISE TO KILL AGAIN

To date, five members of the Class of '72 killed again while on parole. One was executed; two knew their victims.

Nine of the 164 inmates who have never been released killed prison guards, prison employees, or fellow inmates; two of those men were again sentenced to death. A prisoner who murdered another inmate was executed in Florida in June 2000; the other, a 79-year-old inmate who killed a prison employee in Ohio in 1984 and was sent back to Death Row, died in January 2005 of natural causes.

More than a handful of killers say they support the death penalty. They say it's a way to eliminate, forever, those who are truly evil.

I am in the waiting room of my doctor, miserable with a temperature of 102. I have bronchitis and I'm looking for "permission" to fly to Houston. I give a brief sketch of my 24-hour round-trip itinerary – four take-offs and four landings with a three-hour drive (roundtrip) from Houston Intercontinental Airport to Texas' Death Row. With antibiotics, a decongestant, and a prescription of cough syrup with codeine, what are my chances that I could keep pneumonia at bay? I ask.

"Honestly? Zero. Do you really have to go?" he responds.

One execution is enough.

I return to my office and call Larry Fitzgerald, the spokesman for the Texas Department of Corrections. "You really think this is a go?" I ask.

"Yep, his appeals are up. It appears we're right on schedule. Tomorrow, 6 p.m.," he answers.

I then cancel my airline and car reservation, following doctor's orders. But I forget about the motel that has my credit card on file.

The man who is scheduled to be executed tomorrow night – Kenneth Allen McDuff – makes a strong case for the death penalty. Unlike almost all the *Furman* parolees, McDuff took his second chance at life and cashed it in. Five more murders. Maybe even nine. It's men like McDuff who make it difficult for the anti-death penalty movement.

I'm a little relieved not to fly to Texas. I never wrote McDuff during his four years on Texas' Death Row. Perhaps it was because he might have agreed to an interview and then I would have had to go back. Back to a place that harbored so many bad memories. Nine years of visiting Walter on Death Row, and that one night in the Death House which is the primary reason I have not slept through the night these past four years.

But it isn't just Texas Death Row that I fear. It's McDuff. I have read almost every newspaper and magazine article[1] about him and the books, *No Remorse* and *Bad Boys From Rosebud*,[2] and I have seen him in various news documentaries.[3] I have done my homework a little too well. I soon realize I fit the profile of McDuff's victims – to a T. Small, petite women. Brunettes. Women like me. Like all of us.

Melissa Ann Northrup was a 22-year-old married mother of two, pregnant with her third, who worked the graveyard shift at the Quick Pik convenience store in Waco, Texas. She was trying to make ends meet to feed her small family when she was kidnapped on March 1, 1992. Two months later, her body was found in a gravel pit in Dallas County.[4]

More than a year later, Colleen Reed, a 28-year-old accountant with the Lower Colorado River Authority, a Texas state agency, was washing her car in a desolate area of downtown Austin on a Sunday afternoon in 1991 during the Christmas holidays.[5] It was the neighborhood where McDuff was cruising by, looking for his next victim. It was the same neighborhood where I had been in 1983, also working for a state agency, as a 26-year-old briefing attorney for the Texas Court of Criminal Appeals. I lived less than a mile from the site where Reed was kidnapped, raped, and stabbed repeatedly.

Perhaps I am too scared to make contact with McDuff. I fear I might become an object of his obsession. That he could escape from Death Row, like the seven inmates did in 1998, from the same prison where I had visited Walter.[6]

Perhaps I am worried McDuff might have a "get even" list like one former Death Row inmate told me he has. Maybe I think McDuff might put me on it.

It's not so far-fetched. In a confession, McDuff admitted he killed Colleen Reed in Austin, the state's capital, to get back at "the state system" that had turned him down for parole 14 times from 1976 through 1988. He was released in 1989, but the board revoked his parole only nine months later after McDuff was arrested on the misdemeanor charge of "making a terroristic threat" – an incident that grew out of a racial confrontation with a group of black teenagers in his hometown of Rosebud, in July 1990.[7] The state didn't have a case after the witnesses refused to testify. On December 6, 1990, McDuff was released. Free to kill again.

And he did. Just two days later, the nude body of 31-year-old Sarafia Parker, a prostitute, was found in a field near Temple, the same area where McDuff's parole officer was based.[8]

And that was only the beginning of his murder spree.

In February 1991, the body of Valencia Johnson, a 22-year-old prostitute, was found in the woods near the campus of Texas State Technical College in Waco, where the then 45-year-old McDuff attended college.

In October 1991, two prostitutes, Brenda Thompson and Regina Moore, who were last seen with McDuff, also disappeared.[9]

Perhaps I fear that even with death sentences for the brutal murders of Colleen Reed and Melissa Ann Northrup, history could repeat itself. McDuff might be able to get out one more time – a third time – to kill again.

Perhaps I don't want to face the truth – not every paroled killer can be rehabilitated. Some, like Kenneth McDuff, do kill again.

I never interviewed the 52-year-old serial killer either by phone, through letters, or in person. But I did talk to someone who did. Gary M. Lavergne, author of *Bad Boy From Rosebud*, poured over stacks of police files, spent countless hours interviewing law enforcement officers, victims' families, and McDuff family friends and acquaintances. Boxes of McDuff research fill every square inch in his small home office.[10]

Two years after McDuff's execution, I write Lavergne and he agrees to meet. I want the 47-year-old journalist to tell me what I had missed. After our two-hour interview, I am glad I had bronchitis and cancelled that trip to Texas.

Lavergne tells me talking to McDuff gave him "the creeps." He shakes his head when I ask to describe his interview with the serial killer.

"I don't think McDuff was murderous as much as he was a true sexual sadist," Lavergne says.

Before he met with the killer, Lavergne said he made a conscious decision not to be intimidated by the 6' 4" and 250 lb McDuff. And to remain patient.

"As long as McDuff was willing to sit there and talk, I'd listen. He laughed a lot. Smiled. He was the biggest coward I've ever seen. And he had the biggest hands I'd ever seen on a person. He played with his big fingers all throughout the interview."

Lavergne, a native of Louisiana and a former stand-up comedian in New Orleans, said the years he spent pouring over documents and reading the gruesome details of the crime, and finally interviewing the serial killer face to face, took its toll. Many nights he has had a hard time falling asleep.

I know what he means.

McDuff is the poster boy for the pro-death penalty movement. He put the spotlight on the inadequate parole oversight of the

Texas prison system and its parole board. He was paroled in 1989 mainly because the Texas prison system was under a federal court order to reduce overcrowding. The same year McDuff was released, the Texas Parole Board reviewed more than 71,000 applications and released an astounding 42,999 prisoners. Prisoners were required to serve at least a third, or in some cases, only a fourth of their sentences. [11]

At the time of his execution, McDuff was the only man in the history of this country to have gotten off Death Row, walked out of prison a free man, only to check right back into the Death House four years later. [12] He's a killer who's had two different Death Row numbers and has been sentenced to die two different ways – electrocution in 1966 and lethal injection in 1998. For 32 years, he escaped his date in the Death House.

"He killed because he liked to kill. Well, I don't think he particularly liked the killing part. But that was his orgasm," Lavergne says.

The question on the eve of his well-publicized execution: Was the number finally up for this 52-year-old killer who was fascinated with fast cars? It was the same question the families of Robert Brand, Edna Louise Sullivan and Mark Dunnam, had been asking for 32 years.

They last saw 16-year-old Edna, her boyfriend Robert, 17, and his cousin, 15-year-old Dunnam, who was visiting from California, on the evening of August 6, 1966 in Fort Worth. Edna, a pretty teenager dressed in a red-and-white striped blouse and cutoff jeans, was standing near a baseball field talking to Robert and Mark when McDuff took a 0.38 pistol from under the seat of his car and walked over. He demanded that the boys hand over their wallets and then he forced all three of them into the trunk of Robert's 1955 Ford. Shortly before he took off, McDuff told the friend who was with him, "They got a good look at my face. I'll have to kill them." [13]

McDuff drove the Ford with the friend, Roy Dale Green, following in McDuff's Dodge. McDuff turned into a field and stopped. He opened the trunk and said: "I want the young lady out," pulling her by the arm. He told Green to lock her in the trunk.

Robert Brand and Mark Dunnam were still in the trunk and they were on their knees begging for their lives when McDuff shot them both in the face. He shot Brand two times and Dunnam three, and then picked up Dunnam by his hair and shot him again. [14]

For some reason the trunk wouldn't close, so McDuff backed the Ford, with the trunk open, against the fence and then he and Green drove away in the Dodge, with the frightened Edna Sullivan a prisoner in the trunk. McDuff drove south, finally stopping along a dirt road about 11 miles from where they had left the bodies of the boys.

McDuff took Sullivan from the trunk, ordered her to take off her clothes, threw her in the backseat, and then raped her repeatedly, stopping only occasionally for his friend Green to rape her. He then drove down a gravel road, stopped, and took her out of the car and told her to sit down on the road. He choked her with the broomstick and when she fought back McDuff told Green, "Grab her legs."

McDuff then strangled her to death and the men threw her body over the fence and drove home, stopping to bury the boys' billfolds and getting rid of their own bloody underwear. [15]

I'm glad I missed meeting Kenneth McDuff.

Other members of the Class of '72 also killed again while on parole.

Jerry Michael Ward was on Texas' Death Row – sentenced to death for the 1965 murder of a high school student who was kidnapped from a shopping center, raped, and shot three times in the head. After the Furman decision, Ward's death sentence was commuted to a life term; in June 1984, the 40-year-old was released from prison to a halfway house in Conroe, Texas, just outside of Houston.

Two years later, in June 1986, Connie Sue Cooke, a 32-year-old divorced mother of two, was reported missing after being seen with Ward at a bar earlier in the evening. Ward told police he was with Cooke but denied having anything to do with her disappearance; he was also a suspect in the strangulation murder 10 months earlier of a woman who was found just a short distance from the halfway house. Three days after being questioned by police, Ward flew to Las Vegas and committed suicide. In a suicide note to an aunt, Ward proclaimed his innocence and said he believed he would have been sent back to prison and suicide was "the only way out." [16]

John McLemore[17] was in prison for 20 years in a Midwestern state, convicted of a 1971 rape and murder. Four years after he was paroled, he was back inside – convicted of murdering a man over a drug debt. Now 56, McLemore maintains his innocence and says the only witness is his disgruntled ex-girlfriend who wanted to end their relationship. He's serving a life term for second-degree murder.

Illinois' Frank Alex Hennenberg was on Death Row for a 1969 armed robbery and murder.[18] He was arrested in St. Louis, Missouri, driving the victim's car. Hennenberg was paroled in September 1983 after serving more than 13 years. In 1987, Hennenberg was convicted of murder and home invasion and given an 80-year sentence. Illinois corrections officials were unable to provide details of the 68-year-old's most recent murder conviction but they did have a new parole date – October 1, 2046.

Leon Holloway of Ohio returned to prison in 1996 on a new conviction of voluntary manslaughter, sentenced to a term of seven years to life. Holloway was first paroled in 1991 after serving 20 years for capital murder. His initial parole was revoked nine months later for possession of criminal tools and drug abuse and he was reincarcerated for three years. He was released in 1994 and reincarcerated in 1996 on charges of voluntary manslaughter. The 59-year-old will be eligible for parole when he is 64. There are no details concerning his new conviction. [19]

Another ex-Death Row inmate, one who was not on parole, but who escaped from an Oklahoma prison in 1992, was convicted of murder in Tacoma, Washington – 2,000 miles away. He had been incarcerated for 20 years for the murders of a convenience store manager, the manager's wife, and their six-year-old son. In 1972, Lawrence "Rufus" Breedlove and three other men[20] robbed the store of $182 and ordered Howard Siler, his wife, and their child to lie on the floor where they were then shot in the head.[21] Breedlove denied being the triggerman.

Breedlove blames the Tacoma murder of 35-year-old Gregory Atkins, who was a guest at a party, on "girlfriend" problems. He says he fatally stabbed the man in self-defense after the victim, who had been smoking rock cocaine, hit him. He said he stabbed Atkins to try to force him off himself, but "he acted like he didn't feel anything," describing the victim as a wild man – "like Superman."[22]

Jurors didn't buy Breedlove's claim of self-defense but they also didn't believe the murder was premeditated.[23] They knew that Breedlove, a certified paralegal who had completed two years of college, was a prison escapee and an armed robber. But the jurors had no idea he was a former resident of Oklahoma's Death Row. Breedlove, 53, is currently back in an Oklahoma penitentiary; his first parole hearing will be in 2009.

And then there are murders that occur inside. Ohio's Wayne Lester Raney and William J. Bradley killed prison employees; South Carolina's Wilson Cornelius Atkinson, Pennsylvania's David Scoggins, and Florida's Benny Demps murdered fellow inmates.[24]

Raney was 21 years old when he was sent to Ohio's Death Row on August 13, 1971, convicted of murdering two people.[25] A source who asked for anonymity said two years later that he'd decided to "get even" with a guard who allegedly had been hassling him. *The Dayton Daily News* reported that another guard smuggled a 0.25 caliber revolver into the Lucasville prison and Raney, who won the gun in a poker game, used it in an escape attempt. Raney murdered one guard and another was killed by a member of a SWAT team that was trying to kill Raney.[26]

The Ohio Department of Corrections won't give any information as to Raney's whereabouts listing it a "Protected

Case." The source said he believes the 55-year-old Raney is serving his time in another state – possibly Arizona – because of the fear of retribution by Ohio prison guards.

In Pennsylvania, a former Death Row inmate lectures me on capital punishment. David Scoggins is a staunch supporter of the death penalty and tells me, in a three-page letter, that I would be too, if I really knew him. And if I knew the men that he has known over the past 31 years.

Scoggins had been on Pennsylvania's Death Row for three years in 1972, for a brutal rape and murder, when *Furman* came down. He was then transferred into the general prison population where he's been for 28 years. And he desperately wants to die. He's tried to get back on Death Row several times. Only his timing is off.

"I believe in the death penalty 100 percent and the people on Death Row also believe in the death penalty, they just don't believe in it for themselves... I should've been put to death," Scoggins writes.

He describes the gruesome details of a Death Row inmate who kidnapped a young girl and drilled a hole into the top of her head and inserted his penis in it while she was still alive. "Are you saying that a man such as him should not die, but be set free so he could do that again to someone else? I hope not. I would like to put him to death myself. And I would do it."

Scoggins has a death wish – he just can't get the state of Pennsylvania to carry it out. When I re-read the opinion in the case of *Commonwealth of Pennsylvania versus David Scoggins*,[27] I am baffled by the similarities. The only difference is that Scoggins' victim is older. In his letter, Scoggins was describing himself.

He has no remorse for his crime and tells of a fellow inmate who has murdered and raped a five-year-old girl who isn't sorry either. The man's death sentence, Scoggins says, was recently reversed and he was given a life sentence.

The 60-year-old killer says the inmate told him that when he gets out he'll "do it again" only " 'the next time I wouldn't let the flies find the girl's body.' Is this the kind of people you would want to live next door to you?" Scoggins asks in his letter, peppered with exclamation points.

The crime that sent Scoggins to the Death House in 1969 was the rape and brutal murder of a 26-year-old woman who he repeatedly struck in the head with his fists, causing extensive brain damage and almost instantaneous death. He then threw her nude body into a nearby creek. Scoggins was arrested two weeks later. [28] In prison, Scoggins killed again.

On May 24, 1972, while still on Death Row, Scoggins murdered Alexander Edinger, a fellow inmate at the Dallas State Correctional Institution, by stabbing him to death. He was charged with first-degree murder but then *Furman* interceded and he was sentenced to the maximum term – life in prison. [29]

Scoggins says he's killed still another inmate but he couldn't get the death penalty then either, because Pennsylvania didn't yet have an enforceable death penalty statute. The legislature passed a death penalty law in 1977. I am unable to verify the second inmate murder through prison officials, but I have no doubt it is true.

In another letter, Scoggins continues his tirade: "So, that should show you that I really didn't care one way or the other but if they had put me to death, than [sic] I wouldn't have been able to take the life of two other people."

He may get his death wish soon. He says the state "shot me up with the HIV a few years ago by mistake and now it is turning into AIDS" and his days are numbered.

After reading his letter, I breathe an audible sigh of relief. I decline his offer to visit. I don't need to be on the visitor's list of a serial killer.

Like Scoggins, a former Death Row prisoner in South Carolina killed a fellow inmate.

Wilson Cornelius Atkinson was originally sentenced to die in the electric chair for the cold-blooded murder of a Charleston, South Carolina, policeman. The officer was shot in the back of the head from the back seat of his patrol car. The policeman only stopped the 27-year-old Atkinson to ask him about a recent car theft. [30] At his trial, the jury asked the judge questions about when the killer would be eligible for parole if his life was spared. Told parole issues were not to be considered, the jury returned a short time later with the death sentence.

The jury had good reason to worry back then. While incarcerated, but not on Death Row, Atkinson killed another inmate, assaulted guards, robbed other prisoners, and had been caught numerous times with contraband weapons or contraband whisky. At Central Correctional Institution in Columbia, South Carolina, Atkinson had been declared a threat to normal and safe operations of the prison and placed in its maximum-security center. He had at least 13 serious disciplinary violations in his 10 years at CCI, including murder, and his placement evaluation specifically recommended against putting him at Kirkland Correctional Institution because of strong psychopathic patterns, including unpredictable and violent outbursts. [31]

Nevertheless, in 1984, Atkinson was transferred to Kirkland and shared a cell with 88-year-old Stroman W. Jackson Sr., who was serving a 20-year sentence for assault with intent to kill. Within three months, Atkinson fatally stabbed his cellmate. [32] The 63-year-old inmate remains incarcerated.

Another former Death Row inmate also killed again. Also in prison. But this time, he was executed. Benny Demps came to Florida's Death Row in 1971, convicted of murdering R.N. Brinkworth and Celia Puhlick and wounding Puhlick's husband, Nicholas, while the three victims were inspecting some land for sale. They came upon Demps in a citrus grove where he had fled with a safe he had stolen from a nearby house. [33] When the Florida death penalty law was ruled unconstitutional in 1972, Demps and the other 99 inmates moved off Death Row. Florida passed a new death penalty law which was upheld by the U.S. Supreme Court in 1976. [34] Two months later, a 23-year-old murderer and alleged jailhouse snitch, Alfred Sturgis, was stabbed to death. Shortly before he died, Sturgis told a prison guard that Demps and another inmate held him down, while the third inmate, "Toothless" Jackson, stabbed him. Because of Demps' prior murder conviction, he received another death sentence; the accomplices each got life. [35]

Demps maintained his innocence even as he lay on the gurney in Florida's execution chamber on June 7, 2000. The 49-year-old former Marine, wounded in Vietnam, told the witnesses that the state's action was not an execution but a "murder." In a seven-minute speech, Demps said: "I am an innocent man. They have knowingly fabricated evidence against me." [36]

Anti-death penalty advocates say there is more than a distinct possibility that Benny Demps was innocent [37] and the Sturgis murder conviction was Florida's way to get a second chance to execute Demps since he cheated death following the *Furman* ruling 18 years earlier.

Still another former Death Row inmate, William J. Bradley, was back on Ohio's Death Row in 1984 for the beating death of a 62-year-old supervisor in the prison sheet metal shop. Bradley beat Eric Bowling to death after Bowling asked Bradley to work longer hours. What is most remarkable is that Bradley was transferred to Lucasville and allowed to work in an open shop even though just two weeks earlier he had beaten an elderly female volunteer at another prison. [38] Bradley was still on Ohio's Death Row when he died of natural causes in January 2005.

———

In 1972, when Bradley moved from the Death House to the general prison population, Ohio prison guards moved another former Death Row inmate as well. Prison officials gave Lester Edward Eubanks an unescorted pass to go Christmas shopping in 1973 at a mall in downtown Columbus as a reward for "good behavior."

When guards returned to the mall to pick him up, Eubanks had vanished.

217

CHAPTER THIRTEEN

A KILLER'S 32-YEAR CHRISTMAS SHOPPING TRIP

There have been 31 AWOLS in the Class of '72; three escaped from prison and 28 are AWOL on parole. In Oklahoma, where 15 men were on Death Row there in 1972, six – including Lawrence "Rufus" Breedlove – escaped from prison. They have all been reincarcerated.

In Florida, Marie Arrington, one of the two women who were on Death Row in 1972, also broke out of prison. On March 1, 1969, the 34-year-old killer slid through a cell window and escaped in her pajamas. Almost three years later, Arrington was arrested in New Orleans where she was working as a cocktail waitress.[1]

One man has never been recaptured. Lester Eubanks of Ohio has been on the lam for 32 years.

"Miss Cheever, I suggest you write to Mr. Eubanks and establish a pen-pal relationship with him and perhaps then he will put you on his visitor's list and you'll be able to interview him in person," says Vince Laguna, staff counsel at the Ohio Department of Rehabilitation and Corrections. I am on my cell phone across the street from the noisy wooden carousel where I am waiting for a retired police detective from Mansfield, Ohio, the town that is now home to Ohio's new Death Row. "I can't promise you anything. But you should go ahead and write to him."

I am starting to pace, on the sidewalk, in front of Brunches Restaurant where I am supposed to meet David Messmore, a retired police captain who devoted many years during his career, and now even in retirement, to finding Lester Eubanks, a convicted child killer and former Death Row inmate.

Ten minutes earlier I had been sitting in an oversized honey-blonde wooden Shaker rocking chair watching a handful of children ride the brightly colored carousel, a main tourist attraction that sits prominently in the town square. Mansfield is part of Richland County, so named for the fertility of its soil, and home to John Chapman, better known as "Johnny Appleseed." With a population of 55,000, the 200-year-old town has 50 active congregations, 20 on one block alone, and is nicknamed the "City of Churches." But prayers weren't enough for this little Ohio town when, in the late 1980s and early 1990s, many lost their jobs as manufacturing plants closed down and local businesses followed, deserting downtown. In February 1995, Death Row moved from the Southern Ohio Correctional Facility in Lucasville to the newly built Mansfield Correctional Institution. The Death House and death chamber remain in Lucasville, the site of a prison riot and 11-day siege in April 1993 that left seven inmates and one hostage dead.[2]

In an attempt to build up the downtown area and attract tourists to Mansfield, the $1.25 million carousel was part of a major redevelopment project, dubbed the "Carousel District." The carousel isn't busy on this warm mid-August day, but that's because it's early. Round and round I watch the 30 horses and 22 menagerie figures – bears, ostriches, cats, rabbits, giraffe, lion, tiger, zebra, and a goat. The music from a Stinson Band Organ can be heard blocks away. I am surprised I was able to hear my phone ringing over the screaming carnival-like noise.

As I scurry to get away from the blaring pipe organ, I listen as Laguna begins the conversation by scolding me for faxing him a "poorly written Freedom of Information request" letter 24 hours earlier. I sent it only after a public relations officer in the Department of Corrections told me to "make sure you include everything you want." His call came just as I was leaving my office, eager to get home for a birthday dinner party my children had been planning all day. I was the guest of honor. And I was irritated that I had to write yet another FOIA letter when the one I sent a year ago, and then last month, had been ignored.

I hoped Laguna wasn't going to give me another lecture; I was ready to give him a tongue lashing.

The phone reception was a little better the farther I walked away from the carousel; it ended up being a one-way conversation.

"Miss Cheever, under the Privacy Act, those records on Eubanks are protected. We really can't give you access to the information you requested and quite frankly we're not required to do your research. You are not entitled to everything you've requested. I do hope you know that. Of course, you can get this information from Mr. Eubanks."

At this point I wanted to scream "how?" Especially since the 62-year-old killer has been on the lam for 32 years. There have been hundreds of law enforcement officers looking for Eubanks since December 7, 1973, the day he failed to return from a Christmas shopping trip at the Great Southern Shopping Center in downtown Columbus. [3]

I keep walking, trying to juggle the cell phone while looking for a legal pad to take notes. I am half a block down the street when I ask Laguna, in a voice dripping with sarcasm, for suggestions how to contact with Eubanks. "That would be great, Mr. Laguna, if I knew where to write to him."

What he says next almost sends the phone crashing to the pavement. It succeeds in dropping me to the sidewalk where I quickly sit down before my knees can buckle. I start to feel dizzy. "Oh, that's easy enough. You can write to him at the Marion Correctional Facility. That's where he is."

At this point, I am sure I'm going to faint.

"Excuse me, sir. What did... you... say...?" I ask, drawing out the question in a Texas drawl.

He pauses. He seems irritated. "He's in Marion. You can write to him," he says brusquely.

I swallow hard and search my purse for the bottle of water I always carry. My throat is dry and my lips are parched. My hand is shaking.

"Mister Laguna. Are you telling me that Lester Eubanks is incarcerated? Is that what you just said?"

"Yes, and actually he has been for quite some time. So, I'm not really sure what's the big deal. Why don't you just write to him?"

Now I feel sick. And stupid. Silently I berate myself for having waited four years to get to Mansfield, an hour from the airport in Columbus. Until today, no one wanted to talk about Eubanks, a man who had been sentenced to death for savagely murdering 14-year-old Mary Ellen Deener on November 14, 1965. After shooting her, the camouflage-attired Eubanks grabbed a brick, hitting Mary Ellen four times on the head to make sure she was dead. She was murdered while walking from a nearby convenience store, where she had gone to get coins to finish the family's laundry. Her 12-year-old sister waited for her that night at the laundromat. When police found Mary Ellen's body, $1.30 in nickels and dimes were found scattered on the ground in the alley behind 325 North Mulberry Street.[4]

Last summer, after finally convincing Messmore to talk to me, I bought a non-refundable plane ticket to Ohio. But then, for some inexplicable reason, he too went AWOL. I never asked him what happened a year ago or why the sudden change of heart. Sometimes, it's better to keep quiet.

But I had to ask this DOC official on the other end of the line how Eubanks could possibly be back in prison. I had searched the Internet for newspaper articles; the most recent one I could find was on July 28, 1991 in *The Columbus Post Dispatch*, "Enhance Photos Help Law Track Escaped Killer."[5]

In my frequent correspondence with Judith Wise, bureau chief of records for the Ohio Department of Corrections, she had always listed Eubanks as AWOL. Her last letter was less than six months ago. In our phone conversations and emails, as recently as yesterday, Captain Messmore said he was still searching for Eubanks during his off hours; he added that the Mansfield Police Department still had no leads. Could it really be that this convicted child killer had been safely incarcerated the whole time and the fugitive listing was merely a bureaucratic paperwork foul-up?

"How do you know he's inside? I mean, incarcerated?" I stammer.

"That's easy, Miss Cheever. I checked the website," he says in a voice almost mocking me.

I stop taking notes. I drop my notepad back in my purse and stand up. I stare at the carousel. I almost start to laugh out loud. I am on my own carousel, but I'm not having near as much fun as the children.

Then I stop laughing inside. Now, I'm more than a bit angry.

"You mean to tell me, Mr. Laguna, that the only reason you have to believe that Lester Eubanks is incarcerated is because that's what it says on the DOC website? Do you mean to say that you do not have any independent verification that he is indeed inside Marion?" I screech.

"That's right. Yes, that's what I'm saying," he answers, abruptly.

"Well, then, it might help you to know that your own records chief has notified me by mail that Lester Eubanks is AWOL, that he escaped from prison in 1973 because some prison official gave him a pass to go Christmas shopping," I say, emphasizing the "Christmas shopping." I'd like to say idiot, instead of prison official. "He's never been captured. Right now I am in downtown Mansfield and I am five minutes away from meeting a police officer who has devoted most of his career to finding Eubanks and bringing him to justice. You should know that the Mansfield police have no idea that Eubanks is back in prison. It will be news to them. Wow. And it's certainly news to me. They still consider him a fugitive. But you *know* that he's incarcerated because that is what it says on the website? Is that what you just said?"

"Yes, that's right."

"Well, I'm willing to bet money that Lester Eubanks is still a fugitive. That he's not in prison now and hasn't been for the past 28 years. In fact, I am willing to bet the farm."

"Fine, let's bet."

"Oh, no. I really don't think you ought to. Not the farm, Mr. Laguna. Perhaps we can settle on dinner."

"That's fine too. I feel very comfortable with my information. Goodbye, Miss Cheever," he says, before hanging up.

I walk into Brunches and wait for Captain Messmore. I open my Eubanks file, which has been stuffed in my purse, and pull out a copy of the page of the DOC's website that Laguna had been referring to.

I printed it out just yesterday. I have been looking at it for the past two years and cringe when I see how Eubanks is described – "Offender Status: Incarcerated." I know he's not in prison because I have talked to police officers who are still looking for him. The newspaper articles refer to him as a fugitive; the DOC chief of records lists him as AWOL.

The information on the website is purposefully misleading, an effort – by the state, I guess – to cover up the embarrassing bureaucratic bungling of state officials. The Ohio prison system has been plagued by successful escapes, murders of prison guards and volunteer civilians, and deadly riots. To date, 43 inmates – including murders, rapists, and armed robbers – are still fugitives, and some have been for decades. Between 1968 and 1978, 18 of the 43 fugitives walked away from the Marion Correctional Institution, home of the state's honor farm and Eubanks' last address.[6]

I still can't understand, though, how a convicted killer like Eubanks earned an "Honor's Pass" to go Christmas shopping, unsupervised, at a mall in downtown Columbus, less than a year after he was on Death Row.

In 1995, a year in which there were a record 15 escapes, prison officials were quoted as saying there "is only one fugitive still on the run" – 31-year-old Donald J. Saffel.[7] Four convicted murderers escaped that same year after commandeering a supply truck and driving it through a fence, and two other inmates serving life terms got out by sawing through the bars of their cells and climbing over two razor wire fences. Saffel – serving a 30- to 75-year sentence for rape, burglary, and robbery – and his accomplice escaped by snipping through two security fences with a pair of bolt cutters stolen from the prison's vocational workshop.

Eubanks had it easier. He just walked away from the mall.

While waiting for Captain Messmore, I continue to stare at the DOC's web page. During my conversation with Attorney Laguna, he questioned me as to whether Eubanks was listed in my records as AWOL or AWL,[8] describing the distinction and implying that Eubanks could have had "permission" to be a fugitive for the past 28 years. I cannot believe Laguna is serious.

Messmore, a 60-ish, tall and lanky police officer, appears and I can barely sit still, waiting for just the right moment to blurt out the details of my Orwellian-type conversation 15 minutes earlier.

But there was something about Messmore that told me to keep quiet. To wait. To listen to the police officer whom I had waited to meet for four years. Perhaps it was because I couldn't see his eyes; they were shaded by the amber tint of aviator glasses. Messmore rarely looks at me as he tells his story of the night Mary Ann Deener was murdered. He seems defeated, embarrassed by the incompetence of prison officials. The small-town police got their man, Messmore explains, and then the bureaucrats turned him loose.

Within hours of Mary Ellen's murder, Mansfield police arrested Eubanks and he signed a written confession. Witnesses identified Eubanks as running from the scene; the 0.32 caliber revolver, thrown behind some garage doors close to the murder, was registered to him and the fingerprints and gunpowder tests on his hands came back positive.

After a two-and-a-half-week trial, a jury returned a verdict of guilty of first-degree murder with intent to commit rape, with no recommendation of mercy. The 22-year-old Eubanks, a member of the 179th Fighter Squadron of the Air National Guard and the son of a prominent Baptist minister in Mansfield, was on his way to the electric chair.

His path, which included six execution dates, hit a detour when *Furman v. Georgia* came down from the U.S. Supreme Court. An "honors assignment" entitling him to an unescorted trip in 1973 to the nearby shopping mall gave him an exit – a permanent one.

For the past 30 years, it seems very few people have been interested in trying to put Lester Eubanks back behind bars. Only a few police officers including Messmore and his partner, retired detective David Shook, have tried to clear up some unsolved homicides. But in this case, the local cops had gotten their man in 1965. The case isn't really unsolved. It is really unresolved.

Messmore knew Lester Eubanks from Springfield South High School where both attended; Messmore graduated a year earlier. They took karate classes together, and Messmore's family owned a grocery store less than a block from Rev. Mose Eubanks' Mount Calvary Baptist Church. That's also how Messmore knew Mary Ellen and the Deener family.

"She and her folks would come in frequently. It's been very frustrating. This is a little girl. A nice, quiet girl and her family were nice people. I feel terrible about what happened."

There are only a handful of articles about the search for Eubanks in the local newspaper, *The Mansfield Journal*, and even less in the much bigger *Columbus Dispatch*. In 1994, Messmore and Mansfield Police Captain John Arcudi, the coordinator for the Eubanks investigation, approached the producers of John Walsh's highly successful television series *America's Most Wanted* for help. On September 10, 1994, the show aired nationally, prompting about 80 telephone calls with tips, but no good leads.[9]

And then seven years later, and just two weeks before my visit, there was a break. A family member had died, Messmore explains, and local law enforcement believed that Eubanks was back in Mansfield, paying his respects. But when police knocked at the home of his father, the Reverend Eubanks, family members refused to let them in without a warrant. They were told to leave the property. And they did, Messmore said, shaking his head in disbelief and, at the same time, trying not to criticize his colleagues.

Based on information he declined to share, David Messmore believes that Lester Eubanks was inside the house that night;

police were the closest they had ever been to capturing a killer who has eluded the law for more than three decades.

Messmore is pained by the failure of police officers to even ask for a warrant. When I press him for more details, he says only: "I've probably told you more than I should."

Then he pushes the folder he had been carrying, over and says: "Look in there. There's a lot of information. All the police reports. Some news articles. Ballistics stuff. A lot."

But there was no current warrant for Eubank's arrest. According to a January 18, 2004, article in *The Akron Beacon Journal*, there was no warrant for Eubank's arrest on police computer databases. A federal warrant for interstate flight was first entered in 1996, according to FBI spokesman Bob Hawk.

In 2003, at the request of *The Beacon Journal*, the Ohio Highway Patrol, one of the agencies most responsible for prison escapes, released the names of all escapees; Eubank's name was among the 14 on the list, but there was no state warrant pending.

Jeff Maute, the patrol's central records supervisor, said the Eubank's case was considered closed. In fact, even up until December 2003, the Ohio Department of Rehabilitation and Correction's website didn't list any of the 43 fugitives as "wanted." They were identified as being "incarcerated" or in some cases "released," according to *The Beacon Journal*.[10]

I find it hard to understand how this small Ohio community isn't outraged that a child killer is still on the loose. It will take me another 24 hours and a trip to the scene of the murder to attempt to understand why.

The police file has no photograph of Mary Ellen, nor was there one in the newspaper articles I've read. While pouring over the police reports in my motel room that night, I miss an important clue: the notation "CF" typed next to the victim's name.

The next afternoon, when I meet Messmore back at the carousel, he asks if I've had time to visit some of the other tourist sites in town such as the Living Bible Museum or the 47 acres of gardens at the Kingwood Center. I tell him I've spent the morning at the town cemetery, looking for the freshly dug gravesite of

Betty Lee Eubanks, Lester's 74-year-old mother.

"How did you know it was his mother who died?"

"I looked it up in *The Mansfield Journal*. In fact, Lester Eubanks is listed as a survivor. The newspaper said he lives in Columbus. Can you believe that?" I don't expect an answer and Messmore doesn't give one. "The only problem was I couldn't find her grave. I drove around and around stopping at each new grave. I guess the cemetery's not segregated, is it?" I ask. He answers only with a raised eyebrow, surprised by my question.

But that was the case in Brenham, Texas when I went, six months after Walter's execution, to visit his grave. The only problem was, I couldn't find it. After spending two hours walking up and down the cemetery in a cold, drizzling rain, I called the director of Hogan Funeral Home, who quickly let me know that he was also a very prominent lawyer in town and that I had just interrupted a meeting with a very important client.

Hogan sounded irritated but nevertheless curious to meet the lawyer of a convicted killer who spent his childhood summers in this historic town of Brenham, population 14,000, and the birthplace of the state of Texas. On March 2, 1836, a delegation of men gathered here and unanimously signed the Declaration of Texas Independence, declaring Texas a "free sovereign and independent republic." That proclamation set off a war between Texas and Mexico. [11]

Twenty minutes after my call, Booker T. Hogan drives his new, luxury-size car right up to the graves, not bothering to park on the gravel road. When he points out that Walter is down in the family plot in the "Colored" section, my mouth drops.

Maybe it's because of the way Hogan, a tall, distinguished looking middle-aged black man, says "Colored," without flinching. This cemetery, just a few hundred yards from the campus of 118-year-old Blinn College, is segregated.

In Mansfield, when I explain to the retired police captain that I was looking for Mrs. Eubanks' grave to see if Lester might have left her a note, buried in the dirt, Messmore raises his eyebrow again and doesn't respond.

After I left the cemetery, I drove around Mansfield, stopping at the house where Mary Ellen lived, not far from the cemetery. I know from reading an old newspaper article that Mrs. Deener has never gotten over her daughter's murder and she has never discussed it publicly, either. Mary Ellen's sister, Myrtle Carter, told a newspaper reporter several years ago that ever since the girl's murder, their mother had placed Mary Ellen's photograph next to a statue of Jesus. "My mother was a young woman when my sister was murdered and I saw her age from that day on." [12]

Last night I called Mrs. Deener hoping she might agree to see me. A man who answered the phone said only: "She's passed on." I was nine months too late.

The way he said "she passed on" and how he said it should have been a clue, but I missed it.

The next morning, I drive by the Deener house, but no one is home. I leave a note for Brenda Deener, Mary Ellen's sister who was there that night at the laundromat, and who is now living in her mother's home. Brenda is a city social worker and works with Captain Messmore's wife. It is a small town. Messmore thinks she might be willing to talk to me.

I also drive by the ranch-style home of Eubanks' father, the Rev. Mose Eubanks, but I don't leave my card. The house looks empty; I decide I won't drop in on any of Lester's sisters either. I know the family is still in mourning and it isn't proper to press Rev. Eubanks on the whereabouts of his son. Not that he would have told me.

From the police reports, I've written down the address of the crime scene and Captain Messmore gives me a quick tour by car. The laundromat is out of business; it's now "Custom Clutch: Joints and Hydraulics." The convenience store has been replaced by Satch's Restaurant and Lounge, although it, too, looks like it's gone bust.

I can't help but notice that the old convenience store is right across the street from Lester Eubanks' former residence – 339

North Mulberry, a rust-colored, two-story multi-family home where two old refrigerators stand guard on the front porch. Forty years ago, this area on Route 39, just minutes from downtown Mansfield, was probably booming. But the years have taken their toll. The area is a mix of multi-family homes in need of repair, and most of the commercial establishments lack foot traffic and remain empty.

It then hits me. It is so obvious. I just haven't picked up on the clues.

"Mary Ellen Deener was black, wasn't she?"

Messmore took off his glasses and when I looked into his eyes, I got my answer. He must have wondered what took me so long. Yesterday at lunch he told me that the Deener and Eubanks families had known each other for years, well before the murder. He also told me that Brenda Deener was very active in the local NAACP.

The "CF" next to Mary Ellen's name in the police report meant "Colored Female" not "Caucasian Female" as I had thought. And blacks usually refer to dying as "passing on." And when I look, again, at the November 16, 1966, newspaper article about the murder, I notice the 9th-grader's school yearbook picture – Mary Ellen Deener is black. And so is her killer.

Almost 35 years after Furman, it is still rare for the killers of blacks to be sentenced to death even though people of color are the victims of more than half of the homicides. As of December 15, 2005, the Death Penalty Information Center reports that 809 inmates who have been put to death since 1976 were convicted of killing a white. Only 18 of the 1,002 executions in the U.S. have been in cases in which the victim was black and the defendant was white. [13]

In the state of Texas, the statistics reflect the racial disparity of the death penalty. If you murder a white person, you are five times more likely to receive the death penalty than if you murder a black person. A study of Texas homicide cases between 1980 and 1988 found that no white offender who killed a black victim has even been charged and convicted with capital murder.

Of the 356 executions in Texas since 1982, only one white offender has been executed for killing a black: Larry Hayes. In that case, there were two victims – one black, one white. Hayes shot his wife five times and then went to a convenience store where he murdered a black female clerk who refused to leave with him. Hayes dropped all his appeals, saying he'd rather die.

On September 10, 2003, Hayes, 54, was executed. On the death penalty website, Hayes is listed as a "volunteer." [14]

On the Ohio prison website, Lester Eubanks is now listed as "escaped." It's been 32 years since he was last seen "shopping" at the Great Southern mall in downtown Columbus.

CHAPTER FOURTEEN

FINDING FURMAN

Of the 322 men who have been released from prison, more than half are no longer on parole. They have successfully discharged their sentences.

"Miss Cheever. I have found William Henry Furman."

Within 30 minutes of that telephone call from Dan Welton, Furman's former parole officer, I have booked a flight to Atlanta and am ready to finally meet the elusive Mr. Furman.

I fly in on a Saturday night and am ambivalent about waiting until sunrise to make the two-hour trek to meet Furman. But when the tall black guard at the Avis Rent-A-Car gate gives me not only directions to my $32-a- night motel room just 10 miles away, but also tacit permission to go with my gut and wait until morning, I feel better. His voice is stern and he's cautious. He bends down so that we are at eye level and looks me squarely in the eye: "Stay on 75 South, young lady, and just keep on going. Don't stop. Just keep driving until you get to Jonesboro."

I have waited for 13 years, I guess I can put this off another 12 hours. I check in to the motel and ask the middle-aged woman behind the counter for directions to a restaurant close by. She points to a pile of Chinese menus and suggests I get it delivered.

"Chinese food in Georgia?" I whisper to myself, and take the menus and find my room. Five minutes later I'm back at the reception desk. "Sorry to bother you again, but I was thinking more like Southern food. Ya know. Ribs and fried stuff? And a beer?"

A smile creeps across her tired face, one of apology for misjudging her guest from New York City.

Tonight I am feeling a bit restless and adventuresome. I don't want to spend the dinner hour locked in a motel room with the television as my dinner companion. I'd rather go people-watching.

She quickly rattles off directions to Sonny's Bar-B-Que Ribs – "a left, a right, and then a left, just five minutes away. You can't get lost."

I chuckle at her misplaced confidence in my sense of direction.

Last year, when I flew to Memphis to interview Monty Powell, a former gang member who was on Death Row in Illinois in 1968, I met him at his African-American art gallery, where he's a part owner.

The store is filled with customers this afternoon in December; there are only 14 shopping days left until Christmas. He apologizes for not being able to get away and give me a tour. We agree to meet tomorrow morning; I tell Monty that I'll do a little bit of touring on my own.

"Will it be Elvis' Graceland or the National Civil Rights Museum?" Powell asks, in a serious tone.

I look at him and laugh. "That's not really a choice, is it?"

I scribble down the directions on the back of an old grocery list I find in my purse and drive to the museum, which is housed in the old Lorraine motel in downtown Memphis, the site where Martin Luther King was assassinated on April 4, 1968.

But I must've taken a left instead of a right. Forty-five minutes and miles later, I realize my mistake when I pass a road sign: "Welcome to Mississippi." I drive another five miles inside the state before turning around so I can add Mississippi to the list of states to which I've traveled. It was a favorite pastime of my mother's; whenever she traveled outside of Texas, Mom would drive an extra couple of hours, in the part of the United States where the states are much closer together, just so she could say she'd "been there."

Monty Powell

Tonight, I manage to find Sonny's Barbeque and only get a little bit lost.

Architecturally, Sonny's is not designed for single dining but for large families, and there are many here. I am seated immediately – smack dab in the center of the restaurant – in the middle of a roomful of families out for dinner on a Saturday night. It makes me miss my own little family back home something awful.

This afternoon getting to the airport was stressful. I almost missed the flight; there are no "standbys" for the "Continental Cool Travel Special." If you miss it, you have to pay full fare.

Speeding down the Henry Hudson Parkway, over the George Washington Bridge (I close my eyes) and through the New Jersey Turnpike, I begin to relax. But five minutes before we arrive at the airport, I have an unpleasant thought. I unfasten my seatbelt and climb into the backseat. And then I start to hug and kiss Luke and

Lily like it'll be the last time. They are confused at Mommy's sudden and unexplained affection.

Dennis senses my fear.

"Are you sure this is okay? It's safe?" he asks, looking at me in the rear view mirror. "You don't have to go. Did you leave me telephone numbers?"

We've been through this before; lots of numbers – motel, cell phone, and the ex-Death Row inmate's home number. This time I left two out of three, but I don't tell him the cell phone isn't working. The battery needs constant recharging.

My thoughts are interrupted when my waitress, Barb, plops down across from me to take my order. She could tell I'm from out of town. Dressed in black, reading the Sunday magazine of *The New York Times*, who else would dine alone on a Saturday night?

She takes the order and returns with my beer. And then Barb sits down. She's been standing up all day and she's exhausted, she explains. I think she wants to talk about more than the five kinds of barbeque sauces. She seems to be curious about what has brought me to Jonesboro. But she's too polite to ask.

Instead, we talk about barbeque – how long it's cooked and the regional differences in ribs. She describes the sauces she has lined up in Ketchup Squirters: sweet, mild, medium, hot, and very hot.

"How hot is very hot?"

"Oh, it'll take more than one beer there to put the fire out, hon,' she says, laughing.

I douse the dry-rubbed ribs with the very hot and notice that Barb is still standing there, staring. She's waiting for an explanation.

"Texas. I like jalapenos, too. The hotter the better," I reply, hoping it's enough of an answer.

"O.K., Darlin'. How 'bout another one of those Buds to wash 'em down with? I think you might need it."

I did. The ice-cold Buds calmed me. The fried okra was crackling hot and the homemade slaw was perfect. I'm so glad I found Sonny's; my dinner was delicious. When I got back in my car, the anxiety set in. I thought about the trip tomorrow morning and hoped this dinner wouldn't be my last. When I turned out the light at the motel, I wondered whether that spicy sauce or the thought of tomorrow's "ambush" interview with Furman was going to keep me up. Both did.

I've never "ambushed" anyone during the two years I'd been interviewing these ex-Death Row inmates. But Furman doesn't have a telephone and his former parole officer tells me he's always been skittish about talking to the press. In fact, he never has. I don't want to give Furman time to think about whether he should talk. I just want him to.

For some reason I feel more tired tonight than ever. I wonder if I have lost my sense of adventure. Before turning out the light, I conduct the same ritual I'd been doing for the past two years, during which time I've stayed in the cheapest motel rooms I can find and rented the smallest cars. The more money I save, the more ex-cons I can visit.

Again I drag what furniture I can move and push it up against the door. I look over at the desk but decide it is too heavy. And the TV, my late-night companion, is on top of it.

I lock the door, turn the deadbolt and check the sturdiness of the chain. It looks like it works.

Last year in Memphis, I moved to three different rooms at an inexpensive motel because of defective chains. In the first two rooms, the hardware – the chain *and* screw ensemble – fell off the door when I shut it. The chain in the third room was screwed in, but loose. I checked out before I really checked in. I upgraded – from motel to "hotel" for $50 more. I ended up at the Marriott, located right in the middle of the airport. At that point, I didn't care. Loose door chains would keep me up. Airplanes landing overhead would not.

The irony of my situation tonight is not lost on me. I am fearful, but I do not live in fear. I am always on guard when I'm on the road and am ever mindful that those men whom I am interviewing are responsible for the fear we all have. This group has left a legacy of pain, despair, and heartache in their wake by the very nature of their murderous acts.

The days of unlocked houses, unlocked cars, and late-night highway driving are over. But I am lucky. I have never been the victim of a crime. I've never been hurt and I've never been robbed. But I have lost something that is priceless: my wide-eyed innocence. I no longer feel safe most of the time. I now know that bad things – very bad things – can happen to very good, decent people. That acts of violence are random. That I and most of us have to work hard at being safe. That takes a lot of energy.

But I can't afford to be naive because it could cost me my life.

I've also lost my freedom. My movements are now usually in "restricted" or "safe" areas. I've developed a sixth sense to know when I may be in danger. And that is not normal.

In fact, it's very sad. And, it makes me angry. Tonight it makes me even more tired. I recheck the lock and deadbolt and put the chain on. Balls of wadded up newspaper lay at my feet. I engage in this ritual with a heavy sigh. I wonder when it will end. Or if it ever will. Is crime just part of our lives?

I move the reading lamp closer to the bed, drag the rather large, red, upholstered wingchair up against the door and throw my small black rollerbag in the mix, for good measure.

The bathroom light stays on; I swallow a Tylenol PM and turn on my noise machine, adjust it to the sound of ocean waves, and turn off the ceiling light. I try to sleep.

In just nine hours I hope to meet Furman.

The next morning is Sunday and, as usual, I am thankful to have survived the night. I put on a navy blue and white polyester dress that travels well but really makes me look more like a parole officer or a social worker. I drive south on I-75.

Two hours later, I'm at McDonald's, looking for Furman's street on a city map. I gulp down a cup of coffee, secretly hoping that it will provide me with both caffeine and courage. One out of two isn't bad.

I smile and wave at the little children, dressed in their Sunday best, dutifully holding onto the hands of their mothers who have stopped at Mickey Ds on their way home from church. On the inside, I'm a mess. Wishing that I, too, could go back home and hold onto the hands of my little ones. I don't want to be here. I don't want to do this.

It's Sunday and here in the South that means a day of churching and visiting the family. I don't think I'll look so out of place if I drop in unannounced. And here, it's not considered rude. But visits like that are usually reserved for good friends or family. I don't know William Furman and he doesn't know me.

I look down at my watch as I pull up to the corner on Furman's street. It is only 9 a.m., but if I show up any later, he might be gone. I don't want to spend hours sitting outside his house on a "stake-out." I really want to get this over with.

I drive slowly down the block, straining my neck to see the numbers. Some houses are marked, most are not. I find his house and keep on driving.

Several of his neighbors are sitting on their front porches hoping to catch an occasional early morning breeze and some local gossip. They are talking to folks across the street, and to those next door. Each time a car passes they stop talking and stare. Stranger or neighbor? Friend or foe?

When I drive by, I can feel the eyes of the neighborhood on me. My white 1998 Sunbird and white skin stick out.

After a few blocks, I make a U-turn, say some quick Hail Marys, and park in front of Furman's duplex. I am nervous, but I know I have my cell phone tucked safely inside the zipped pocket in my purse.

On my birthday, as a joke, I asked for a gun. Just a little bitty thing that fits in a purse.

I really hate guns; I've only shot a rifle once, and it was under duress.

I was 10 years old, sitting with my mother in a small deer blind on Tom Cunningham's ranch outside Goliad, Texas. She was armed with a 0.243 caliber rifle. I was there to keep her company, trying to read a Nancy Drew book in the fading daylight, while Mom looked out over the parched South Texas land, hoping a deer would walk into her line of fire. She was hell bent on bagging a buck, knowing that the venison would feed her family for months.

"Mom, it's getting dark. I think it's time to quit."

"No way. I'm not leaving here without my deer. I don't hear much shooting and I don't think your Dad or brothers have gotten anything. You and me, sister, are getting a buck. That's it."

Just then, something moved in the brush.

"Okay, here we go. Keep quiet," she whispered.

"Mom, I think that's a cow. Don't shoot!"

"Hush. It's a buck if I ever saw one!" But she couldn't see a thing; it was too dark.

She pulled the trigger and the rifle recoiled with such force that the scope knocked her glasses off and ended up cutting her above the eye. Blood was dripping down her face. I thought she had shot herself in the eye. That's how much I knew about rifles.

"Hell's bells," she whispered, wiping the blood with a soiled tissue she kept in her pocket for emergencies like this. She shoved the gun into my arms, warning me it was loaded and cocked.

"Oh, no. I don't hunt, Mom. I'm here for company. Remember?"

"You *will* shoot. We *will* get that deer. Now go on. Shoot!"

"You can't see a thing. Look at all this blood. I don't think it's a deer, Mom. I think it's a cow. And Mr. Cunningham is going to be really mad at you if you shoot one of his cows."

"Shoot. It's a deer. Shoot."

I did as I was told, even though the fear of a similar recoil sent the bullet into the sky; we were lucky it didn't come back down on top of us.

I was mad at my mother for making me shoot the rifle, but it was hard to stay mad for long. "Deer. Cow. Who the hell cares? Venison or steak, honey. We'll get something."

We both started laughing so hard, we had to use the latrine. But we couldn't leave the blind until Dad and Mr. Cunningham came to pick us up. She was still bleeding. Now she was using her shirt to mop up the blood. She assured me that she hadn't blown her eye out; she said if she put enough pressure on the wound, the bleeding would stop. It did.

When Mr. Cunningham drove up in his pickup with Dad, Mom and I practically crawled out of the blind; we were doubled over laughing. She squeezed in next to Dad and I sat on my father's lap. My brothers were sitting in the back.

My mother grew up on a ranch in West Texas – she spent a lot of time sitting in deer blinds with her own father and little brother, Hancie. They taught her how to shoot and to respect the firepower of a rifle. In Texas, as well as other parts of the South and western United States, hunting is part of almost every kid's childhood experience. Many states, including Texas, require that kids take a hunting education safety course and obtain a license. While many children have their own rifles, not many – I would say – get to experience the sport of hunting with their mother. But then, not many mothers were like Sally.

"What the Sam Hill happened to you, Sally?" Cunningham asked, when he saw the bloody shirt.

"Oh, hell, nothing. Charlie's new gun kicked like a donkey. That's all."

"Well, did you get anything? I'll tell one of my boys and he'll go git it."

"I don't know, Tom. You missing any cows this evening?" she roared.

And then Mom and I squealed with laughter, wiggling around, telling Mr. Cunningham to hurry up and get back to the ranch house because we had to go to the bathroom something awful.

We left a cloud of dust behind and I quietly prayed that we left that cow alive, too. That was the first time I'd ever shot a rifle; I wasn't about to try again.

A cell phone is all I can handle this morning.

I drop the car keys into my pocket, and suddenly I feel the eyes of the neighborhood upon me. With a fingernail baring into my left thumb, to give me a self-inflicted pinch for courage and to keep from turning right around and bolting for the car, I walk right up to the door.

I am startled. It's open.

I knock on the wooden door frame and a tall, thin black man appears.

"Mr. Furman?" I say extending my hand, "I'm ..." but before I can get it out, he stops me.

"Miss Cheevah. Right? Come on in. I've been waiting for you!"

Dressed in an Atlanta Braves T-shirt, blue jeans, and dark-brown work boots, Furman ushers me into the small living room in this old, run-down, three-room, $137-a-month duplex and points to a chair. The room is dark; there's a burgundy sheet and a blue and yellow plaid blanket covering the windows. Cautiously I sit down.

I think we are alone but then I see some movement in the corner of the room; I jump a little when a heavy-set 30-ish black man, a cane by his side, extends his hand. "Hi. I'm Boonie." He's one of Furman's roommates; the second is Furman's "lady friend" who is working the early morning housekeeping shift at the Holiday Inn down the road.

When Furman closes the door, I flinch. I've been trying to conduct these interviews in public. Or at least, in a position where I can make a quick exit. I know I have my cell phone and earlier I had been practicing, while the phone is off, touching the numbers 9-1-1 and hitting the send button.

I slip my hand, discreetly, into my purse to locate the phone. But I can't find it. I fling my hand wildly, clutching pens, lipsticks, loose change. But no phone.

Suddenly, I realize that in my haste and nervousness to meet Furman, I have left my only link to the outside world in my car. There's no way I can leave, go out to my car for the phone, and return without putting this interview in jeopardy. I just hope for the best.

My fear quickly dissolves when Furman begins to speak, slowly and with much effort, as he holds my crumpled letter that really does look as though it has been in someone's back pocket for the past nine months.

"I called you last night on that 800 number on your letter. But I couldn't get you. Nice to see you now, Ma'am."

He shuffles over to the old wooden table in the corner of the room and moves the pot of black-eyed peas that had been soaking. I sit down on a hard wooden chair and he sits across from me, on one of the two battered couches that have been covered with old sheets.

The pale blue paint on the living room walls is peeling and the walls are bare. I can see it is a three-room house – like a railroad flat apartment in Manhattan. The middle room is painted a mustard color and several ice chests are stacked on top of each other. A military-style cot is in the corner with a blanket rolled up where the pillow should be. The bed is next to a refrigerator but I don't think it's working.

I can't see the third room.

Furman looks uneasy as he watches me assess his dismal living conditions; I think I am being discreet. After an awkward start, he doesn't hesitate to answer my questions.

We are interrupted occasionally by a movie on the TV; I am competing with *In the Heat of the Night* and it looks like the TV and I are in a tie for Furman's attention. Later this afternoon, it will be the San Francisco 49ers and the Atlanta Falcons.

Furman, who has never married and never had children, says little, but the answers are more than the "Yeses" and "Nos" that I expected after talking to his former parole officer. He says more with his eyes as they tear. He turns away; his hands cradle his face and his lips quiver.

"It's still rough on me. I think about it a lot. Once or twice I thought I would be executed. I came close to death. I try to put it in the back of my mind," he says. "I think to myself – I'm here. I have more time. And time is standing still."

He knows he's lucky. "I got a second chance at life and I'm trying to make it last. As long as possible." He tells me his philosophy of life is simple. "Life is short and I took me a long walk." The memories are painful and I can see that he is tired.

I tell him I am going to check into my motel but that I will return to take him and Boonie to lunch.

I drive by the motel that I booked on the Internet; the room is being held with my credit card. I need to cancel by 4 p.m. or I will be charged. After driving past the motel, I call the toll-free number. I need a break from "the furniture against the door" routine. My mission has been accomplished. I have found Furman. Tonight I want a good night's sleep. I drive by three other motels close to Furman's house and decide on a Best Western. It's an extra $10 but the rooms are only accessible on the inside – via the lobby – and there is no extra charge for a non-smoking room. The keys are electronic and unmarked. I can only see one entrance and everyone has to pass by the front desk clerk to get to their rooms. I feel safe.

A few hours later I return, and this time only a few of Furman's neighbors bother to look up.

He and Boonie are waiting outside and they are wearing their Sunday best. Furman is in gray polyester slacks and a short-sleeve pale pink button-down shirt. The strong whiff of aftershave is refreshing compared to the smell of the blue carpet in the living room.

I am glad we are going out to lunch. "Pick a place, Mr. Furman. Anywhere," I say as we pass a Bennigans, Texas City steakhouse, Dennys, and an Apple Restaurant.

He picks Mr. D's Seafood – a fast-food joint on a main thoroughfare, two blocks from my motel. He assures me the seafood at Mr. D's is as fresh as that you'd get back home in Savannah. Mr. D's is more like a Long John Silver's; the most expensive meal is a combination platter for $5.98. I add fried okra to their orders and walk over to the bright orange Formica booths.

Furman stops me in my tracks.

"Um. Miss Cheevah. I'm hoping you don't mind. Me and Boonie here was talkin and I'm wonderin' if we might get our lunch 'to go,' ya know? See, the 49ers is playing at 2 and then the Falcon's at 4. Dat be alright with you, Miss Cheevah?" he asks, with great hesitation.

"No problem. I love football!" I answer enthusiastically, cringing when I realize I've just agreed to return to Furman's dark house, instead of spending this sunny, warm October afternoon taking a walk through some of the beautiful parks in this quaint Southern town.

But, after all, it's a Sunday in the South and football is king. Furman has been waiting all week to see these two games. I have been waiting 13 years to meet him. And I still have a lot of questions.

Fifteen minutes later we are back in his living room and now the house smells like fried food.

We are in front of the TV; the Styrofoam containers of fried shrimp, fried okra, "mean greens," and sweet tea are sitting precariously on our laps and the game has started. I grew up eating lunch in front of the TV on Sundays in a house full of diehard Dallas Cowboy football fans; an afternoon of pro football is not unusual. In this case, the company is.

At 56 years old, William Henry Furman is in bad shape – both physically and mentally. He seems slow. He doesn't know his own telephone number and has to bring me the phone book. In the corner, on the book's cover, Furman's number has been scribbled in pencil. He has trouble with his eyes. I don't know if he can write.

At his 1968 trial, doctors at the Georgia Central State Hospital diagnosed Furman as "mental deficiency of mild to moderate, with psychotic episodes associated with convulsive disorder," which meant that he had periods of insanity related to epilepsy. [1] He doesn't seem insane to me, but maybe in the past alcohol triggered those periods of insanity.

Since his release from prison in 1984, Furman has had two mild heart attacks and is on daily heart medication. He's given up the booze because, he says, it's not good for his heart. He wants to live.

He cannot walk for long periods of time because he has difficulty breathing; he had to quit working in construction because of his health. His right eye is off kilter so he rarely looks at you while speaking.

It turns out the reason I couldn't find him for 13 years is because he's moved around. "I stayed on the street for a while, living in cars and abandoned houses. But I like this house just fine. I'm staying put."

He keeps busy, picking up aluminum soda cans, walking to the corner grocery store for Coca Colas, and volunteering at the soup kitchen at the Mulberry Methodist Church. He gets disability and welfare checks and spends his days watching television. The TV looks brand new and it's in the middle of the room.

Sometimes Furman goes to church, if only to please the well-dressed older woman who drops in while we're having lunch.

"I'll be goin" with you tomorrow. Right now I have a guest, Ma'am," he tells the woman wearing a black and white dress with a matching wide-brimmed black and white hat.

Furman returns to the living room and gives Boonie a "high five."

"Oh, yeah. She be back. Bet on that."

The men giggle at the not-so-private joke.

She's the church lady, Furman explains, and she walks up and down the neighborhood every Sunday morning trying to get the "men folk" into the "House of God." This is her calling and you can hear her from a block away. She's talking to all the neighbors. It seems that every man on this block has some sort of an excuse.

She usually fails in her mission, Furman reports, but she gets an "A" for effort.

The church lady doesn't like to take "No" for an answer. She wants to know when I'm leaving and at what time he'll be ready tomorrow.

I ask if he's really going.

"Oh, yeah. Just to shush her up. And it's not all that bad, ya know. I gets me a meal."

It isn't religion that has kept William Henry Furman out of trouble since his release from prison more than 21 years ago. It is the memories. Ones too painful to share.

He became eligible for parole in 1980, but the parole board wouldn't approve of his parole plan. He wanted to move back to his childhood home – Savannah – which is also the city where his victim, William Micki, was murdered. Micki's relatives still live there and they talked the parole board into barring Furman from the city, for life. He relocated to the town where he now lives.

Furman isn't exactly clear as to how his case came before the United States Supreme Court. And his lawyers weren't clear, either. His case was one of six that were appealed; the Supreme Court picked his, fellow Georgia Death Row inmate Lucious Jackson (aggravated rape – no murder), California's Aikens (two brutal rape-murders) and the Texas case of Elmer Branch (a non-aggravated rape). All four were black; their victims, white.

Furman says he remembers the morning of June 29, 1972, the day the historic ruling that bears his name came down. Looking through the bars of the 163-year-old Central State Hospital in Midgeville, Furman saw a large number of newspaper, radio, and television reporters descend on the hospital grounds.

He knows how he arrived on Death Row – but insists the August 11, 1967, murder was an accident. He's been nicknamed "the Bungling Burglar" and for good reason.

In his 1978 book, *Death Penalty: The Case of Life vs. Death in the United States*, author Leonard A. Stevens writes about the historic case, describing the 24-year-old as drunk when he left Ruby's Two Spot and decided to burglarize the home of one of the poorest families in the neighborhood. Hoping to "to pick up a radio or two," Furman made so much noise breaking in that he woke up the victim, William Micki, who had only gotten home an hour earlier from his second job as a waiter at the Tiffany Lounge. He was a machinist's mate 2nd class with the U.S. Coast Guard and was living with his wife and children in a small, white frame house on West 63rd Street in Savannah.[2]

Furman says Micki rushed toward him in the kitchen.

"I thought he was going to shoot me," Furman explained later. "He come after me. I knew he was going to shoot." He said he backed away from Micki, pulled out his gun and tripped on a wire from the washing machine and fell backward. When he lost his balance, the gun discharged. He said he had no idea the bullet struck Micki.[3]

He fled into the woods and ran to his Uncle James' house. Police followed his fresh footprints (it had been raining) and found him hiding in a crawlspace underneath his uncle's porch. Furman surrendered and admitted that he had been in the Micki's home and had fired his gun but said he had no idea that Micki had been killed.

Micki was murdered the day before his 30th birthday and was buried with full military honors. Survivors included his wife, Lanell, their infant child, three children from his previous marriage, and six children from Lanell's first marriage that had ended with the death of her first husband.[4]

B. Clarence Mayfield, one of three black lawyers in Savannah, was appointed to represent the "Bungling Burglar" and try to keep him out of the electric chair. Mayfield was paid a grand total of $150.

Furman, who lived with his mother, had already been convicted and incarcerated four times for burglary, and was working as a handyman at the Superior Upholstery Company in Savannah. At the time of the murder, he was on parole. Whether it was an accident or not, whether it was intentional or unintentional, William Henry Furman was accused of capital murder, a charge that carried a death sentence because it happened during another felony – in this case, burglary.

Both jury selection and the trial began on September 20, 1968. And they ended the same day, as well.

The prosecution brought in nine witnesses, including the twice-widowed Lanell Micki. The defense had no witnesses.

Furman wanted to testify but Attorney Mayfield told him he wouldn't hold up under cross examination. So they compromised – Furman made an "unsworn statement" that couldn't be subject to questioning.

At 3:35 p.m. the trial was over and the jury began deliberations. Thirty-five minutes later they were back; they asked who was to decide Furman's punishment.

Judge Dunbar Harrison told them "it's up to the jury." They returned to the courtroom just an hour later, with a verdict of guilty – no mercy.[5]

Judge Harrison then sentenced Furman to die in the busiest electric chair in the country. From 1924 to 1964, 414 men and one woman had been executed in Georgia; they included 343 murderers, 66 rapists, and 6 robbers.

Judge Harrison also set a date – Furman was to die on November 8, 1968, less than six weeks away.

Like Furman's, Walter's jury returned in less than an hour with a sentence of death. In the 13 years he was on Death Row, Walter was given five execution dates. But Furman's appointment in the Death House was permanently postponed. As were execution dates of 588 others.

After years of looking for him, I couldn't believe I was now sitting in the living room of the man whose name is synonymous with the abolition of the death penalty. I cannot count the number of times I read the Furman decision or the thousands of legal opinions that referred to the historic ruling that bears his name. Sometimes it's easy to forget that there are real people behind the names of these famous cases. And I am sitting right next to him.

I pinch myself to make sure I'm not dreaming. I've been waiting years to ask, "Mr. Furman, how do you feel about your contribution to the abolition of the death penalty?"

He seems startled at my "golly, gee whiz" enthusiasm. Maybe he doesn't understand the question. I rephrase it: "Mr. Furman... uh, you... um... I mean, your case... hmm... is the one responsible for saving the lives of 588 people on Death Row. And probably hundreds more. How do you feel?"

He looks at me and shrugs. There is an uncomfortable silence. Furman rubs his eyes; he looks tired.

Then he leans closer.

"I didn't do nuthin' back then but try to stay alive. I just wanted... to stay alive."

William Henry Furman is not the same man who sat on Georgia's Death Row in 1968 waiting to die. He's older now. And much wiser than I had expected for a man who was said to be mentally retarded with periods of insanity related to epilepsy.

William Henry Furman is a Death Row survivor. All he wanted was just to stay alive.

———

It took a while, but I found Furman. There was one more person I needed to meet. I had put it off for too many years.

It was time to meet the mother of the young man Walter had murdered, in cold blood, more than 13 years ago.

The question was: Did Lea Liepold want to meet me?

CHAPTER FIFTEEN

FINDING FORGIVENESS

Of the 505 killers in the Furman group, 163 knew their victims; 342 did not.

Journey of Hope ... from Violence to Healing is an organization that is led by murder victim family members that conducts speaking tours and addresses alternatives to the death penalty. [1]

Murder Victims' Families for Reconciliation (MVFR) and Murder Victims' Families for Human Rights (MVFHR) are national organizations whose members have lost a relative to murder or state execution. The groups oppose the death penalty in all cases; members travel with the Journey of Hope. MVFR was founded in 1976, shortly after the death penalty returned to the United States, four years after *Furman*. MVFHR is an international organization, based in the U.S., and was founded in 2004.

"**I** want to talk to that nun."

That's all Lea Liepold asked of me when we met the first time. She wanted to talk to Sister Helen Prejean, the nun who's been the spiritual adviser for men on Louisiana's Death Row and author of the books *Dead Man Walking* and *The Death of Innocents*. [2]

I know Sister Helen – we met briefly at a death penalty fundraiser in Washington, D.C. honoring Justice William Brennan, just a few weeks after Walter's execution. She found me in the crowd that day, apologizing for not being able to return my call that frantic afternoon in Texas before I was to talk to Walter for the last time.

"I'm so sorry, Joan, that I wasn't there for you. I was out of town, on a book tour. Are you okay? Are you sure you're okay?" she said, holding my hand tightly, tears welling in her eyes. "Gosh, I am so sorry. Is there anything I can do for you?"

No, I assured her. Not at that time. But 11 years later, there was.

———

After interviewing more than 125 former Death Row inmates, I knew there was a meeting I couldn't put off any longer. It was time to visit the mother of the young man Walter shot – at point blank range – in the back of the head. Never once during the nine years I represented Walter, nor during the four years since his execution, had I tried to make contact with Mrs. Liepold. I had read her testimony more than a hundred times during those years, desperately trying to find some sort of reversible error that would give Walter either a new trial or a new sentence.

In the black and white pages of the transcript, Mrs. Liepold's pain is great. I can't imagine what it will be like to hear it in person.

Finally, I summon up the nerve and write. I am kind of hoping it will go unanswered. It has been 18 years since she buried Daniel, one of five children. The local newspaper described his funeral, where more than 900 mourners packed the chapel at Lackland Air Force Base to say their goodbyes. Many were strangers to the Liepold family, but not to Daniel. They knew him as a helpful neighbor, a nice young man who pumped gas at the station down the street and who cheerfully stocked the shelves at the Circle K convenience store and rang up their purchases, handing them their change with a warm smile. He had touched their lives and now his was over.

Even though it's been a long time since the funeral, I now know, as a new mother, that Mrs. Liepold's pain is still great and it runs deep. I need to see her. I want to see how she is doing. And to find out if Walter's execution eased her sorrow.

But our meeting, thanks to a foggy rainy morning and a cancelled flight from New York, will be postponed. I secretly hope it will be permanently canceled. But Lea Liepold is one tough cookie. I am not going to get out of it that easily. When I call to update her about the weather and the delay, she suggests meeting the following afternoon.

I try to buy some more time. "If this isn't a good time, I could meet you when I come back to San Antonio again. That might be better," I say, trying not to sound too nervous or upbeat at the prospect of a postponement.

She doesn't take the bait. "No, Miss Cheever. I'll see you tomorrow. I have a funeral to get to, but perhaps sometime in the afternoon. Let's say 6 p.m. You have directions to my home," she says in a gravely voice; its pitch has probably changed over the years because of cigarettes.

The car I rent at Enterprise for $14.95 is a compact, a four-door Neon; its color is bright red. When I stop at my parents' house to drop off my luggage, I get a tongue-lashing about the car's color and its size. To Mom, anything smaller than a station wagon is a "sports car."

"Hell's bells. What are you thinking driving to that poor woman's house in that car? Who do you think you are? Looks like a damn sports car to me! And red, too. Don't you have better manners?" she asks, before leaving the house in a cocktail dress, heading downtown for a charity fundraiser dinner in her beat-up 1991 Ford Taurus station wagon.

I pull up to the Liepold's house and park behind Mr. Liepold's truck and their son Darren's blue van. The sun is still up. There is a fence around the front yard with a sign: "Beware of Dogs."

As I walk to the front door, I see remnants of Christmas – a string of outdoor lights are carefully bundled and left on a bench. I take a deep breath and ring the doorbell. I look down and see the Madonna and Child staring at me, a foot-tall ceramic statue in the picture window. The drapes are drawn.

I don't have long to linger on the figurine, wondering if the windowsill is its permanent home or whether it was left out purposely to remind me that the mother inside can never hold her child again.

Mrs. Liepold opens the door. She's dressed in brown slacks and a plain, long-sleeved chestnut-brown blouse that matches her eyes. She looks me over – up and down. I wonder what she expects to see. In her eyes, I am the "devil's" lawyer, the woman who kept her son's killer alive an extra 13 years.

She brings me back to the family room where Roger, her husband and Daniel's father, and Daniel's little brother, Darren, now 28, are waiting. She sits in a dark brown Lazy-Boy to my left; Daniel's high school graduation picture, the same one that had been introduced at Walter's trial, stands in a picture frame on the end table that separates Mrs. Liepold and me. I take my seat on the couch and sit next to Joyce, a long-time family friend. I suspect Joyce is there out of a mix of curiosity and to relieve some of the tension in the room. She is to be the buffer. During the next three hours, the 50-ish woman says little, and only at times when the tension runs high or when members of the family are unable to speak through the river of tears that fill the dark wood-paneled den. Joyce is warm and friendly. I can tell by her pointed questions that she has gone through a lot of the mourning with the Liepolds. But her questions don't have the same ring of emotion and she never points an accusatory finger. Joyce always brings the family back to the issue of capital punishment. And my book. And me.

Nervously, I begin the meeting and state my purpose. I don't deviate from the letter I'd sent a week earlier. I explain my role as Walter's attorney; the conflicting feelings I have now as a mother and, despite those feelings, my continued opposition to the death penalty.

And then, remembering the advice of an attorney friend, who I frantically called on my cell phone just minutes before this meeting, I just keep quiet.

"Joan, just shut up and listen," Kathleen had said. "There's nothing you can say or do. This isn't a debate. It's a condolence call. Make sure you say how sorry you are for their loss. And make sure you listen."

So I do. During the next three hours I hear bits of the 18 years of the life of Daniel Liepold. He was a loving son and a "gentle and good boy" who eagerly helped the older people in the neighborhood with their yard work. Daniel was a hard-working student who managed to graduate from high school despite his severe dyslexia.

"I remember the day I took Daniel to the DMV [Department of Motor Vehicles] so he could take the test for his license," Mrs. Liepold says. "He was so determined to pass it. He worked so hard at everything he did, 'cause of his dyslexia," she says, looking down, as the tears roll down her face.

She wipes her eyes with a tissue and continues. Daniel had failed the test three times because it's hard for a dyslexic to pass a written test in the time allotted. On the next try, Mrs. Liepold asked the police officer if Daniel could take it verbally.

Of course, was the answer. On the first try, he passed, Mrs. Liepold recalls, beaming. The driving part was a breeze, she says.

"The instructor, Officer Patrolman, can you believe that name? Patrolman Patrolman. I'm not making it up. Anyway he told me he'd never been with such a safe driver."

But he had to be safe, because the dyslexia always put him at a disadvantage, Mrs. Liepold says. At the gas station one night, he had mistakenly charged $1.25 when the pump read $5.21, because that's what he saw. But his customers looked out for Daniel and paid the correct amount, gently pointing out the numbers on the pump.

One night Daniel closed the station and left without shutting the pumps off. He was so well liked in that neighborhood that the owner of the competing gas station across the street walked over and attached padlocks to the pumps so that Daniel would not get in trouble with his boss.

Daniel left the gas station to work at Circle K, the convenience store where he was murdered. He was careful, there, too, Mrs. Liepold says, and because of his dyslexia he was ever mindful that he had to put in extra hours to make sure the shelves were properly stocked and that reorders were filled out correctly.

The hours were long and the work was difficult, but Daniel stuck to it. Then he decided it was time to move on. He gave his heartbroken employer the requisite two weeks notice. He was three days from leaving his job at Circle K when Walter walked in during the early morning hours of February 11, 1981.

The two knew each other – they'd worked together months earlier during the day shift at the convenience store. That was just before Walter began working days and evenings at the San Antonio Country Club. Daniel considered Walter his friend; he'd installed a stereo in Walter's car for free and had sent him a birthday card.

Daniel had always been careful while he was driving, when he restocked the store shelves, and when he pumped gas. He was cautious while working the late night shift at the convenience store, but he wasn't afraid.

When he saw the familiar face of Walter Williams walk into the store that night, he had no reason to be scared even though Walter seemed to be high on something and his breath smelled like alcohol. Daniel knew Walter was in bad company; he walked in with a known troublemaker, Ted Edwards. They were both acting weird.

But Walter was his friend. He'd been at Daniel's house. Daniel didn't have to be cautious, because, after all, he was in the company of a friend. It seemed natural then for Daniel Liepold to turn his back while Walter and Ted Edwards were in the store. He never turned back around. The last sound he heard was the explosion of gunfire. His friend, Walter Williams, shot him in the back of the head. In cold blood.

"*Why?* Did you ever ask Walter Williams why he murdered my brother? Did you ever ask?" Darren says, shaking his right index finger at me, wiping his tears with his left hand. "You wanna know something? I not only lost my brother. I lost my best friend. Can you even understand how it feels? Huh? Can you? So why did he do it? Or did you ever even *ask?*"

By now, Daniel's father, Roger, is awash in grief. Every time he sees Darren cry, Roger weeps openly. He doesn't care that a stranger is in the room. It is too hard to hold in. I look at Mrs. Liepold; her eyes are red and puffy. I don't think she has many tears left. She's been crying for 18 years. Mrs. Liepold wants answers. From me. Tonight. And that's why I'd been let in the front door. Against her better judgment. And that of both of her husband and Darren.

"Yes, I did ask him. Several times. But I don't think you're going to like the answer. I'm not into excuses. But you asked. He was so messed up on drugs and alcohol, I don't think he knew what he was doing. His wife was gang-raped about five days earlier. Walter went on a drinking and drugging binge. It doesn't excuse what he did. The horrible crime he committed. That he killed your brother..."

"Yeah, drugs and alcohol? I've done drugs and gotten pretty damn drunk. And I don't blow people away. *That's* what you're telling me?"

"Darren, it doesn't excuse it. But you asked," I whisper. Darren returns a cold stare.

Mr. Liepold senses my discomfort and quickly jumps in: "Now, son. I've seen you drunk. And it's not pretty. You can be a pretty mean drunk. Mighty mean."

"But I don't go around killing people," Darren quickly replies.

"But you can be mean," his father says, quietly.

Mrs. Liepold puts up her hand, a signal to stop this kind of talk. This isn't about Darren. This is about Walter Williams. He is on trial here.

Mrs. Liepold tells me she was bothered by Walter's lack of remorse.

"I wasn't for the death penalty before Daniel was killed. But I am now. And one of the reasons is that Walter Williams never showed the slightest bit of remorse. He just sat in the courtroom with that look on his face. As if he was laughing. At all of us."

I tell her that I didn't know the Walter Williams of 1981. Only the Walter of 1985. And the Walter of 1994. But that I'm sure at his trial he was unrepentant and cocky. The Walter Williams I knew *was* remorseful, I tell her.

"We talked of it often. We talked of the pain he inflicted on your family. He asked for forgiveness."

"How do you know? How do you *know?*" Mrs. Liepold asks.

"Because I was there. I stood five feet away from him when he was executed. His last words were asking you and your family for forgiveness." By now I am shaking. "You didn't know that?"

I squeeze the tissue in my right hand hard and roll it in a ball. My fingernails dig deep into my palm. I am trying to focus. But the mere question brings me back to that horrible night. The memories are jarring. I am now in the Death House, tightly holding onto the rail in front of me – the metal bar that separates Walter and me.

Mrs. Liepold clears her throat. The noise brings me back. We look at each other and I see the color leave her weathered and wrinkled face. And then the tears fall.

"No one ever told us that. The [newspaper] reporter who called right after the execution never said anything like that. This is the first I've heard of it. Oh, God."

Silently, I am angry. At my fellow journalists. I know they'd heard Walter's last words. He did ask for forgiveness. Why didn't they write that down?

Why didn't the chaplain – a man of God – tell this heart broken family?

It shouldn't have surprised me that the Liepolds never knew Walter had changed. How could they have known? I didn't tell them.

"I was there, Mrs. Liepold. I heard it. So did Chaplain Pickett. I asked him to write it down. I'm sorry. I thought you knew. I visited Walter in the holding cell a few hours before he was executed. We talked. I asked if he wanted me to leave so he could pray on his prayer rug. He may have been into Islam – he had a new name and a new religion. But I told him that he was still Walter; I wasn't going to call him anything else. As to the Islam thing, I told him that we were both baptized Catholic. And he was still, in my eyes, Catholic. And in those last hours, he asked me to pray with him. And he asked you, your family, and God to forgive him. I'm sorry. I thought you knew that."

And then I begin to cry. Quietly. Openly.

The pain in that room was greater than I could ever have imagined. It had not lessened in the 18 years since Daniel's death.

It was a different kind of grief. It's the kind of pain you carry each and every day; the kind that temporarily numbs you. The kind that causes the tears to fall, in the middle of the day, out of the blue. The kind of pain that makes it hard, sometimes, just to breathe. Your heart races and your pulse quickens.

You never forget. You know you will live with this pain forever because you have to.

Mrs. Liepold is now a grandmother and she has grandchildren to feed, to bathe, to help with homework; to pick up from religious instruction classes at the Catholic Church in the neighborhood. She has to go on living for the others who are living.

I cry tonight because I realize that I have, in some way, prolonged the pain. That I have kept Walter's message asking for forgiveness from these good people for more than four years. I had assumed that they knew. I had assumed that it still didn't make a difference.

But it does.

Lea and Roger walk me out to the car and never even look at it. They are focused on me. I had arrived as the devil, Mrs. Liepold says, and I leave as an "angel" with a message, she whispers, as she takes her calloused hands and caresses my face. Then she kisses me on the cheek and wraps her arms around mine. She squeezes me tightly.

"Now, get home and back to your little kids. I'm sure they're missing their Mama. Make sure you give them a kiss. Lots of kisses. Because –" and suddenly she stops.

I know what she is about to say. You can never kiss them enough because one day they may be suddenly gone, victims of a brutal, senseless murder.

Her eyes fill with tears again as she opens my car door.

"God bless you, Joan. And thank you," she says, and she and Roger walk back into the fenced front yard. They turn around and wave goodbye.

A few weeks later, Mrs. Liepold sends me an email, thanking me again for the visit. And she repeats her earlier request – she'd like to speak to Sister Helen Prejean, and she'd like for me to arrange it.

I promise I'll try, but I don't have much luck. During the next few years, Sister Helen continues her journey witnessing executions and writing about it; she's the spiritual adviser and witness to the execution of Dobie Gillis Williams of Louisiana and Joseph Rodger O'Dell of Virginia, two men she believes are innocent. She's been forced to cut down on her speaking engagements to focus on writing *The Death of Innocents: An Eyewitness Account of Wrongful Executions.*

And a few years later, I move to Ireland.

But in October 2005, I'm back in San Antonio when Sister Helen and the Journey of Hope... from Violence to Healing comes to Texas. Murder victim family members lead the nonprofit group and they conduct speaking tours across the U.S. to address alternatives to the death penalty. Sister Helen is scheduled as the keynote speaker Monday evening at a local university – she'll be in San Antonio for less than 24 hours.

I write Mrs. Liepold to let her know that I haven't forgotten my promise; I've been able to set up a meeting with Sister Helen for Tuesday morning in a private room at a local bookstore. I ask Mrs. Liepold to call me to confirm. But she doesn't respond. I send her two emails, and still no reply. I know she got the letter 10 days ago, because she signed for it.

I could call her, but I don't want to intrude. I don't want to inflict any more pain on the Liepolds. The meeting is off.

On Tuesday morning, I'm at Holy Cross High School with a large group of high school students listening to the personal stories of members of the Journey of Hope: Juan Melendez, exonerated in 2002 from Florida's Death Row after 18 years; and Bill and Desiree Babbitt, the brother and daughter of Manny

Babbitt, a decorated Vietnam veteran who was executed in California in 1999.[3]

My cell phone buzzes. I leave the school library and quickly walk outside. Sister Helen is on the line; an employee from the bookstore just called. The Liepolds are there, waiting.

I run to my car, fumbling for the keys while stumbling over an apology.

"Don't you dare apologize," Sister Helen says abruptly, in her distinctive Louisiana accent. "This is a good thing. This is a really good thing. I'll see you there."

When I walk into the bookstore, I find Lea and Sister Helen sitting at a table, holding hands. Roger and Joyce, the family friend, are there too. Sister Helen is silent; she's listening to Mrs. Liepold tell a story about Daniel. And then another. And then the driver's license story. Sister Helen asks her a few questions; mostly, she just listens.

For a moment there is silence. And then Mrs. Liepold takes a deep breath. The tears begin to fall. She talks about the morning the Circle K managers came to the Liepold home at 3 a.m. to tell them about Daniel. She says she'll never forget the sound of the doorbell. She heard it continuously as friends came by to offer their condolences. The chime was a constant reminder "of the worst day of my life." Within weeks, the doorbell was removed.

A few months later the weather turned warm and the ice cream truck returned to the neighborhood; music blared from the truck's loudspeakers. When it played "Danny Boy", Mrs. Liepold stayed inside, paralyzed by grief. Finally, a neighbor told the ice cream man to stop playing that song. And why.

"I just can't understand why Walter would have murdered Daniel," Mrs. Liepold says, stopping for a moment to wipe her eyes. "I forgive him, Sister Helen. I do. But I'll never forget."

Sister Helen looks over at Roger who has been crying.

"Oh, Lea. No one is asking you to forget Daniel. He is your son. He is a part of you. And will always be. But you forgive him? Walter? Well, that's big. That's really big," Sister Helen says, softly.

A few minutes later, Mrs. Liepold congratulates Sister Helen on her speech last night. "I was there, you know. Joan sent me tickets. I wanted to hear what you had to say." But, she says, it was the large number of relatives of murder victims from the Journey of Hope that left a lasting impression.

"I couldn't believe that there were so many people just like me. And the woman whose child was murdered when she was seven [Marietta Jaeger-Lane]. She knows exactly how I feel. And she's forgiven him [the murderer]," Mrs. Liepold says. "There were so many [family members of murder victims] there last night. Like me."

———

Marietta Jaeger-Lane, a founding board member of Murder Victims' Families for Reconciliation and a cofounder of Journey of Hope, spoke that night at St. Mary's University.[4] She told the audience about Susie, who was kidnapped from a family camping trip in Montana in 1973. During the next year, the family had no information about Susie. Shortly before the one-year anniversary, Marietta was quoted in a Montana newspaper as saying she "would give anything for the chance to talk to the kidnapper myself." He called in the middle of the night, one year to the day that Susie disappeared, taunting the mother of five by asking: "So what do you want to talk to me about?"

They talked for an hour and the killer revealed enough details about himself so that he was arrested a short time later. Marietta pushed for a life term, instead of the death penalty.

During the year of Susie's disappearance, Marietta said she struggled to balance her rage against her need for forgiveness. She calls it the year she had "a wrestling match with God."

"God was patient and persistent, and eventually I gave God permission to change my heart," Marietta told the group. "I came to realize that to kill somebody in my little girl's name would be to violate and profane the goodness and sweetness and beauty of who Susie was."[5]

———

An hour and many tears later, Sister Helen leaves; Roger goes back to work.

I've kept my promise. Mrs. Liepold got her talk with "that nun." Now she says she wants to talk to me.

Once again, she wraps me in her arms and kisses me. She tells me she prays for me all the time. I start to cry. Soon, I am weeping.

Hugs and kisses. Prayers. And, 24 years later, forgiveness.

EPILOGUE

"**M**om, why are they going to kill him? Why do they have to kill him? Didn't he change?"

I was flipping through the television news channels – MSNBC, CNN, and the Fox Report – immersed in the pre-execution media frenzy as the state of California prepared to execute Stanley "Tookie" Williams, a convicted murderer, co-founder of the Crips gang, and author of nine children's books.

I was hoping to buy some time. I didn't know what to tell Lily, now 14. I kept looking at the TV, ignoring her. But teenagers are persistent. Unrelenting. "Hello? Mom, are you there? I said, why are they going to kill him?"

I looked up and began to stammer. "Hmm. I don't know. I really do not know."

Lily glared at the TV. Then, in a momentary flash of anger, she snarled: "I cannot believe this country still has the death penalty."

But that may soon change.

In March 2006, executions in California, Florida, Pennsylvania, Missouri and Maryland have been halted until the issue of whether executions by lethal injection are "cruel and unusual punishment" is decided. A "triple federal execution" scheduled in May 2006 has also been postponed.

In May 2006, a California federal judge will hear arguments concerning the constitutionality of the lethal injection procedure, after stopping a February 21 execution because prison officials could not find a medical doctor who would agree to monitor a new injection protocol. The judge's action, in effect, has imposed a temporary de facto moratorium in California, sparing the lives of 649 Death Row inmates. His ruling came just two months after the execution of Stanley "Tookie" Williams.

In February 2006, Florida Governor Jeb Bush promised not to sign any more death warrants until the case of a Florida inmate is decided, granting a temporary reprieve to the 388 inmates currently on Florida's Death Row. The Florida case will be argued in the U.S. Supreme Court on April 26, and a decision is not expected before mid-summer.

In January 2006, the State of New Jersey decided to suspend all executions until at least 2007 while it studies the fairness and expense of the death penalty. There is no death penalty in the states of New York and Kansas, after state supreme courts there ruled it was unconstitutional in 2004. There is no death penalty in 12 other states, plus the District of Columbia (Washington, D.C.)[1]

Texas – the state with the most active death chamber continues to stick to its execution schedule despite the stays in other states. But a new Texas law, as of June 2005, will allow jurors to impose an alternative sentence to death, Life Without Parole (LWOP). Death penalty opponents say LWOP will drastically reduce the number of death sentences in Texas, pointing to North Carolina, which cut its death sentences by 65 percent.[2]

In 2005, the U.S. Supreme Court abolished the death penalty in cases involving juveniles, citing the violation of several international treaties and "the overwhelming weight of international opinion against the juvenile death penalty." The court added: "The opinion of the world community, while not controlling our outcome, does provide respected and significant confirmation for our own conclusions."[3] In June 2002, the court ruled it was unconstitutional to execute the mentally retarded.[4]

Public support for the death penalty in America has declined in recent years – from 80 percent in 1994 to 64 percent in 2005, according to a recent Gallup poll.

The stay of execution in the case of Clarence Hill in Florida is responsible for stopping executions across most of the United States and has given anti-death penalty opponents another reason to be hopeful. But it was a close call for the 48-year-old Hill. He was already strapped to the gurney with IV lines running into his arms when a telephone call came from the U.S. Supreme court stopping it. The issue before the court is a procedural one: whether a lower court erred in denying Hill's claim that the method of lethal injection violated his civil rights.[5] All but one of the 38 states with the death penalty use lethal injection, a combination of three chemicals: sodium thiopental (for anesthesia), pancuronium bromide (to induce paralysis), and potassium choloride (to stop the heart).[6]

The Hill case has forced another "holiday" for the death penalty across most of America, albeit a short one, until the summer of 2006. Until then, the majority of the 35 inmates who had execution dates between January and June, have had their appointment in Death House postponed.

Some inmates will be spared, but not all. The latest winners of the "Death Row Lottery" can attribute their good luck to timing, geography, and a public increasingly uncomfortable with the death penalty.

Florida's Clarence Hill, sentenced to die for the 1982 murder of a police officer during a bank robbery, is lucky to be alive.[7] His 11th-hour appeal was heard by Anthony Kennedy, who, as a justice of the U.S. Supreme Court, oversees the Death Rows of Florida, Alabama, and Georgia. Justice Kennedy is the author of the majority opinion that abolished capital punishment for juveniles and the justice who acknowledged the anti-death-penalty influence of the European Union.[8]

Hill's case will be argued on April 26 and a decision is not expected until the end of the court's term in late June. While the

Supreme Court says it will not consider the constitutionality of the administration of lethal injection in the Hill case, the issue of the death penalty and how Americans put people to death, is being debated in the most influential court in the world – the court of public opinion.[9]

The Hill decision is expected to coincide with the commemoration of the 30th anniversary of *Gregg v. Georgia*, the 1976 Supreme Court ruling that brought capital punishment back to the U.S., four years after the court freed the "Furman 589." The summer of 2006 may be the time when Americans are forced to reevaluate capital punishment and determine if, as the Supreme Court ruled in *Furman*, a sentence of death is reserved for "the worst of the worst."

If Americans believe that only the "worst of the worst" are currently on Death Row, just because the post-Furman death penalty statutes mandated the use of "proceedural safeguards" to ensure that the death penalty not be used in a "wanton or freakish manner,"[10] then America has been sorely misled.

For the past eight years I have studied the cases of the 505 killers, 80 rapists and 4 armed robbers in the Class of '72. I have read the gruesome details of the crimes as well as information about the character and background of the criminals themselves. Prior to our meetings, I read everything I could about these former Death Row inmates. I probably knew too much, which may explain why I was afraid most of the time. But, like many people, I believed that the "Death Row Club" was a bit more exclusive – it was reserved for those who are incapable of rehabilitation and who we, as a society, are sure will kill again. In that context my fear seems both reasonable and healthy.

The same kinds of horrendous crimes that sent the members of the Class of '72 to Death Row back then are represented on Death Row today. And those men are now free.[11]

Statistically, the racial makeup of the killers in the Class of '72 is almost the same as the same group in 2006. In 1972,

47 percent of those who were on Death Row were white; today 45 percent of the Death Row population is white. In 1972, 51 percent of the Death Row population was black, versus just over 42 percent currently. There were only 0.02 percent non-black minorities in 1972 on Death Row; now there are 13 percent. Two percent of the current Death Row population are women, as compared to just two women on Death Row in 1972. There were 80 men on Death Row in 1972 sentenced to die for rape; there are no inmates currently on Death Row for the crime of rape without a murder.

The Death Rows of 1972 and 2006 are not made up of only the "worst of the worst". While there are the serial killers and the "kill for the thrill" murderers, there are also men and women who are capable of rehabilitation and who most probably will not kill again.

With the December 13, 2005, execution of Stanley "Tookie" Williams in California and the earlier executions of James Allridge and Karla Faye Tucker in Texas, the issue of rehabilitation has, once again, taken center stage. Many Americans believe the death penalty should be imposed in cases in which an inmate is incapable of rehabilitation and who is someone who, most likely, will kill again if released.

The best prediction of future dangerousness can be found in the 33 years of prison and parole records of the men in the Class of '72. The best evidence of rehabilitation can be found in the success of these former Death Row inmates.

I began my search for the Furman group because I had to find the answer to a disturbing question: If I had helped get Walter off Death Row and if he was eventually released from prison, would he have killed again?

The answer came from the 1972 graduates of Death Row.

There are many good arguments against the death penalty. I found 589.

POSTSCRIPT

Newsday's Bill Falk is now editor-in-chief of *The Week*, a magazine digest of the best reporting and writing from the U.S. and international press. Shortly after our meeting, psychic John Edward produced and hosted a nationally syndicated television show, *Crossing Over*. He is the author of several best-selling books, including *Crossing Over: The Stories Behind the Stories*.

Bobby Hill died of cancer on December 1, 2000, in Savannah at the age of 59. "Comfort to the Poor, Conscience for the Rich" was the headline in the December 10, 2000, issue of *The Savannah Morning News* describing Hill's life and death.

Lawrence "Bubba" Hayes was released from a New York state prison on June 7, 2005, after serving 10 months because he missed an appointment with his parole officer. Hayes, 54, a founding member of the Campaign to End the Death Penalty, lives in New York City. In November 2005, he was among the featured speakers in CEDP's "Voices from Death Row" tour.

Hayes' nephew and co-defendant, Cornelius Butler, has never been reincarcerated since his release from prison on August 7, 1995. Butler also managed to escape the World Trade Center on the morning of September 11, 2001 – he worked there as a cook.

Chuck Culhane returned to prison in May 2002, after 8 years on parole, for a substance abuse parole violation; he was given 12 months but a parole commissioner increased it to 36 months, which was appealed. Culhane left prison on June 26, 2003.

Two years later, Culhane checked into a drug rehab program where he was arrested, after again testing positive for cocaine. At a hearing in September 2005, Culhane was sentenced to 14 months; recently a parole commissioner reviewed his case and increased the term to 24 months. Despite two heart attacks and severe arthritis, Culhane is upbeat about life on the outside and on the prospects for a successful appeal.

On November 19, 2001, Culhane's best friend and co-defendant Gary McGivern died in the Wende penitentiary of cancer, after serving six years for possession of drugs – a violation of his parole. McGivern had just turned 57.

Calvin Sellars still lives in a small Texas town where he works with several attorneys on civil cases only.

Less than six months after Rusty Holland's application for clemency was denied, he and Vicki separated and then divorced. Vicki has remarried; her daughter Jeannie is now 23, married, and in the Army; the youngest, Karen, is on the high school dance team.

Rusty is back in prison – a federal penitentiary in South Carolina – on charges of "possession of a firearm by a convicted felon." He was arrested in North Carolina in September 2003 and is serving the federal and state sentences concurrently. He will be eligible for parole in 2011.

In Florida, Wilbert Lee has retired as corrections counselor from Miami-Dade County and spends much of his free time playing dominoes. His friend Freddie Lee Pitts is working, driving a shuttle bus from the Miami Airport to the Florida Keys; he and Betty are still married. Pitts is active in anti-death penalty work, serving on the board of the Innocence Project.

Gene Miller, author of *Invitation to a Lynching* and winner of the Pulitzer Prize that secured Pitts and Lee's freedom, died of lung cancer on June 17, 2005.

Monty Powell left the art gallery in Memphis and moved to

California and stayed only a year, deciding it was too expensive to live there. Now divorced, Powell moved to Minneapolis to be closer to his then teenage son. For the past six years he has worked for a medical supply firm.

Moreese Bickham's wife, Ernestine, died in December 2002. Moreese continues to live in Klamath Falls, Oregon with his daughter, Vivian, a few of his grandchildren, and several great-grandchildren and a great-great-grandchild. When he can sneak out of the house, Moreese goes fishing.

Wilbert Rideau, Bickham's friend on Louisiana's Death Row, was released from prison in January 2005 for time served, after jurors in his fourth murder trial found him guilty of the lesser offense of manslaughter. Called the "most rehabilitated prisoner in America" by *Life* magazine in 1993, Rideau was released from Angola after spending 44 years in prison. He is living in an undisclosed location and trying to earn money to pay the $127,000 bill he owes the state for the costs of his trial.

Leroy Johnson continues working as a landscaper in a small Southern town. No member of the Death Row Five has ever been reincarcerated.

Mike Turczi moved from Gary, Indiana, to a small town in Michigan where he is married and has a daughter. He still drives 18-wheelers.

Joseph Cerny of Washington died on September 30, 2003, just a week after he was released from prison.

Utah's Bennett Belwood died on May 5, 2005, at the age of 60.

Elmer Branch is still in a Texas prison, now serving the sentence for the rape conviction that first sent him to Death Row in 1967. He has glaucoma and is in poor health, but his outlook remains positive – he writes weekly letters and maintains his "piddling" privileges in the prison shop where he continues to build exquisite and custom-made shipping vessels. Branch maintains his innocence, a reason the parole board keeps rejecting his application for parole. He will be up for review again in 2008. Branch has been in prison for a total of 31 years.

Kenneth McDuff was executed by the State of Texas in 1998; six weeks before his execution, a confidential "informant' told authorities where to find the bodies of three of McDuff's victims: Colleen Reed, Regina Moore, and Brenda Thompson.

Marie Arrington of Florida, who was sentenced to death in 1968 for the brutal murder of her lawyer's secretary, escaped in 1969 and remained a fugitive for more than three years. Arrington, now 72, will die in prison.

Police say they believe Lester Eubanks returned to Mansfield, Ohio, in July 2001, after his mother died. Upon arriving at Reverend Eubanks' home, they were refused entry without a warrant, the source says. In Mrs. Eubanks' obituary, Lester was listed as a surviving son and a resident of Columbus. On January 18, 2004, after the *Akron Beacon Journal* published an embarrassing story on Eubanks' shopping trip escape on its front page, law enforcement officials issued both a state and federal warrant for his arrest. Now 62 years old, Eubanks is still on the lam.

William Henry Furman lives in anonymity in Georgia.

In 2006, Roger and Lea Liepold celebrated their 50th wedding anniversary.

Sister Helen Prejean is traveling in Europe and across the U.S. to talk about her new book, *The Death of Innocents: An Eyewitness Account of Wrongful Executions*, and continues to share her message of the need for reconciliation and abolition.

While I was living in Ireland, my mother, Sally, died unexpectedly before she had a chance to read *Back from the Dead*; the publication date and the anniversary of her death just happen to coincide. Even though she was supportive of my journey and believed in the possibility of redemption and rehabilitation, Sally believed in capital punishment. I'd like to think that if she had read *Back from the Dead*, Sally would have changed her mind.

NOTES

PROLOGUE

1. *Gregg v. Georgia*, 428 U.S. 153 (1976)
2. Facts and Figures on the Death Penalty, Amnesty International, Dec. 2005
3. Prisonersoverseas.com, "The Death Penalty," and Amnesty International
4. "North Carolina Carries Out Nation's 1,000th Execution" *Associated Press*, Dec. 2, 2005
5. Kenneth Mentor, *College Courses in Prison*, New Mexico State University, draft submission to be included in the *Encyclopedia of Corrections* (Editor, Mary Bosworth)

CHAPTER 1

1. *De La Rosa v. State*, 743 F2d 299 (5th Cir. 1984)
2. In their affidavits, the doctors wrote "there is insufficient evidence of symptomatology that would support a diagnosis of Antisocial Personality." (Exhibit 6 of Williams' Petition for Writ of Habeas Corpus.)
3. Affidavit of Dr. John Sparks, chief psychiatrist for Bexar County (San Antonio, Texas).
4. In "Fatal Defense," an award-winning series in *The National Law Journal* on the death penalty in the U.S., capital punishment in the South was described as "more like a flip of the coin," adding "Who will live and who will die is decided not just by the nature of the crime committed but equally by the skills of the defense lawyer appointed by the court. And in the nation's Death Belt, that lawyer is too often ill-trained, unprepared, and grossly underpaid." Marcia

Coyle, Fred Strasser, and Marianne Lavelle, *The National Law Journal*, June 11, 1990

5. Deborah Fins, *Death Row USA*, Death Row Population Figures, NAACP Legal Defense and Education Fund (Jan. 1, 2006); McKinnon, Jesse, *The Black Population in the United States: March 2002* U.S. Census Bureau, Current Population Reports, Series P20–541. Washington, D.C. (2003)

6. Amnesty International USA, *Killing with Prejudice: Race and the Death Penalty in the USA* (2004)

7. Sophy Burnham, *Book of Angels: Reflections on Angels Past and Present and True Stories of How They Touch Our Lives* (Ballantine Books: 1992). Co-counsel Robert Hirschhorn was not present at Walter's execution because he was still grieving over the recent death of his wife, jury consultant, Cathy "Cat" Bennett, who died at 42, after an eight-year battle with cancer.

8. "Execution Database," Death Penalty Information Center, Washington, D.C. (Feb. 15, 2006)

CHAPTER 2

1. The article "Is John Edward Communicating with the Dead?" was published in *Newsday* on Jan. 5, 1997. In it Falk wrote that because it was so difficult to believe that a 27-year-old guy in blue jeans could talk to the dead, he decided to bring in someone who would be a difficult read. Falk wrote: "The test I devise to resolve my lingering doubts is an obvious one. If Edward can do a successful reading for Joan Cheever, he's got to be the real item." After the reading "Cheever told *Newsday* 'I was certain 100 percent Walter came through.' " Bill Falk wrote: "As for me, I'm left a tiny fraction short of 100 percent convinced, perhaps only because I'm afflicted with the occupational hazard of not being completely sure of anything... But I am convinced that all the rational explanations have been eliminated. The dozen clients I've seen and interviewed are real people, not actors. Edward couldn't possibly uncover the very personal details he relates in readings through some furtive investigation. And even if he did depend on investigative research, then he would have certainly flopped when I brought him Joan Cheever, which he did not."

2. In "John Edward is the Oprah of the Other Side," *The New York Times Sunday Magazine*, July 29, 2001, Falk describes that evening, saying

that during the reading, Edward not only channeled Williams, but also nailed a number of unusual details, including mentioning a name "that sounds like 'Hirsch.' "

CHAPTER 3

1. Deborah Fins, *Death Row USA*, Death Row Population Figures, NAACP Legal Defense and Education Fund (Jan. 1, 2006)
2. While there are differences in earlier published reports as to the exact number of inmates who were on death rows across the U.S. as of June 29, 1972, the number used in *Back From The Dead* – 589 was compiled from a variety of sources: corrections officials, parole records, newspaper accounts, law journal articles, and books. The primary source of the data is "A National Study of the Furman-Commuted Inmates: Assessing the Threat to Society From Capital Offenders," and much appreciation goes to its authors James Marquart and Jonathan R. Sorensen of Sam Houston State University. Marquart and Sorenson's figure of 558 (in addition to the list of 31 inmates on Illinois' Death Row they said they were unable to obtain from Illinois corrections officials) is consistent with my number of 589. Marquart and Sorenson's 1989 study was reprinted in *The Death Penalty in America*, edited by Hugo A. Bedau (Oxford University Press: 1997), pp 162–175 (published in *Loyola of Los Angeles Law Review*, vol. 23, no. 1 Nov. 1989, pp 5–28). *See also* J. Marquart, S. Ekland-Olson, & J. Sorensen, *The Rope, The Chair, and The Needle: Capital Punishment in Texas, 1923–1990, 39* (University of Texas: 1994) and *Execution Data Sheet, May 14, 1971*, dubbed "The Lyons List." Source: Citizens Against Legalized Murder, Douglas H. Lyons, Chairman.
3. *Furman v. Georgia*, 408 U.S. 238 (1972)
4. Michael Meltsner, *Cruel and Unusual: The Supreme Court and Capital Punishment* (Random House Inc.: 1973) and Jack Greenberg, *Crusaders in the Courts: How a Dedicated Band of Lawyers Fought for the Civil Rights Revolution* (Basic Books: 1994).
5. Id. Interview with Michael Meltsner (Northeastern University School of Law), Anthony Amsterdam (New York University Law School), and Hugo A. Bedau (Tufts University). The NAACP joined several other organizations, including the International Labor Defense, the legal arm of the Communist Party, in creating The Scottsboro Defense Committee. the teens' convictions were reversed in the landmark case of *Powell v. Alabama* on the basis that the boys

lacked adequate trial counsel. *Powell v. Alabama,* 287 U.S. 45 (SCt. 1932). Eventually, after retrials and plea bargains, four of the teens were sentenced to prison terms ranging from 20 years to life imprisonment. Rape charges against the other four were dropped.

6. In 1967, Luis Monge was executed in Colorado's gas chamber after being convicted of murdering his wife and three of their children.

7. Interview with Michael Meltsner and *Cruel and Unusual.*

8. Amsterdam had a "dress rehearsal" just two weeks earlier when he argued the death penalty issue in a separate murder case before the California Supreme Court – the case of Robert Page Anderson, who was sentenced to die for the murder of a pawnshop employee during a robbery and the attempted murder of two police officers and another man. Interview with Anthony Amsterdam and *Cruel and Unusual.*

9. *Furman v. Georgia,* 408 U.S. 238 (1972)

10. By March 15, 2006, Texas set a national record – executing 360 of the 1,013 inmates who have been executed nationwide since the death penalty returned to the U.S in 1976. Death Penalty Information Center, Washington, D.C.

11. In the early 1980s, Hill was accused of using his law practice to obtain fees from "unsophisticated and trusting people" for services he did not provide. In October 1984, Hill was disbarred by a unanimous Georgia Supreme Court. Less than two years after we met, Hill would no longer be living in that boarding house; instead he moved to a cell in a federal penitentiary. On May 28, 1992, Hill was sentenced to serve one year in prison and to three years of supervised release after having been convicted of 34 counts of fraudulently obtaining $9,000 in federal job-training money intended for poor and displaced workers. Erik Tryggestad, "Comfort to the Poor, Conscience for the Rich," *The Savannah Morning News,* Dec. 10, 2000; Tom Barton, "Bobby Hill Climbed Peaks, Hit Valleys," *The Savannah Morning News* (Dec. 6, 2000); David Morrison, "Bobby Hill Decides to Come 'Out of Exile' in Surprise Bid for Lieutenant Governorship", June 16, 1986.

12. Interview with Bobby Hill, October 1990, Savannah, Georgia.

13. One of Hill's clients, Carl Junior Isaacs, an escapee from a Maryland prison who was convicted of murdering six members of the Alday family, has been on Georgia's Death Row since 1973. *Isaacs v. Georgia,* 226 S.E. 2d 922 (Ga. 1976). In April 2003, Isaacs lost his appeal before the U.S. Supreme Court. He was executed on May 6, 2003. Mark Passwaters, "Genesis of a Killer" *The Albany Herald,* May 5, 2003.

14. *Williams v. State,* 668 S.W.2d 692 (Tex. Crim. App. 1983).

15. Id.
16. Death Penalty Information Center, Washington, D.C. (January 2005), "Execution Database" 1976–1994.
17. After Furman, the Texas Legislature rewrote its flawed death penalty law; the constitutionality of the new death penalty law was tested in *Jurek v. Texas*, 428 U.S. 262 (1976), and approved by the U.S. Supreme Court.
18. *People v. Aikens*, 450 P.2d 258 (Cal. Sup. Ct. 1969), *Aikens v. California*, 406 U.S. 813 (1972)
19. Id.
20. J. Marquart, S. Ekland-Olson, & J. Sorensen, *The Rope, The Chair, and The Needle: Capital Punishment in Texas, 1923–1990*, 39 (University of Texas: 1994)
21. "Burger was upset by the California decision. It deprived the Court of the most brutal of the five cases that had been argued: a cold-blooded rape-murder. If there was an argument for capital punishment, it was in such a case," referring to *Aikens v. California*. Bob Woodward and Scott Armstrong, *The Brethren: Inside the Supreme Court* (Simon & Schuster: 1979) p. 250–251. Four cases – Furman, Branch, Jackson and Aikens – were argued that day. See Meltsner, *Cruel and Unusual*, p. 267.
22. For an excellent look into the inner workings of the Court during the Furman era, read Bob Woodward and Scott Armstrong's *The Brethren: Inside The Supreme Court* (Simon & Schuster: 1979) and Edward Lazarus' *Closed Chambers: The First Eyewitness Account of the Epic Struggles Inside the Supreme Court* (Random House: 1998).
23. *Furman v. Georgia*, 408 U.S. 238 (1972)
24. The decision that upheld slavery in the U.S., *Dred Scott v. Sandford*, 60 US 393 (1857), was 109,163 words; more recently, a federal campaign finance reform case, *McConnell v. Federal Election Commission*, was 89,694 words. 540 U.S. 93 (2003)
25. Meltsner, *Cruel and Unusual* at p. 289.
26. All five justices agreed that the Eighth Amendment prohibited capital punishment when it was imposed so rarely that it could not serve any valid social purpose – either deterrence or retribution.
27. *The New Orleans' Times-Picayune*, June 30, 1972
28. *The New York Daily News* urged state legislators to readopt the death penalty with all of its "old time" severity in order to see "what the Supreme Court does about that." In his *New York Times* column, Tom Wicker predicted "a flurry of state laws requiring, for instance, mandatory death sentences' for vicious rapes, the killing of police officers, or prison guards.

29. *Cruel and Unusual*, p. 290.
30. The legislators and the state supreme courts had, with their new death penalty statutes, alleviated most of the concerns of two members of the Furman majority – Justice White and Justice Stewart. Justices Marshall and Brennan continued to oppose the death penalty in all cases. At the time *Gregg* was argued, Justice Douglas died and was replaced by Justice John Paul Stevens who joined the majority in upholding the new statutes. The changes in the law included banning the death penalty in cases of rape or robbery in which the victim did not die. And, most importantly, another crime in addition to the murder had to take place. That is, the murder had to occur at the same time a serious felony was being committed – such as rape, robbery, kidnapping, or arson. And at his trial, the defendant had to have a separate sentencing procedure to determine punishment. There had to be a finding of aggravating factors before a jury could impose death. The aggravating factors could arise just from the heinous nature of the murder, or the defendant could have had a prior and violent criminal history. The aggravating factor evidence could be supplied by a psychiatrist who would testify that the defendant posed a serious threat to society if he got out, and thus execution was the only way to protect society. If those factors were met, the court reasoned, the imposition of death, in and of itself, was not a cruel and unusual punishment.
31. The constitutionality of the death penalty statutes of five states were before the court – North Carolina, Georgia, Florida, Louisiana, and Texas. On July 2, 1976, the Supreme Court took a further step in bringing back capital punishment to the United States in the decision of *Gregg v. Georgia*, 428 U.S. 153 (1976).
32. *Brooks v. Estelle*, 697 F2d 586 (5th Cir. 1982)

CHAPTER 4

1. I call Professor Amsterdam after hearing that there is a list of the names of all those who had been on Death Row in 1972 when he argued the case before the high court. A list of names will save a lot of time – as I later find out, about two years' worth. The list Amsterdam had referred to was called "The Lyons List" named after NAACP Legal Defense Intern Doug Lyons who put it together. The names of every inmate on Death Row, identified by each state's

Death Row, is on that list. When I called Lyons, a practicing attorney in California, he too was unable to locate it.

2. In *Closed Chambers*, Author Edward Lazarus writes that the most famous Amsterdam tale involves a case he argued before the District of Columbia Circuit Court of Appeals as a prosecutor. When Amsterdam answered a question from the bench by citing from memory the case, complete with volume number and the page on which it could be found, the judge called for the book but was unable to find the case on the page Amsterdam said it was on. Upon being upbraided for his incorrect citation, Amsterdam immediately responded: "Your Honor, your volume must be misbound." It was. See Notes *"Sand in the Machine,"* p. 342, footnote 11 from *Closed Chambers: The First Eyewitness Account of the Epic Struggles Inside the Supreme Court*, (Random House: 1998).

3. In Texas, the *The Dallas Morning News* reported that a death penalty case costs about $2.3 million more than a noncapital murder trial. C. Hoppe, "Executions Cost Texas Millions," *The Dallas Morning News*, March 8, 1992. *The Wall Street Journal* reported that taxpayers in Jasper County, Texas ran up a huge bill after the capital murder conviction of three men accused of killing James Byrd Jr. who was dragged to death in 1998. The cost – $1.02 million to date, with other expenses expected – has strained the county's $10 million annual budget, forcing a 6.7 percent increase in property taxes over two years to pay for the trial. Russell Gold, "Counties Struggle With High Cost of Prosecuting Death-Penalty Cases; Result Is Often Higher Taxes, Less Spending on Services; 'Like Lightning Striking'." *The Wall Street Journal*, Jan. 9, 2002.

4. In June 2005, Texas passed a "Life Without Parole" law after decades of rejecting the law that would give juries a third option in death penalty cases. New Mexico is the only state in the U.S. without a LWOP option. Unfortunately, Professor Wright never saw Texas' LWOP law. On July 7, 2000, the legendary "King of Con Law" died at the age of 72. He'd been teaching at the University of Texas Law school since 1955.

5. Death Penalty Information Center, Washington, D.C. (January 2005), "Execution Database," Executions in 1999.

6. My co-worker Ed Frost left the *The National Law Journal* in 1996 for a new career as a private investigator at New York City-based The Mintz Group.

7. Michael T. Kaufman, "Queens Grocer, 65, Chases 2 Robbers, Kills One of Them," *The New York Times*, Aug. 26, 1971.

8. *People v. Butler and Hayes*, 320 N.E. 2d 870 (NY Ct. App. 1974)

9. *The New York Times*, May 13, 1972, p. A1.
10. Corky Siemaszko, "Last Man Executed in New York in 1963," *The New York Daily News*, June 7, 1998.
11. The murder and death sentence of Darrell Harris was reversed July 9, 2002 by the New York Court of Appeals on the grounds that Harris was tried at a time when the death penalty statute still contained plea-bargaining provisions that later were held to be unconstitutional by the Court of Appeals in another case, *Hynes v. Tomei*.
12. "Parole Official Guilty of Perjury," *The New York Daily News*, Aug. 4, 1999.
13. There was no response to a written request for an interview.
14. A year later, McSherry, the parole board commissioner responsible for sending Lawrence Hayes back to prison, was also behind bars, convicted of perjury and obstruction of justice charges arising out of an investigation into allegations that Governor Pataki's campaign aides promised campaign contributors early paroles for their relatives in return for the contributions. In November 1999, McSherry was sentenced to two years in prison.

CHAPTER 5

1. Patrick A. Langan and David J. Levin, "Recidivism of Prisoners Released in 1994," Bureau of Justice Statistics, Department of Justice, June 2002. Within three years from release, the recidivism rate was 67.5 percent. Released prisoners with the highest rearrest rates were robbers (70.2 percent), burglars (74 percent), and those in prison for possessing or selling stolen property (77.4 percent). The lowest rearrest rates were those in prison for murder (40.7 percent) and rape (46 percent).
2. The dark-brown wooden cabin was built in 1936 shortly after the church was founded by activists involved in the Sacco-Vanzetti murder trial of 1921 in Massachusetts, one of the most sensational trials in U.S. history. Despite worldwide protests concerning the defendants' innocence and the confession of another man to the crime, both Sacco and Vanzetti, Italian immigrants, were executed by electrocution on Aug. 23, 1927.
3. Polls did then show that support for the death penalty was rising, but more recently – again according to polls – support for it has fallen. An October 2005 Gallup poll shows that 64 percent of

Americans are in favor of the death penalty, much lower than the 80 percent in favor during the heyday of executions in the 1980s and 1990s. In 1966, the percentage of Americans in favor of capital punishment was at its lowest at 42 percent.

4. *State of New York v. Charles Culhane and Gerald McGivern*, 305 N.E. 2d 469 (NY Court of Appeals 1973).

5. Craig Wolff, "The Murderer of a Sheriff Wins Parole," *The New York Times*, March 16, 1989.

6. *People v. Culhane*, 380 N.E. 2d 315 (NY Court of Appeals 1978).

7. Florida spent an average of $3.2 million per execution from 1973 to 1988. During that time period, Florida spent an estimated $57 million on the death penalty to achieve 18 executions; *The Miami Herald*, July 10, 1988. See also *Costs of the Death Penalty and Related Issues*, Testimony of Richard C. Dieter, Jan. 25, 2005, New York State Assembly. Death Penalty Information Center, Washington, D.C.

8. When Cole made that statement, public support for the death penalty was on the rise. In a June 1997 *Newsweek* poll, conducted during the Tim McVeigh–Oklahoma City bombing trial, more than 84 percent of Americans were in favor of the death penalty. Recently, after the execution in California of Stanley "Tookie" Williams, support has declined. See also note 3 above.

9. On April 1, 1999, the New York Parole Board denied McGivern's bid for freedom, citing his "involvement in a felony murder wherein a deputy sheriff was murdered during an escape attempt." In its denial, the board said: "The panel also told McGivern that he needed to attend further programs in the 'area of substance abuse' " – even though the inmate successfully completed the only such course offered at Wende years earlier. "In view of your violent and serious history interwoven with substance abuse, this panel must determine that you still present a threat to community safety and welfare," the panel wrote in closing.

10. On Jan. 5, 2000, the State of New York agreed to settle the civil suit the inmates brought against prison officials for $8 million. Blyden was one of the plaintiffs in the suit. Herb Blyden died Sept. 21, 1997 at the Kresge Hospice in Cheektowaga, N.Y. where he'd been a resident for the past eight months. In his obituary, *The New York Times* called Blyden "a jail-hardened, prison-educated, civil rights activist who gave an eloquent voice to 1,200 beleaguered inmates as their chief negotiator during the 1971 Attica prison uprising." He became "an impassioned advocate for prison reform, campaigned for feminism and equal rights for gay people, and seconded Ramsey Clark's nomination for the United States Senate

nomination at the 1974 New York State Democratic Convention." The 220-pound six-footer "read Schopenhauer, Santayana, and Hermann Hesse, not to mention all the works of B.F. Skinner and enough legal texts to make him a recognized jailhouse lawyer long before Attica helped make him a legend."

11. Neely Tucker, "Study Warns of Rising Tide of Released Inmates," *The Washington Post*, May 21, 2003.

12. From Culhane's poem "Last Christmas For Death Row."

13. Janine Pommy Vega, ed. *Candles Burn in Memory Town: Poems From Both Sides of the Wall* (Segue Books: 1988) and Bell Gale Chevigny, ed. *Doing Time: 25 Years of Prison Writing* (Arcade Publishing: 1999).

14. "The Story of the Capeman," www.wbr.com.

15. "Daughter's Killing Led Dad to Oppose Capital Punishment," *The Arizona Daily Star*, Feb. 27, 2000.

16. "A Voice Against the Death Penalty" *The Philadelphia Inquirer*, Oct 1, 1999.

CHAPTER 6

1. Joseph Johnson was the last offender to be executed by electrocution on July 30, 1964. Death Row Facts, Texas Department of Criminal Justice, see http://www.tdcj.state.tx.us/stat/drowfacts.htm.

2. Laura Buchanan, "Texas History 101" *Texas Monthly*, May 2003.

3. The story was told to the author by her grandfather, Hance W. McKinney, who died in 1985.

4. Brian Wice, "Fall From Grace" p. 36, *Houston Metropolitan*, July 1991.

5. *Sellars v. State*, 400 S.W. 2d 559 (Tex. Crim. App. 1965) and *Ex Parte Young*, 397 S.W. 2d 74 (Tex. Ct. Crim. App. 1969).

6. *Hoover v. State*, 390 S.W. 2d 758 (Tex. Ct. Crim. App. 1969).

7. "Fall From Grace,' *Houston Metropolitan*, July 1991 at p. 36.

8. Tom Moran, "Death Row Graduate" *The Houston Chronicle*, July 20, 1980 and "Conviction Ruled Illegal after 14 Years in Prison," *The Fort Worth Star Telegram*, May 6, 1978. Calvin Sellars is one of six Texans on a list of 343 inmates who two professors – Hugo Adam Bedau of Tufts University and Michael L. Radelet of the University of Florida – say in a 1985 study have been wrongfully convicted of capital offenses in the United States since 1900. Bedau, Radelet, and Constance E. Putnam, *In Spite of Innocence: Erroneous Convictions in Capital Cases* (Northeastern University Press: 1992). See also

Tom Moran, "Not Guilty: 6 Texans put on list of 343 wrongfully convicted in U.S." *The Houston Chronicle*, Nov. 14, 1985.

9. *Sellars v. Estelle*, 536 F2d 1104 (5th Cir. 1976).

10. Although they are brothers, Wesley chose to spell his name differently from Calvin – as Wesley Sellers rather than Sellars. *Sellers v. State*, 492 S.W. 2d 265 (Tex. Ct. Crim. App. 1973).

11. *Sellars v. Estelle*, 450 F. Supp. 1262 (S.D. Tex. 1978) and Zarko Franks, "Sellars Held Illegally 14 Years, Judge Rules," *The Houston Chronicle*, May 5, 1978.

12. Id.

13. *Sellars v. Estelle*, 450 F. Supp. 1245 S.D. (Texas 1977) and Zarko Franks, "Death Row to Freedom's Brink on 'Jailhouse Law'," *The Houston Chronicle*, March 19, 1978.

14. "Former Death Row Prisoner in Schepps Case Wins Freedom," *The Dallas Times Herald*, May 6, 1978 p. 22A.

15. Id. On April 11, 1978, the 5th Circuit ordered the state of Texas either to retry Sellars or dismiss the charges. *Sellars v. Estelle*, 571 F2d 1314 (5th Cir. 1978).

16. The court ruled that Sellers was denied his right to due process because police reports allegedly favorable to him were withheld during his trial. *Sellers v. Estelle*, 591 F2d 1208 (5th Cir. 1978).

17. "California Kid killed in Arizona after long crime record here." *The Houston Chronicle*. Nov. 25, 1986, p. 10.

CHAPTER 7

1. Not its real name.

2. Their names have been changed.

3. *State v. Holland*, 201 S.E.2d 118 (S.C. 1973).

4. David Plotz, "Busted Flush" *Harper's Magazine*, Aug. 1999. A year after my visit to Town Bingo, the incumbent governor, conservative Christian Republican David Beasley, an ardent foe of gambling, was defeated for governor. The new governor, former Democratic state legislator Jim Hodges, was also opposed to video gambling but was not as vocal. Once in office, however, Hodges imposed several restrictions including requiring the poker operators to pay $130 million in taxes. He also imposed a moratorium on casinos and made sure that felons were barred from owning video-poker machines.

5. Their names have been changed.

6. Barry Mayson, *Fallen Angel: From Hell's Angel to Heaven's Saint* (Doubleday 1982).

CHAPTER 8

1. For an in-depth look into the lives of Pitts and Lee and the crime that sent two innocent men to Florida's Death Row, read Gene Miller's *Invitation To A Lynching* (Doubleday: 1975), p. 83.
2. Id.
3. *State v. Lee*, 141 So.2d 257 (Fla. 1963).
4. Interview with Freddie Lee Pitts. See also *Invitation To A Lynching*.
5. Gene Miller, 76, died on June 17, 2005. An editor and reporter at *The Miami Herald* for 48 years, Miller won two Pulitzer prizes for his reporting that spared the lives of four innocent inmates on Death Row. In addition to Pitts and Lee, Miller's reporting freed Joe Shea and Mary Katherine Hampton in 1967. Upon hearing of Miller's death, Wilbert Lee described him as "family." Lee said he didn't know if he could attend Miller's funeral because "I'm not sure my heart can take it." He added: "I think about all those nights and weekends, over all those years, Gene spent working on my case when he could have been home with his wife and children. He was a very great person. He believed in justice and he was a fighter for justice." Jim DeFede, "Journalism will miss "Fighter for Justice" Miller," *The Miami Herald*, June 21, 2005; Martin Merzer, "Gene Miller. Newsman, Champion." *The Miami Herald*, June 18, 2005.
6. Karen Branch and Tom Fiedler, "Nightmare Ends for Two Wrongly Accused," *The Miami Herald*, May 1, 1998, page 1A.
7. Charles Lee was executed on July 18, 1963. Source: Execution List: 1924–1964, Florida Department of Corrections.
8. Death Penalty Information Center, Washington, D.C. Cases of Innocence: 1973 to present (March 1, 2006).
9. Adam Liptak, "Fewer Death Sentences Being Imposed in U.S." *The New York Times*, Sept. 15, 2004, citing a 2004 study by the Death Penalty Information Center in Washington, D.C. And see DPIC, Cases of Innocence: Exonerations by Race (Nov. 18, 2005).
10. Miller, *Invitation to a Lynching*.
11. Sydney P. Freedberg, "Freed From Death Row," *The St. Petersburg Times*, July 4, 1999.
12. Both men were executed on the same day – May 12, 1964. Blake went first. "Execution List," Florida Department of Corrections. *Blake v. State*, 156 So. 2d 511 (Fla. 1963). They were the last men to be executed in Florida until the state resumed executions in 1979. On May 25, 1979, John Spenkelink, 30, was the first to be executed under Florida's new death penalty law.

13. " 'Not Mad' Says Slayer Just Before Death Chair," *The Florida Times Union*, May 13, 1964 p. 25.

14. *Dawson v. State*, 139 So. 2d 408 (Fla. 1962).

15. Studies strongly suggest that Dawson was innocent. See *In Spite of Innocence: Erroneous Convictions in Capital Cases*, by Michael Radelet, Hugo Adam Bedau, and Constance E. Putnam (Northeastern University Press: 1992).

16. Miller, *Invitation to a Lynching*.

17. Richard Wallace, "Court: Pardoned Felon Shouldn't Have Lost Job," *The Miami Herald*, Dec. 24, 1987 p. 1D.

18. The Florida Senate was prepared to award each man $1.5 million but House Speaker Dan Webster sent word: $500,000 or nothing. "Pitts and Lee Railroaded Again" in Viewpoints, *The Miami Herald*, April 30, 1998.

19. Karen Branch and Tom Fiedler, "Nightmare Ends for Two Wrongly Accused," *The Miami Herald*, May 1, 1998, p. 1A. See also "Pitts and Lee: It's Finally Over," *The Miami Herald*, July 14, 1998 p. 11A.

20. "Attendees Assail Capital Punishment: Former Death Row Inmates Honored at NU Conference," *The Chicago Tribune*, Nov. 14, 1998, p. 4.

21. Death Penalty Information Center, Washington D.C.

22. Don Terry, "Survivors Make the Case Against Death Row," *The New York Times*, Nov. 16, 1998.

23. On Jan. 12, 2006, the state of New Jersey imposed a moratorium on executions, suspending capital punishment while a study commission examines the fairness and expense of the state's death penalty law. The moratorium will remain in effect until Jan. 15, 2007. In 2004, the death penalty laws in New York and Kansas were determined to be unconstitutional and have not been remedied. But in Dec. 2005, New York Governor George Pataki called a special session to pass legislation permitting the death penalty for those convicted of murdering a police officer. "Pataki Wants Death Penalty for Killers of Police," *The New York Times*, Dec. 19, 2005.

CHAPTER 9

1. James Marquart and Jonathan R. Sorensen, "A National Study of the Furman-Commuted Inmates: Assessing the Threat to Society From Capital Offenders," reprinted in *The Death Penalty in America*, edited by Hugo Bedau (Oxford University Press: 1997) p. 173.

2. Viva LeRoy Nash is 90 and on Arizona's Death Row. Nash was convicted, at age 67, of murder of a Phoenix coin store clerk during a robbery in 1982. *State v. Nash*, 694 P2d 222 (1985); Florida Department of Corrections, "Active Death Row Population Information," March 8, 2006.

3. Kevin Sack, "After 37 Years in Prison, Inmate Tastes Freedom," *The New York Times*, Jan. 11, 1996.

4. David Isay with Wilbert Rideau and Ron Wikberg, "Tossing Away the Keys," *National Public Radio: Weekend All Things Considered*, April 29, 1990.

5. Sack, "After 37 Years in Prison, Inmate Tastes Freedom."

6. At the time of the murders, Ernestine and Moreese were separated.

7. "Active Hate Groups in the U.S. in 2004," The Southern Poverty Law Center's Intelligence Project.

8. *State v. Bickham*, 121 So. 2d 207 (La. 1960).

9. Sack, "After 37 Years in Prison, Inmate Tastes Freedom."

10. Bickham did spend two nights in jail for drunk driving.

11. Wilbert Rideau and Ron Wikberg, *Life Sentences: Rage and Survival Behind Bars* (Times Books: 1992).

12. Wilbert Rideau was released from prison on Jan. 15, 2005, after his fourth trial on charges that he murdered bank teller Julia Ferguson. He has never denied his guilt but said it was not a premeditated act and that he panicked. An 8th-grade drop out, Rideau was convicted of murder in 1961 and spent 11 years on Death Row at Angola. A jury found Rideau guilty of manslaughter and he was released because he had already served more than the maximum sentence for that crime – more than 44 years. Rideau had been the editor-in-chief of the prison newspaper, the *Angolite*, since 1975 and has been the recipient of numerous national writing awards including the American Bar Association's Silver Gavel Award, the George Polk award, the Robert F. Kennedy Journalism Award, and the Thurgood Marshall Award. In 1993, *Life* Magazine called him the "Most Rehabilitated Prisoner in America." Rideau was co-director of *The Farm: Angola, USA*, which was nominated for an Academy award for best full-length documentary. *The Farm* won the Sundance Grand Jury Prize in Documentary in 1999. In an interview with the Associated Press, Rideau described his freedom as waking up "in heaven every morning." "Freed Prison Journalist 'Wakes Up in Heaven Every Morning'," *Associated Press*, Jan. 11, 2006.

13. Sack, "After 37 Years in Prison, Inmate Tastes Freedom."

14. *Cripps v. State*, 259 La. 403 (La. Sup. Ct. 1971).

15. Rideau and Wikberg, *Life Sentences.*
16. David Isay and Harvey Wang, *Holding On: Dreamers, Visionaries, Eccentrics, and other American Heroes* (WW Norton: 1996).
17. Id.
18. Sack, "After 37 Years in Prison, Inmate Tastes Freedom."

CHAPTER 10

1. Not her real name.
2. Turczi's friends, Sunny Hudkins and George Bobis, accompanied Turczi to the murder scene. At trial, Bobis testified against Turczi and received immunity and Hudkins was acquitted of the charges against him in a separate capital murder trial.
3. *Turczi v. State,* 301 N.E. 2d 752 (Ind. Sup. Ct. 1973).
4. Not his real name.
5. Leroy was with a relative the night of the murder.
6. *State v. Martineau,* 196 A 2D.54 (NH Sup. Ct. 1963).
7. Complaint of Violation of Parole, State of New Hampshire, signed by Parole Officer Robert A. Johnson. Martineau's parole was revoked several times from 1973 through 1982, first for being charged with attempted burglary, for which he served an 11-month term. Once released, Martineau's parole was revoked three times from 1973 to 1982 for violations that included: "failure to abstain from intoxicating liquors," "failure to conduct himself as a good citizen" by associating with three men who had felony convictions, and "failure to submit payroll stubs."
8. Martineau is back in prison, this time for a federal offense of possession and distribution of heroin and cocaine in Rhode Island and Massachusetts. *US. v. Hyson et al,* 721 F2d 856 (1st U.S. Cir. Court of App. 1996).
9. "No Joy In Canon City," *The Denver Post,* June 29, 1972, p. B4.
10. *Manier v. Colorado,* 518 P2d 811 (1974).
11. *Cerny v. State,* 480 P2d 199 (Wash. Supreme Court 1971).
12. *State v. Belwood,* 494 P2d 519 (1972).
13. L. Kay Gillespie, *The Unforgiven: Utah's Executed Men* (Signature Books 1991).
14. On Jan. 17, 1977, Gary Gilmore was taken from his cell on Death Row to a vacant cannery on the grounds of the Utah State Prison, tied to a chair, and blindfolded. Moments later he was executed by a firing squad. Like Belwood, Gary Gilmore had a death

wish. But Gilmore was successful. Just three months after the 36-year-old Gilmore, a career criminal, was released from prison in April 1976, where he had been serving time for an assault conviction, he shot and killed a gas station attendant during a robbery attempt and then repeated the crime the next night when he killed a 25-year-old motel manager. With a new death penalty statute on the books, Gilmore was tried, convicted, and sentenced to death in October 1976. In November, he received a stay of execution by the Utah Supreme Court so that he had time to appeal his conviction. But Gilmore wanted to die. He fired his own lawyers and those from the American Civil Liberties Union and the NAACP Legal Defense Fund, including *Furman* appellate lawyer Anthony Amsterdam. Within days, Gilmore's stay of execution was lifted. Norman Mailer, *The Executioner's Song* (Warner Books: 1980).

CHAPTER 11

1. Not her real name.
2. *The Wichita Falls Times-Record News*, Feb. 11, 1997.
3. The "Allen Charge" gets its name from a U.S. Supreme Court decision in 1896, *Allen v. United States*, 164 U.S. 492, 501–02; the language in the charge is direct and intended to encourage jurors to reach a unanimous verdict.
4. Wichita Falls CVB "Historical and Cultural," www.wichitafalls.org (copyright 1995)
5. The Chihuahuan Desert is the largest in North America and covers more than 200,000 square miles. In the U.S., it extends into parts of New Mexico, Texas and Arizona. In winter, temperatures are cool and in the summer, it is extremely hot. "The Chihuahuan Desert," from www.DesertUSA.com.
6. Laura Buchanan, "Texas History 101" *Texas Monthly*, May 2003.
7. Susan Blaustein, "Witness to Another Execution: In Texas, Death Walks An Assembly Line," *Harper's Magazine*, May 1994.
8. *Branch v. State*, 447 S.W. 2d 932 (Tex. Cr. App. 1969).
9. Id.
10. Branch had been found to be a "borderline mental deficient and well below the average IQ of Texas prison inmates... He had a 'dull intelligence' and was in the lower fourth percentile of his class." From the concurring opinion of Justice William O. Douglas in *Furman v. Georgia*, 408 U.S. 238 at p. 251 (1972).

11. Brief of the Respondent The State of Texas, *Elmer Branch v. State of Texas*, No. 69–5031, "Statement of Case" p. 1.
12. A "no lo" plea means one will not plead either guilt or innocence, but in criminal law it has the effect of entering a guilty plea.
13. Nancy Hess, Ombudsman, FDCJ-Parole Division and Letter From Elmer Branch, Aug. 5, 1999.

CHAPTER 12

1. Gary Cartwright, "Free to Kill," *Texas Monthly*, August 1992
2. Bob Stewart, *No Remorse* (Pinnacle Books: 1996) and Gary M. Lavergne, *Bad Boy From Rosebud: The Murderous Life of Kenneth Allen McDuff* (University of North Texas Press: 1999).
3. Bill Kurtis, A&E Network, American Justice series *Free to Murder Again: The Kenneth McDuff Case* and *The Prosecutors* on the Discovery Channel.
4. Mike Cochran, "Victims' Families, Authorities Fear Killer Will Take Secrets to Grave," *The Dallas Morning News*, Nov. 29, 1996 and Tommy Witherspoon, "Family of Slain Waco Clerk Awarded $4.5 Million Settlement," *The Austin American Statesmen*, Oct. 3, 1992.
5. *Bad Boy From Rosebud*, p. 154.
6. In November 1998, seven Death Row inmates attempted an escape from the Ellis Unit, near Huntsville. One of them, Martin Gurule, was successful, becoming the first person to escape Death Row in Texas in 64 years. Gurule drowned shortly after the breakout, but it took a week before his body was discovered. In June 1999, the Department of Corrections began transferring all Death Row inmates from the Ellis Unit to the new Death Row at the Terrell Unit, in Livingston. "Inmates Are Moved," *The Houston Chronicle*, March 4, 2000. See also Michael Graczyk "Autopsy shows death row inmate drowned," *Associated Press*, Dec. 5, 1998
7. Gary Cartwright, "Free to Kill," *Texas Monthly*, August 1992
8. "Kenneth Allen McDuff: Trail of Death," *The Dallas Morning News*, Nov. 16, 1998
9. Id.
10. Lavergne, *Bad Boy From Rosebud*. Gary Lavergne also wrote *A Sniper in the Tower: The Story of Charles Whitman* (University of North Texas Press: 1997). On Aug. 1, 1966, Charles Joseph Whitman climbed to the top of the University of Texas Tower and committed what was

then the largest simultaneous mass murder in U.S. history. Whitman gunned down 45 people inside and around the Tower before he was killed by two Austin police officers. The night before, Whitman murdered his wife and mother, bringing the total to 16 people dead with 31 wounded.

11. In 1991, the Texas Legislature passed a law requiring capital murderers to serve a minimum of 35 years before being considered for parole; two years later the legislature raised the minimum period to 40 years. For a history of the Texas parole process, read "Board of Pardons and Paroles," *The Handbook of Texas Online* (A joint project of the General Library at the University of Texas at Austin and the Texas State Historical Association, 2001). See also Jim Phillips, "Inquiries Trace Parole Process in McDuff Case," *The Austin American Statesman*, July 19, 1992.

12. California's Robert Massie was sentenced to death for the 1965 murder of Mildred Weiss and the attempted murder of Frank Boller and the robberies of Boller, Frank Muccia, and Archie Bolivar. *People v. Massie*, 428 p. 2d 869 (Cal. S. Ct. 1967). His sentence was commuted to life by the California Supreme Court when it decided, two months before the ruling in *Furman*, that the California death penalty statute was unconstitutional; *Anderson v. State*. 493 P2d 880 (1972). In 1978, Robert Lee Massie was paroled; on Jan. 3, 1979 he murdered a man during a liquor store robbery and wounded another store employee: *People v. Massie*, 709 P2d 1309 (Cal. S.Ct. 1985) and *People v. Massie*, 967 P2d 29 (Cal. S.Ct. 1998). On March 27, 2001, 60-year-old Robert Lee Massie was executed at San Quentin.

13. *McDuff v. Texas*, 431 S.W. 2d 547 (Tx. Ct Crim App. 1968), *Ex Parte Roy Dale Green*, 548 S.W.2d 914 (Tex. Ct Crim. App. 1977), Gary Cartwright, "Free to Kill" *Texas Monthly*, August 1992, Bob Stewart, *No Remorse* (Pinnacle Books: 1996), and Gary Lavergne, *Bad Boy of Rosebud* (University of North Texas Press: 1999).

14. *McDuff v. Texas*, 431 S.W. 2d 547.

15. Gary Cartwright, "Free to Kill," *Texas Monthly*, August 1992, p. 128.

16. Former Texas Death Row inmate Jerry Ward, 40, was paroled in June 1984. He is believed to have murdered his girlfriend a year later and then committed suicide. Melinda Miller, "Dead Man Suspect in Woman's Disappearance," p. 1, *The Houston Chronicle*, June 25, 1985. According to the same article in *The Houston Chronicle*, Ward was described by a county psychiatrist in 1965 as a "sexual psychopath who will commit the same crime over and over

again" in an evaluation conducted shortly after his arrest in the rape-murder of the high school student. Ward was 19 years old when he was convicted in 1965 of the brutal rape and murder of an 18-year-old high school student whom he kidnapped from a shopping center in Houston. *Ward v. Texas*, 427 S.W.2d 876 (Tx. Ct. Crim. App. 1968).

17. Not his real name.
18. *Illinois v. Hennenberg*, 302 N.E.2d 27 (1973).
19. *Holloway v. Ohio*
20. Breedlove was convicted along with Ray Charles Carolina, Karrole Donnie Wayne Draper, and Wayne T. Glover. Both Carolina and Draper are still incarcerated in Oklahoma. Glover was never on Death Row.
21. *Breedlove v. State*, 525 p. 2d 1254, (Ok. Ct. Crim. App. 1974).
22. On June 9, six weeks before the Tacoma murder, Breedlove escaped from the Jess Dunn Correctional Center in Taft, about 50 miles southeast of Tulsa. L.A. Johnson, "Man Arrested in City Slaying is Murderer on the Lam," p. A1, *The News Tribune* (Aug. 5, 1992)
23. Breedlove said he went to the apartment of Teresa Jackson the morning after a party there, to retrieve his belongings because Jackson had told Breedlove earlier that his presence was causing friction between her and Atkins. The escapee told the jury that after the two men fought Breedlove left quickly, without his belongings, because he believed that the victim would attack him again. "Suspect Claims Self-Defense: Fatal Stabbing Result of Unprovoked Attack, Jail Escapee Says," *The News Tribune*, Dec. 19, 1992, p. B2. Breedlove's conviction and sentence of 21 years and 6 months was reversed by the Washington Court of Appeals because the trial judge had refused to allow Breedlove to represent himself. *State v. Breedlove*, 900 P2d 586 (Aug. 25, 1995). On remand, and before the second trial, the State offered Breedlove a plea bargain with a maximum sentence of 20 years. He appealed that sentence, as well, which was affirmed on appeal. *In Re The Personal Restraint Petition of Lawrence Breedlove*, No. 66425–1. (Wash. S.Ct. June 24, 1999).
24. James Marquart and Jonathan R. Sorensen, "A National Study of the Furman-Commuted Inmates: Assessing the Threat to Society From Capital Offenders," reprinted in *The Death Penalty in America*, edited by Hugo Bedau (Oxford University Press: 1997), p. 169. In addition to the prisoner homicides in Florida and Pennsylvania, Marquart and Sorensen report two additional homicides in Louisiana and Alabama.

25. John Switzer, "50 Killers Hope to Dodge The Chair," *The Columbus Dispatch*, March 19, 1972, p. 14A. "Prisoner Admits He Killed Guard," *Sunday Chronicle Telegram*, Aug. 15, 1973.
26. Tom Beyerlein, "Walls Fail to Stop Smuggling Drugs and Weapons Often Available in Prison," *The Dayton Daily News*, Nov. 12, 1995
27. *Commonwealth v. Scoggins*, 304 A 2d 102 (1973).
28. Id.
29. *Commonwealth v. Scoggins*, 353 A2d 392 (Pa. Supreme Court 1976). Several times during the days preceding the murder, and again at breakfast on the morning of the murder, the victim verbally insulted Scoggins in front of mutual friends. Shortly after breakfast, Scoggins found the victim in his cell and stabbed him six times. He died a week later. Scoggins claimed self-defense but a photograph introduced at trial showed that the victim had a "claw left arm" and was physically incapable of attacking Scoggins in the manner in which Scoggins testified.
30. *State v. Atkinson*, 172 S.E. 2d 111 (1970).
31. *Jackson v. South Carolina Department of Corrections*, 390 S.E. 2d 467 (Ct App. 1989).
32. *The State*, p. B3, Dec. 12, 1989. (Knight-Ridder newspapers)
33. *Demps v. Florida*, 272 So. 2d 803 (Fla. S. Ct. 1973).
34. *Proffitt v. Fla.*, 428 U.S. 242 (U.S. S.Ct. 1976).
35. *Demps v. State*, 395 So. 2d 501 (Fla. S. Ct. 1980), cert denied. 454 U.S. 433 (1981) At the sentencing phase, the judge overruled the jury's recommendation of death for Demps' co-defendant, "Toothless" Jackson, the inmate who stabbed Sturgis, and changed the sentence to life imprisonment.
36. Michelle Pellemans, "Proclaiming Innocence, Demps Put to Death By Lethal Injection," *The Tampa Tribune*, June 8, 2000, p. 2; Robert Anthony Phillips, "Fla. Court Rejects Execution Appeal: Killer Set to Die After 2nd Stay on Death Row," *APBnews.com*, June 6, 2000
37. Steve Mills, Maurice Possley, and Ken Armstrong, "Shadows of Doubt Haunt Executions: Three Cases Weaken Under Scrutiny," *The Chicago Tribune*, Dec. 17, 2000
38. *State v. Bradley*, 538 N.E. 2d 373 (1989).

CHAPTER 13

1. Pat Leisner, "Fast, Easy Money in Rackets Still Exciting to Murderess," *Associated Press*, March 18, 1973

2. "Ohio Prison Talks Hit Lull: Death Toll Rises to 7," *The Chicago Tribune*, April 14, 1993, "Inmates End Prison Siege," *The Chicago Tribune*, April 21, 1993

3. Doug McInnis, "Killer's Shopping Trip Led to Escape," *The Columbus Dispatch*, July 14, 1991, p. 5F.

4. Donn Gaynor and George Constable, "Man, 22, Charged With Killing Girl," *The Mansfield News Journal*, Nov. 15, 1965

5. FBI Spokesman Nestor M. Michnyak confirmed that the bureau had made a computer-enhanced photo of Eubanks to show what he might look like 17 years later. The FBI used three photographs of Eubanks – from 1959, 1965, and 1972.

6. Since 1950, 30 inmates have escaped from Ohio prisons, including seven convicted murderers who, in 1987, remained at large. In 1995, administrators from the state's 28 prisons met to determine how a record number of inmates – 15 – had escaped that year. "They're Always on the Run – Mystery Surrounds Whereabouts of Ohio's Escaped Inmates," *The Columbus Post Dispatch*, Feb. 22, 1987, p. 2B.

7. Michael Miller, "Prison Escapes on the Rise in 1995," *The Cincinnati Post*, Oct. 10, 1995

8. According to the Punitive Articles of the Uniform Code of Military Justice (UCMJ), AWOL means absence without leave; AWL means absence with leave.

9. Jodi Andes, "TV Show Brings in New Leads," *The Mansfield Journal*, Sept. 12, 1994

10. Phil Trexler, "Among Them Are Murderers, Rapists And Armed Robbers. Who Are They, The 43 Inmates On the Run From Ohio Prisons? But The Real Question: Where Are They?" *The Akron Beacon Journal*, Jan. 18, 2004, p. A1.

11. Handbook of Texas Online, "Washington County," www.tsha.utexas.edu.

12. *The Mansfield Journal*, Sept. 12, 1994

13. David Baldus, "The Unedited Death Penalty Forum," Spring 1997, Volume XII, Number 2. *The Death Penalty*, the American Bar Association: "The data collected by Watt Espy indicates that in the pre-Furman period, which I define here as the 1920s to the 1960s, nearly 70 percent of the people executed for murder in the South were black." See also "Executions in the U.S. 1608–1987: The Espy File," Death Penalty Information Center, Washington, D.C.

14. Offender Information, Larry Hayes, Texas Department of Criminal Justice, and Execution Database, www.deathpenaltyinfo.org, Death Penalty Information Center, Washington, D.C.

CHAPTER 14

1. *Furman v. Georgia*, 408 U.S. 238, 253 (1972)
2. Leonard A. Stevens, *Death Penalty: The Case of Life vs. Death in the United States* (Putnam Pub Group Library: 1978). See also Michael Meltsner, *Cruel and Unusual* (Random House: 1973) and Burton Wolfe, *Pileup on Death Row* (Doubleday: 1973).
3. Id. For an excellent and carefully researched book on background of *Furman v. Georgia*, the trial in Savannah, and its path to appeal before the U.S. Supreme Court, read Stevens' book: *Death Penalty: The Case of Life vs. Death in the United States*. For an overview of the pre-*Furman* years and how Furman's case wound up in the U.S. Supreme Court, one of the most authoritative books on the subject is Michael Meltsner's *Cruel and Unusual*.
4. Stevens, *Death Penalty: The Case of Life vs. Death in the United States*.
5. *Furman v. State*, 167 S.E. 2d 628 (1968).

CHAPTER 15

1. Journey of Hope... From Violence to Healing, P.O. Box 210390, Anchorage, AK, 99521–0390 USA, www.journeyofhope.org. Murder Victim's Families for Human Rights is an international organization of family members of victims of murder, execution, terrorist killings, extrajudicial assassinations and "disappearances." www.mvfrh.org
2. Helen Prejean, *Dead Man Walking: An Eyewitness Account of the Death Penalty in the United States* (Random House: 1993) and *The Death of Innocents: An Eyewitness Account of Wrongful Executions* (Random House: 2004).
3. Manuel "Manny" Babbitt was executed by the state of California on May 4, 1999 for the 1980 robbery of a 78-year-old Sacramento woman. Although Babbitt was convicted of her murder, the coroner ruled that the victim died of a heart attack brought on by the beating. At the time of the attack, Babbitt, a Vietnam veteran, may well have been suffering from post-traumatic stress disorder. In March 1998, while on Death Row, Babbitt was awarded the Purple Heart, 30 years after he was wounded in Vietnam, *California Department of Corrections and Rehabilitation*. "Dramatic Plea to Save Killer: Ex-cop Says Death Row Inmate Rescued Him in '68," *The San Francisco Chronicle*, March 29, 1999

4. Maro Robbins, "Healing Seen In Between Bonds Kin, Killer," *The San Antonio Express-News*, Oct. 24, 2005
5. Journey of Hope... From Violence to Healing. St Mary's University, Oct. 24, 2005. See also Carol Sowa, "Parents of Victims, Condemned Join Sister Prejean in Opposing Death Penalty," *Today's Catholic*, Nov. 25, 2005.

EPILOGUE

1. Those states are: Alaska, Hawaii, Iowa, Maine, Massachusetts, Michigan, Minnesota, North Dakota, Rhode Island, Vermont, West Virginia, and Wisconsin.
2. The Death Penalty in 2005: Year End Report, Death Penalty Information Center, Washington, D.C., December 2005.
3. *Roper v. Simmons*, 03–0633.
4. *Atkins v. Virginia*, 00–8452.
5. Hill's claim is based on a study published in the April 16, 2005, issue of *The Lancet*, a respected British medical journal, that suggests that inmates executed by lethal injection experienced pain and "unnecessary suffering," therefore violating a Death Row inmate's right not to be subjected to "wanton and unnecessary pain."
6. Nebraska has the electric chair. The chemical pancronium bromide has been banned by the American Veterinary Medical Association. The constitutional claim of cruel and unusual punishment and lethal injection was successful in temporarily halting the executions of Michael Taylor in Missouri and David Nelson in Alabama.
7. On Jan. 25, 2006, less than 24 hours after Hill's life was spared, Marion Dudley was executed in Texas; his appeal was based on an innocence claim. And on Jan. 27, 2006, after the U.S. Supreme Court overturned a federal appeals court stay of execution, the state of Indiana executed Marvin Bieghler. Death penalty lawyers say one reason Hill's appeal was successful was because Florida has never ruled on the constitutionality of the lethal injection procedure which has been the execution method for only six years. Previously inmates were executed in the electric chair, but that was challenged on grounds of cruel and unusual punishment after two botched executions during which the inmate's body was set on fire.
8. Justice Kennedy's stay was temporary; on the following day, the full court agreed to hear the appeal. Clarence Hill was fortunate to have had Kennedy as his circuit justice. The justice who oversees the

death rows of Texas, Louisiana, and Mississippi, is the pro-death penalty justice Antonin Scalia. Likewise, Death Row inmates in Missouri, Arkansas, and Nebraska would have better luck rolling the dice than getting a stay from that circuit's justice, Clarence Thomas.

9. On Feb. 17, 2006, the state of California was ordered to change its lethal execution protocol or face a delay in the Feb. 21st execution of Michael Morales. U.S. District Judge Jeremy Fogel told prison officials that they had to put an anesthesiologist in the execution chamber to make sure that Michael Morales does not feel pain before administering the two chemicals that cause paralysis and cardiac arrest, or the execution would be postponed. The California Department of Corrections said it would provide an anesthesiologist to monitor the inmate's consciousness, but the doctors refused to do so on medical ethics grounds.

10. While those new death penalty laws did include a requirement of a two-proceeding to determine guilt–innocence and sentencing; the requirement of the commission of another felony in addition to the murder; requirement of the jury to reflect a cross-section of the community and to follow guidelines in assessing aggravating and mitigating factors, the fact remains that the initial decision of whether a murder is a capital one or not is left to the local prosecutor, and the quality of legal representation is a study in economics.

11. Parolee Herbert Steigler of Delaware murdered three members of his family, including his six-year-old daughter, in 1968 by setting his house on fire; he was paroled in 1980. Eugene Armstrong of Illinois killed a police officer in 1967 and has been paroled. In February 1968, William "Sarge" Wallen returned from Vietnam for a brief visit with his family; within two months he was charged with murdering a man in a fight over a girlfriend. Wallen, who had no prior record when he was sent to Death Row, was paroled in 1980 and in 1985 was reinstated with full voting rights and the right to carry a firearm; he never returned to prison. Meanwhile, in California, Manny Babbitt, also a Vietnam veteran – and who, like Wallen, had no prior record – was convicted of capital murder following the death of an elderly woman who died of a heart attack after Babbitt broke into her apartment. The court rejected Babbitt's claim that his actions were caused by post-traumatic stress disorder; he was executed by the state of California in 1999. See Note 3, Chapter 15.

THE HISTORY OF THE DEATH PENALTY IN THE UNITED STATES

December 1, 1607: The execution of Captain George Kendall in Virginia is the first recorded execution in the new colonies; he was accused of being a spy for Spain.

Late 1700s: The abolitionist movement in the United States begins.

1800s: Many states in the U.S. reduce the number of capital crimes and build prisons.

1823–1837: Great Britain eliminates more than 100 of its 222 capital crimes.

1834: Pennsylvania is the first state to eliminate executions in public and moves them inside correctional facilities.

March 1, 1846: Michigan abolishes the death penalty for all crimes except treason.

1888: New York builds the first electric chair; in 1890, William Kemmler is executed.

1907–1917: Nine states abolish the death penalty for all crimes or strictly limit it.

1930s: Executions are at the highest level in U.S. history (an average of 167 per year).

December 10, 1948: The United Nations General Assembly adopts the "Universal Declaration of Human Rights" proclaiming a "right to life."

1950–1980: Defacto abolition of the death penalty becomes the norm in western Europe.

July 1, 1966: Support of the death penalty hits an all-time low in the U.S. of only 42%.

June 2, 1967: Luis Monge of Colorado is the last person to be executed in the U.S. before a nationwide moratorium is declared; it remains in effect until 1977.

June 3, 1968: The Supreme Court says a juror's mere reservations about the death penalty are insufficient grounds to strike him/her from the jury (*Witherspoon v. Illinois*).

May 3, 1971: The Supreme Court says a jury's unrestricted discretion and a single guilt/sentence trial is not unconstitutional (*McGuatha v. California; Crampton v. Ohio*).

June 29, 1972: The Supreme Court abolishes the death penalty in the U.S. in *Furman v. Georgia*, saving the lives of 587 men and two women. In its 5–4 decision, it rules that a jury's absolute discretion results in arbitrary sentencing and therefore the punishment is "cruel and unusual" in violation of the Eighth Amendment.

July 2, 1976: The Supreme Court reinstates the death penalty in *Gregg v. Georgia*, declaring it constitutional under the Eighth Amendment and approves rewritten statutes with sentencing guidelines that allow the admission of aggravating and mitigating factors. Other procedural reforms include: separate deliberations for the guilt and penalty phases of the trial, automatic appellate review of convictions and sentences, and a proportionality review, a practice to identify and eliminate sentencing disparities.

January 17, 1977: Gary Gilmore is executed by a firing squad in Utah, ending a 10-year moratorium on executions in the U.S. Gilmore did not challenge his death sentence.

December 7, 1982: Charlie Brooks of Texas is the first person in the U.S. to be executed by lethal injection.

November 2, 1984: Velma Barfield (North Carolina) is the first woman to be executed since 1962.

1986–1993: The Supreme Court rules: the executions of insane persons is unconstitutional (*Ford v. Wainwright*); intentional racial discrimination must be shown (*McCleskey v. Kemp*); the execution of juveniles aged 15 and younger is unconstitutional (*Thompson v Oklahoma*); 16- and 17-year-olds can be executed (*Stanford v. Kentucky*); executing mentally retarded persons is allowed (*Penry v. Lynaugh*); and evidence of innocence is no reason for a federal court to order a new trial (*Herrera v. Collins*).

April 28, 1999: The U.N. Human Rights Commission passes a resolution supporting a worldwide moratorium on executions.

June 2002: The Supreme Court rules that death sentences in which a judge finds the aggravating factors violate the right to a trial by jury *(Ring v. Arizona)* and the execution of the mentally retarded is unconstitutional (*Atkins v. Virginia*).

January 12, 2003: Illinois Governor George Ryan abolishes the death penalty and grants clemency to 167 death row inmates.

June 24, 2004: New York's death penalty is unconstitutional.

March 1, 2005: The Supreme Court bans the execution of juveniles *(Roper v. Simmons)*.

March 2006: De facto moratorium in California spares lives of 649 inmates while a federal judge reviews how lethal injection drugs are administered.

May 2006: A California federal judge schedules hearing on constitutional claims.

Late June 2006: The Supreme Court is expected to rule on a Florida inmate's right to bring a claim that lethal injection is cruel and unusual punishment (*Hill v. Crosby*).

Source: *History of the Death Penalty*, The Death Penalty Information Center, Washington, D.C., 2006.

BIBLIOGRAPHY

BOOKS

Banner, Stuart. *The Death Penalty: An American History*, Harvard University Press, 2002

Bedau, Hugo Adam, ed. *The Death Penalty in America: Current Controversies*, Oxford University Press, USA, 1997

Bowers, William J. *Legal Homicide: Death as Punishment in America 1864–1982*, Northeastern University Press, 1984

Greenberg, Jack. *Crusaders in the Courts: How a Dedicated Band of Lawyers Fought for the Civil Rights Revolution*, Basic Books, 1994

Isay, David and Wang, Harvey. *Holding On: Dreamers, Visionaries, Eccentrics and other American Heroes*, WW Norton & Co., 1995

Lavergne, Gary. *Bad Boy From Rosebud: The Murderous Life of Kenneth Allen McDuff*, University of North Texas Press, 1999

Lazarus, Edward. *Closed Chambers: The First Eyewitness Account of the Epic Struggles Inside the Supreme Court*, Random House, 1998

Mailer, Norman. *The Executioner's Song*, Warner Books, 1980

Marquart, James, Ekland-Olson, Sheldon and Sorensen, James. *The Rope, The Chair, and The Needle: Capital Punishment in Texas, 1923–1990*, University of Texas, 1994

Meltsner, Michael. *Cruel and Unusual: The Supreme Court and Capital Punishment*, Random House, 1973

Miller, Gene. *Invitation To A Lynching*, Doubleday, 1975

Prejean, Helen. *Dead Man Walking: An Eyewitness Account of the Death Penalty in the United States*, Random House, 1993 and *The Death of Innocents: An Eyewitness Account of Wrongful Executions*, Random House, 2004

Rideau, Wilbert and Wikberg, Ron. *Life Sentences: Rage and Survival Behind Bars*, Random House Trade, 1992

Stevens, Leonard A. *Death Penalty: The Case of Life vs. Death in the United States*, Putnam Pub Group Library, 1978

Stewart, Bob. *No Remorse*, Pinnacle Books, 1996

Von Drehle, David. *Among the Lowest of the Dead: The Culture on Death Row*, Crown, 1995

Wolfe, Burton H. *Pileup on Death Row*, Doubleday, 1973

Woodward, Bob and Armstrong, Scott. *The Brethren: Inside the Supreme Court*, Simon & Schuster, 1979

STUDIES

Marquart, James, and Sorensen, Jonathan R. "A National Study of the Furman-Commuted Inmates: Assessing the Threat to Society From Capital Offenders," *Loyola of Los Angeles Law Review*, Vol. 23 No. 1 (November 1989), reprinted in Bedau, Hugo A., ed., *The Death Penalty in America*

Vito, Gennaro F. and Wilson, Deborah G. *"Back From The Dead: Tracking the Progress of Kentucky's Furman Commuted Death Row Population,"* Urban Studies Center, College of Urban and Public Affairs, University of Louisville (December 1986)

Cases of Innocence: 1973 to present. Death Penalty Information Center, Washington, D.C. (Nov. 18, 2005); *Execution Database: 1976–1994.* Death Penalty Information Center, (January 2005); *Executions in the U.S. 1608–1987: The Espy File,* Death Penalty Information Center

Execution Data Sheet, May 14, 1971, Citizens Against Legalized Murder, Douglas H. Lyons, Chairman

Killing with Prejudice: Race and the Death Penalty in the USA. Amnesty International USA, 2004

TABLE OF CASES

U.S. Supreme Court

Aikens v. California, 406 US 813 (1972); *People v. Aikens*, 450 P.2d 258 (Cal. Sup. Ct. 1969)

Furman v. Georgia, 408 U.S. 238 (1972) and *Furman v. State*, 167 S.E. 2d 628 (1968)

Gregg v. Georgia, 428 U.S. 153 (1976)

Jurek v. Texas, 428 US 262 (1976)

Maxwell v. Bishop, 398 F2d 138 (8th Cir. 1968); 398 U.S. 262 (1970)

Powell v. Alabama, 287 U.S. 45 (1932)
Proffit v. Florida, 428 U.S. 242 (1976)
Witherspoon v. Illinois, 391 U.S. 510 (1968)
Woodson v. North Carolina, 428 U.S. 280 (1976)

State Cases

Branch v. State, 447 S.W. 2d 932 (Tex. Cr. App. 1969)
Breedlove v. State, 525 P. 2d 1254, (Okla. Crim. App. 1974)
Cerny v. State, 480 P2d 199 (Wash. Sup. Ct. 1971)
Commonwealth v. Scoggins, 304 A 2d 102 (1973); 353 A2d 392 (Pa. S. Ct. 1976)
Demps v. Florida, 272 So. 2d 803 (Fla. S. Ct. 1973); 395 So. 2d 501 (Fla. S. Ct. 1980)
Ex Parte Young, 397 S.W. 2d 74 (Tex. Ct. Crim. App. 1965)
Illinois v. Henenberg, 302 N.E.2d 27 (Ill. 1973)
In Re Breedlove, No. 66425–1,. (Wash. Sup. Ct. 1999)
Lee v. State, 141 So. 2d 257 (Fla. 1963)
Manier v. Colorado, 518 P2d 811 (Colo. Ct. App. 1974)
McDuff v. Texas, 431 S.W. 2d 547 (Tex. Ct. Crim App. 1968)
People v. Massie, 428 P. 2d 869 (Cal. S. Ct. 1967)
People v. Butler, 320 N.E. 2d 870 (NY Ct. App. 1974)
People v. Culhane, 305 N.E. 2d 469 (NY Ct. App. 1973)
Sellars v. State, 400 S.W. 2d 559 (Tex. Ct. Crim. App. 1965)
State v. Atkinson, 172 S.E. 2d 111 (S.C. Ct. App. 1970)
State v. Belwood, 494 P2d 519 (Utah 1972)
State v. Bickham, 121 So. 2d 207 (La. 1960)
State v. Bradley, 538 N.E. 2d 373 (Ohio 1989)
State v. Breedlove, 900 P2d 586 (Okla. Ct. Crim. App. 1995)
State v. Holland, 201 S.E.2d 118 (S.C. Ct. App. 1973)
State v. Lee, 141 So.2d 257 (Fla. 1963)
State v. Nelson, 175 A2d 814 (N.H. Sup. Ct. 1963)
Turczi v. State, 301 N.E. 2d 752 (Ind. Sup. Ct. 1973)
Ward v. Texas, 427 S.W.2d 876 (Tx. Ct. Crim. App. 1968)
Williams v. State, 668 S.W.2d 692 (Tex. Crim. App. 1983)

INDEX

303